BLOOD LIFE COMPENSATION PENALTY IN SOUTH SUDAN

PROF MADHEL MALEK AGEI

The publisher wishes to acknowledge and thank Dr. Douglas H. Johnson for his invaluable help and support for Africa World Books and its mission of preserving and promoting African cultural and literary traditions and history. Dr. Johnson and fellow historians have been instrumental in ensuring that African people remain connected to their past and their identity. Africa World Books is proud to carry on this mission.

Cover design, typesetting and layout: Africa World Books
Unit 3, 57 Frobisher St, Osborne Park, WA 6017
P.O. Box 1106 Osborne Park, WA 6916

CONTENTS

ABSTRACT

The blood life compensation has been popularly promoted through a judicial process emerging in recent road accident occurrences in South Sudan. This book is an exploratory investigation of understanding the connections between compensation, road accidents and what causes road accidents to happen, legal implications, processes of law, culture, and mourning rituals together with cultural differences that may exist between one's home country or clan and the country of concern undertaking. Both legal systems and cultural priorities come out of the history of a country or state or clan. Culture affects legal systems just as processes of laws and regulations affect changes in culture. There has been a substantial review of exploration on the impact of accidents on cultural mourning, beliefs, values, grief, and communication about property damage in a community setting. There has been very little on the role of customary law practice. In this book, I will be focusing mostly on issues of compensation, understanding road accidents and how they happen, impact consequent on the survival, and prevention measures for its happening. Nilotic or Bantu ethnic classes of peoples with different clans and subclans[1], and in particular ethnic Jieng, have established specific traditional customary rules and regulations whereas Azande speakers, have fewer regulations about compensation claims. These practices come out of cultural priorities and the meaning of the compensation benefitting survival.

The available literature outlines the different types of road accidents, mourning, bereavement, rituals, and practices of various ethnic groups in South Sudan and Africa performed in the event of the death of a loved one. These include slaughtering an animal, morning prayers, special burial for the death of a master of fishing spears, mourning periods and the cleansing ceremonies. While some of the death rituals and practices are still adhered to in rural homes and cities of South Sudan, others are adapted and new practices have emerged. One such is the practice of the 'blood life wealth' penalty, payable in monetary or money equivalent after the death of victim in accident. Within a Nilotes context in South Sudan, the dead are regarded as ancestors and they are treated with great respect, as they are believed to have a special relationship with the living. Proper rites and ceremonies performed following the death of a loved one, particularly the master of fishing spear and divinity deities, reflect this belief. Any deviation from the above could be marked as a sign of disrespect for the ancestors and Natural Laws from Heavenly *Nhialic*-god, and bad luck could befall anyone in the family who does not adhere to the stipulated practices.

The investigation was carried out among rural inhabitants who practice strict cultural mourning rituals. Individual persons and focus clans were interviewed on their experiences and the meaning they attach to the practice of the apuk riem, apuk weng or apuk wong riem, which is translated as "blood life wealth price" or blood life compensation payable in cattle herds according to Jieng culture. I have described the gathered findings, the current highlighted perceptions, meanings and feelings about the blood life compensation prices payable in cattle after the burial; fatal road accidents, mourning and rituals. Though the cause of blood life fatality is interpreted as tragic and part of the mourning ceremony, the important functions of this blood life compensation prices payable in cattle herds were indicated as comforting and supporting the bereaved as well as helping those who survived, to cope with the impact of loss life of a loved one. On the other hand, other community members condemned the practice as disproportional and felt that it was insensitive to compensate for a boychild or loved one killed recklessly, while other people are still in mourning. It can be argued such disproportionality hurts the bereaved and delays the chances of forgiveness, reconciliation, healing and recovering from grief. Symbols, heroes, and rituals are the tangible or visual aspects of the practices of a culture. The true cultural meaning of the practices is intangible; this is revealed only when the practices are interpreted by the insiders.

The blood life compensation prices payable in cattle equivalent of a monetary amount, can be an effective coping strategy if it has been initiated in line with the reconciliation of cultural differences and with sustainable judicial practice custom. The experiences in compensation after road accidents penalty and meaning attached to blood life compensation could serve as guidelines to explore the spiritual needs of the bereaved in rural home communities.

CHAPTER ONE

INTRODUCTION

Introduction

South Sudan has many ethnic groups who inhabit the country and fulfill the country's unique economic requirement for inexpensive migratory labour. These ethnic groups and clans of different nationalities of South Sudanese are under distinct classifications, defined by a host of ethnical, cultural, historical and linguistic factors as follows; (1) Nilotic ethnic classes of people with different clans and subclans, (2) Central Sudanic[2] or Nilo-Sahara to Kordofanian ethnic classes of peoples with different clans and subclans,[3] (3) Nilo-Hamitic or Afro-Asiatic ethnic classes of peoples with clans and subclans, and (4) Bantu ethnic classes of peoples[4] with different clans and subclans.[5]

These ethnic groups were managed using insensitive and violent

---

2   Westermann, Diedrich, 1922a. *Die Sprache der Guang*. Berlin: Dietrich Reimer.

3   Encyclopedia Britannica, Inc.

4   *The Chronological Evidence for the Introduction of Domestic Stock in Southern Africa* Texas State University. Retrieved December 17, 2007.

5   Evidence against the "early split" scenario shown here is presented in E. Patin et al., "Dispersals and genetic adaptation of Bantu-speaking populations in Africa and North America", Science, Vol. 356, Issue 6337, pp. 543-546 (5 May 2017), doi:10.1126/science. aal1988.

policing systems and colonial municipal administrative traditions. The clans have been classified into sixty-four ethnic classes of people or more narrowly distinct categories, according to clannish classifications, that reflect a mixture of common interests, customs, ethnicities, and practices. As a result, many South Sudanese became urbanized, and urbanization changed much of the world view, values, rituals, customary courts and traditions of such people.

Loss of human life is a universal human hardship for the ones who remain behind.[6] Among all forms of experiences that occur in any given culture,[7] for Azande clans or Apuk clans, Bantu or Nilotic, society or community, death seems to be the one that transcends them all.[8]

The current book covers the information about road accidents, their causes and the blood life compensation prices payable in cattle herds to be collected immediately 'after the burial of deaths' of a loved one. It is a traditional ruling decision which has become popular in small towns and big cities of South Sudan.

Blood life compensation price payable after the burial of dead or after an injury, is a frequent occurrence in South Sudan's small towns and cities because of the violent accidental deaths caused by narrow roads in towns, with the highest number of road accident traffic deaths occurring between 2007 and 2011. Car accident fatalities and *boda boda* accident fatalities were common occurrences in cities of Juba, Torit, Yambio, Wau, Warrap and other rural roadways. Pedestrians and motorbike cyclists known as *boda boda riders* or Senke riders, are the victims in 44 percent of all fatal roadway accidents and collision crashes in South Sudan, compared to a

---

6   Bonnano, G. A., & Kaltman, S. (1999). *Toward an integrative perspective on bereavement.* Psychological Bulletin, 125(6), 760-776.

7   Hockey, J., Katsz, J., & Small, N. (2001). *Grief, mourning and death ritual.* Philadelphia: Open University Press. Kastenbaum, R. J. (2004). *Death, society and human experience* (5th edn.). Boston: Allyn & Bacon.

8   Rosenblatt, P. C., Walsh, R. P. & Jackson, D. A. (1976). *Grief and mourning in cross-cultural perspective.* New Haven, Connecticut: Human Relations Area Files Press.

global average of about 26 percent for those types of road users[9].

Juba city, Yei town, Wau city and Torit city lead in the number of road accidents that have occurred countrywide between 2007 and 2009, even though the number decreased compared to last two years by 2020.

People learned to use animals like donkeys, horses, and camels as well as water canals for transportation prior to 4000 BC to 3000 BC. Around 3500 BC, a wooden wheel was used for land transportation, while a wooden sailing canoe, boat or logboats, were used for water transportation[10].

Whether movement was for migration motives, hunting or food gatherings, escape from predators or any other motives, peoples found one way or the other to transport themselves to wherever they wanted to move or reach or connect with. The first tracks were created by people carrying goods and often followed feeder roads, waterways transport or footprints. Tracks would be naturally created at points of high traffic density.

In the past Colonial period of the 1900s, South Sudan's roads (or Southern Sudan's roadways) generally were neglected and hard to travel. People usually walked on footpaths and feeder roads. The British colonial administrators rode horses and others were carried in sedan chairs. Others used pack animals. The colonial Governors and Commissioners built good roads for military purposes. The South Sudanese civil war started in 1956 and began to use the same colonial military roads, and they continued doing so from 1983 to the current period 2020.

Boda boda is a word used to describe motorcycles and originated from Uganda border from 1960s to 1970s. Small traders who took illegal goods between the Ugandan and Kenyan border as smugglers or contrabandists

---

9   Christopher J.L. Murray and Alan D. Lopez, eds., *The Global Burden of Disease: A Comprehensive Assessment of Mortality and Disability from Diseases, Injuries, and Risk Factors in 1990 and Projected in 2020* (Boston: Harvard School of Public Health, 1996).

10   David W. Anthony, *The Horse, the Wheel, and Language: How Bronze-Age Riders from the Eurasian Shaped the Modern World.* Princeton University Press, 2010 ISBN 140083105 Page 46

would use motorcycles. They coined this word *boda boda,* which can be translated as 'border to border', but in short pronunciation as *boda boda* riders[11].

Pedestrians, bicyclists, and motorcycle riders, commonly called Senke riders or boda-boda riders, are the most vulnerable and the heaviest users of roads in South Sudan. Most people who use public transportation, bicycles, *boda boda*[12] riders or who routinely walk highway roads in rural roadway settings are poor people, clarifying the higher risk suffered by less privileged people.

There are many modes of transport and few roads that are not narrow and overcrowded. The heavy flow of traffic, habitual rushed driving and frequent breach of safety rules and road traffic risks result in ever-increasing fatal injuries, disabilities, severe head injuries and killings or deaths. Such accidents often result in loss of life and materials.

I hear of them and read about them in newspapers almost daily. All drivers have a legal duty of care to drive safely. This means Bantu speaking driver Jackson Gelua Anthony must follow local traffic laws, maintain a proper lookout for other drivers and pedestrians or children, and keep his car in working order and in road path. When driver Jackson Gelua Anthony violated his duty of care, it was because of his negligence, carelessness, and reckless driving.

Hypothetical Experiences

In emotional terms, death is equated to a disaster because it is a stressor that forces an individual to act in response and adapt or try to adopt strategies to cope with its impact[13]. In many cases, the Jieng community, Azande community or many other communities, struggle to find ways to avoid

---

11   Ugandan riding boda boda in Juba city explained to Madhel Malek Agei, February 2021.

12   Two-wheel motor cycles used by many people for transport in South Sudan.

13   Fischer, C. T. (2006) (Ed*). Qualitative Research methods for psychologists: Introduction through empirical studies.* New York: Academic Press.

the various impacts of a violent, slow, or painful death and the powerful effects of death[14]. Grief is a normal, healthy condition and an expression of bereavement caused by loss of life[15]. Often, when death occurs, communities or people or individuals who're close to the deceased, tend to act in response using the same coping strategies that the person has used with other powerful emotions in the past. The awareness of death in Nilotic, Bantu, Afro-Asiatic or Nilo-Sahara to Kordofanian ethnic communities or any other communities is a basic aspect of the human condition that gives significance to living. There is a universal reaction that individuals who lose loved ones go through in a struggle to find meaning in the event of unexpected death.

All communities or societies have their own customs and beliefs surrounding death and each culture has its own approaches to dealing with loss life in human action and / or accident. Compensation price for violent accidents can be more or less standardized but almost always involve a core of compensation prices, punishments, understandings, customary court procedures, spiritual beliefs, rituals, preventions, customary law systems, expectations and etiquette[16]. In Jieng (or Jaang Rek), Azande, Balanda Bviri, Balanda Boor and some cultures in South Sudan, the dead are venerated in different ways; usually celebrated as ancestral worship through the use of divinity high priest chiefs and deity spiritual powers.

In African culture, death does not alter or end the life or the personality of an individual, but only causes a change in its condition[17]. The deceased member of the family becomes an important extension of the

---

14   Bento, R. F. (1994). When the show must go on: Disenfranchised grief in Organisation, *Journal of Managerial Psychology, Pages* 9, 35-44.

15   Frisch, N. C., & Frisch, L. E. (2006). *Psychiatric mental health nursing* (2nd edn.). Canada: Thomson Delmar Learning.

16   Parkes, C. M., Laungani, P. & Young, B. (Eds.) (1997). *Death and bereavement across cultures.* London: Routledge.

17   Mbiti, J. S. (1975). *Introduction to African religion.* South Africa; Heinemann International Literature & Textbooks.

living in ancestry world of spirits. Hence, they are called the 'living dead' or ancestors[18].

Mourning rituals have been a constant phenomenon throughout history. But accident injuries and deaths are more and more numerous, without adequate records and reporting. This narrative explains why and how different cultures perform death rituals, depending on the meaning they attach to death[19] based on whether the death was a violent accident, a slow death, a peaceful one or painful.

Most of the rituals are based on the traditional and spiritual belief systems of those communities in focus. In ethnic Jieng cultures and Zande family cultures, together with all those South Sudanese cultures, these death rituals can include: cleansing, a burial ceremony, the slaughtering of an animal, wearing mourning robes, removal of ornaments on a neck, wrist, ankle or body, barring of a drum to play, and restriction of the mourners so that they cannot participate in social functions for a specified period. The specific details of grief and rituals can also be unique, from ethnic Azande family to Apuk branch of ethnic Rek family, to another even in the same society due to influences of spiritual, and divinity spirit beliefs, education, and wealth status, among others.

A ritual is a specific behavior or activity that gives symbolic expression of certain feelings or thoughts of different ethnic communities and individuals. Rituals after blood life loss and blood life compensation prices represent a symbolic confirmation or affirmation of values by means of culturally standardized utterances, blood life prices collections and actions. From this perspective, rituals seem to perform specific functions in a given society or culture. The burial sacraments like fire smoke, burn ache applications and stepping feet on ache after death burial cleansing, the most common rituals, are a source of valuable sustenance to the society and to those who have been bereaved.

---

18   Mbiti, J.S. (1969). *African religions and philosophy*. London: Heinemann.

19   Rosenblatt, P. C., Walsh, R. P. & Jackson, D. A. (1976). *Grief and mourning in cross-cultural perspective*. New Haven, Connecticut: Human Relations Area Files Press.

Each society has prescribed rituals, and blood life wealth price numbering cattle ceremonies that can help families in resolving their grief. Rituals and blood life wealth price numbering cattle herds serve particular functions, but primarily, blood life wealth prices help the families to accept the reality of life loss, to express the feelings related to blood life loss and accomplish the task of grief work.

Death to ethnic Rek branch of Jieng family classification communities is not an event which just occurs, handled and then forgotten about. When one dies, there is a series of events which usually take place. These include a period of at least forty-five days of mourning before the actual burial cleansing after death, feasting and gatherings accompanying the burial cleansing after death. Evening prayers may also be held through divinity deities in some families, depending on their family traditions. Family members usually prepare food for friends and neighbours; inform visiting mourners about the cause of death of the deceased. They also enhance the expression and containment of strong emotions for the family members and friends of the deceased person. The repetitive and prescriptive nature of rituals usually ease feelings of anxiety in that they provide structure and order in times of chaos and disorder in the family that is mourning. It is mentioned earlier, within communities, they may reaffirm ethnic or religious identity. Rituals also provide the opportunity for public display of grief.

Like other traditional communities in South Sudan, in traditional Jieng cultures, burials and bereavement rituals help in the purification of the mourners who are believed to be polluted from contact with the curse life and the dead. Community members participate in ceremonies that are considered to be essential for the removal of contaminated and cursed spirit and allow the mourners to re-enter society and return to the process of living. In addition to common rituals, the Apuk clan branch of Rek family speaking people together with the Jieng ethnic traditional way of life and divinity spirits observe the pre-burial rituals and post-burial purification rituals. This is especially important when it comes to issue of supernatural spiritual powers, divinity spirit powers and masters of the fishing spear family elders. This is due to the belief that death floats over them like a shadow until such a time that they undergo a purification practice. The purpose is to show that boundaries that separate life and death are every now and then not very clear and indefinite. Nobody who can tell when the life ends, and when it starts. Failure to cleanse or purify as required by clan tradition is believed to bring bad luck (i.e. misfortune) or evil to the family members or people close to the deceased and deceased family members.

It is believed that when a driver fatally injures a pedestrian while driving at even just a low speed of 10 miles per hour and dies, it is bad luck for the driver who accidentally crashed pedestrian, and that the deceased person who died in violently will become an evil spirit. Rituals offer comfort, relief, and wellbeing into communities. Such rituals may act as a psychological means of adjustment in the face of misfortunes.

Commonly in indigenous Apuk cultures, failure to cleanse or purify new road network passing through ancestry land of Apuk homeland, as required by traditions, has caused road accidents and human error. Personal errors sadly happen when they are preventable through rituals and cleansing. The processes for specific accident causes and common types of accidents are described, and this shapes the process of proving liability, obligation, legal responsibility and proving fatal compensation claims taken to court hearings.

Mistakes were the factors that cause those drivers and some people to make those errors, which cause devastating injuries or even fatalities leading to death of victims. In fact, the most publicized type of driver error has been drink driving, which is liable for more fatal collision crashes in South Sudan roadways than any other cause. Truly, a person who consumes alcohol and then gets behind the wheel can await to suffer from reduced reaction interval and attentiveness or vigilance, as well as impaired vision and thinking abilities. For this reason, struggling to handle some undertakings while you are driving also has an impact comparable to drink driving, reducing the reaction interval and attentiveness.

Common accidents and collision crashes happen because of personal errors, and common behavior of people, resulting in accident, such as: speeding; drunken driving; distractions to the driver; traffic light jumping; avoiding safety equipment like seat belts and helmets; and non-adherence to lane driving and overtaking in a wrong manner, at a corner or junction, have been found as most common behavior of road drivers, which leads to accidents to fatal deaths.

Motivation for the Study

I was invited to investigate a roadway accident death involving a three-year-old boychild Mangong Akol Akot Anei who died in collision on July 15, 2019 and to investigate causes of road traffic accidents (RTAs) in South Sudan involving children, pedestrian roadway users, drivers, passengers, and traditional practices on bereavement, grief and mourning practices. Particular emphasis will focus on the legal compensation claims for blood life lost after road accident surrounding circumstances and outcomes of these accidents discussed by the special committee comprised of court personnel, local administrators, traditional chiefs and community leaders of Apuk Rek branch of ethnic Jieng communities in Warrap State in South Sudan.

This book explores a variety of ways of road accidents and how they happen, how road accidents can be prevented, processes of law and judicial procedures in which culture experts make cultural argument about blood life compensation price practices. Both legal systems and cultural priorities come out of the history of a society or community or country. Culture affects legal systems just as laws affect changes in culture, through legal implications, processes of law and compensation penalty verdict after court hearing.

Traditional court chiefs, court of law clerks and bereaved family members were invited to call in and give input and opinion about life lost for the blood life compensation payable in cattle prices for the bereavement, to forgive and reverse curses, impacts and effects of accident deaths on those who are still alive. This was an eye-opening one for me because I realized the importance of taking reconciliation rules, cultural differences, road accident occurrences, and rural community practices into perspective.

The controversial type of blood life compensation called apuk *riem* or *apuk hook riem or riim* or *hook apuk riim or riem,* translated as 'blood life wealth' or 'compensation payable in cattle equivalent prices after death mourning', which is practiced in the Jieng rural communities throughout South Sudan, featured in discussions in that stage. That stage and the Wanhalel Dinka Traditional Customary Laws used in Apuk Law Court hearing generated interest for me to explore the phenomenon of the blood life wealth payable in cattle equivalent prices after mourning the dead in road accidents in South Sudan. I believe that the blood life compensation payable in cattle equivalent prices after road accident processes of law practice is perceived differently by Azande people and many different ethnic people across the country. Again, people pay their blood life compensation wealth and mourn their dead differently. This also motivated me to write this book in a thorough examination of customary ways.

Statement of the Problem

Numerous accounts of human life show that South Sudan is facing immense challenges. When the civil war ended, few roads were improved in big cities and every road accident which happened resulted into potentially fatal injuries. An accident happens in no time. A pedestrian dies in a motor vehicle accident every month and each year, motor vehicle accidents kill hundreds of people across the country.

Preferences are all different when it comes to mode of transportation, yet at one time or another everyone is a pedestrian. Sadly, there was an increase in the number of pedestrians who died in roadway crashes between 2006 and 2019, raising the death toll.

Road incidences involving children or minors usually occur when they are moving on the roadway, unable to know the sizes and speeds of vehicles or Senke motorcycles from the sound or noise of the engine, Children tend to move towards whichever way a sound or noise is coming from and therefore, whichever way a vehicle or a *boda boda* cycle is coming from. Immature children are full of life, robust, and frequently reckless and easily distracted, which may lead them to suddenly run into the roadway. Speed and distance are difficult for a child to judge but are crucial for crossing a roadway safely. "The concept of left and right" as positions relative to the body develop slowly and is only well established after the age of about seven to nine or eleven years in life.

The people of South Sudan are equally disadvantaged, particularly minors and children, persons with disabilities and elderly citizens who have no access to basic health insurance services including accident insurance which covers qualifying injuries, death, adequate judicial procedures and nutritional care.

Legal protection insurance which facilitates access to law and justice by providing legal advice and covering legal costs of accident, protects the life of the pedestrians involved in road accidents regardless whether the case is brought by accident victims against the actors, by exposing roadway users violating traffic rules to law.

In South Sudan, car collision crashes are on the rise on its old and new roadways as there are many modes of transport and those new roadways are narrow, and overcrowded by *boda boda* riders. I hear of car accidents and read about hundreds of car accident victims on the radio and in newspapers almost every week. These car accidents always result in loss of life, damage and severe injuries. These accidents are caused by the carelessness of drivers and their ignorance and negligence of road rules. Accident victims suffer from soft-tissue injuries. Other accidents have led to many deaths. The force of impact, even at low speeds, can result in compression of your body, for instance, spine and the disks in the lower body part of the spinal column experience pain and soreness for weeks or years.

My most vivid moments I can still remember from accidents are of a head-on collision, of terrifying impact which was massive, scary, and horrific to see. It happened when one lorry driver bypassed my lorry driver to overtake the next lorry driver, travelled the wrong way down one roadway and crossed the midpoint on the highway, to rush rockets, ammunitions and combatants of Koryom II Battalion to battles targeting Bor city in Jonglei operation zones and Juba city to capture in 1992[20].

The driver next to my lorry took it as a challenge as he was far behind. God knows why people take risks in such situations. None of the drivers was ready to compromise.

Both lorry drivers began to run parallel on the curve road. All the passengers, who were all combatants, were extremely horrified because it was really very risky. Soon the lorry driver tried to apply the brakes, to turn the lorry aside at a juncture. It was too late. Within seconds, I saw the clutch wire break and the vehicle went out of the driver's control, while between the other lorry and the bush trees. The lorry driver tried to overtake other lorry drivers and failed to judge the speed of the other lorry drivers. He ran his lorry into a bushy tree and his lorry hit the big tree, from less than 5 seconds before the lorry collision crash accident to the time of impact, smashing it completely.

All of a sudden, I heard a loud noise. I saw a man rolling on the ground. The lorry killed nine combatants who were passengers and injured sixteen combatant passengers on the spot. Their pathetic cries went up in the air. I, along with other combatants, rushed to the spot. The combatants occupying another lorry, came down faster too and we all rushed them to Torit Hospital. The road accident resulted in the dead bodies of nine combatants buried in Torit Military Cemetery in northwestern Torit town. Those who were passengers with minor injuries, were given first aid and

---

20   The word *Koryom* originated in *Thuongjang* language of ethnic Jieng, which is translated as 'locust' in English. Kuol Manyang Juuk recruited more than 30,000 people from the ethnic Jieng branch of Padang in Bor sections whom he named as *Koryom* Battalion that were trained in military combats in Torit Training Center, where I joined them in May 1991. Kuol Manyang Juuk named *Koryom* II in honor of the first *Koryom* Division, which has been annihilated in battles fought. Unfortunately, the second *Koryom* II got almost annihilated, but a few of us survived the battles fought in Bor and Juba city from March to August 1992.

those with severe born fractures, were operated while others had their limbs amputated. I feel pained whenever I am reminded of the road accidents and the fatal injuries that I have seen. I will never fail to recall the last month of March 1992. It was the month I witnessed a big lorry accident between Bur Base and Torit city.

I will also never fail to recall June 4, 1992, the time I witnessed the second road accident. It was another sad story about Mother '*Koryom*',[21] translated as *meen Koryom* in Thuongjang languages, which was involved in road accident with a full load of heavy ammunitions. I was sitting on assorted weaponries next to my colleagues who were also combatants on top of the Mother '*Koryom*' car. It happened in the middle of narrowed feeder road. The driver tried to apply brakes to turn that old Mother car around, and in few seconds, I saw one passenger flying on air jumping out aimlessly, then, I saw a front clutch broken and a tire running in another direction. The driver ran the car into a bushy forest with tall grass and banked his car in the ditch, it hit big tree, in less than a second, from the time of the Koryom crash to the time of impact, it was smashed completely. The 'Mother *Koryom*' car was loaded with the most explosive bomb shells, ammunitions and big artillery shells which were being urgently rushed to combat zones.

---

21   The name of 'Mother Koryom', which can be translated as 'Men Koryom' in Thuongjang was coined by former Koryom Division combatants who used this pickup car or vehicle first. The name Koryom was first issued to the Division, by Dr. John Garang de Mabior to symbolize locusts - that is, mass movement to conquer and liberate as much as the territories they could seize and capture on their ways from 1985 to 1990. The 'Mother Koryom' car was loaded with the most explosive bomb shells, ammunitions and big artillery shells to urgently rush them to combat zones when it crashed on the roadway on June 1992. Commander Kuol Manyang Juuk was ordered to evacuate Torit city immediately Dr. Garang Mabior, C-In-C of SPLA transferred to me in Torit city to transport first Koryom Division were either killed or disabled in those battles they fought, they are not around any longer and Commander Kuol Manyang Juuk gave Mother Koryom car to me in Torit town on March 27, 1992, when SPLA was ordered to vacate Torit town by to transport assorted ammunitions to Juba operations.

Although I was seated on top of those explosive assorted bombs and big shells, but I survived the deadly bomb shell explosions and from those from assorted dangerous ammunitions. This filled me with great horror, and I remained upset for three weeks. I saw death very close to life at that moment.

Who knows what is in store for me? Or you? Who knows what is going to happen the next moment? Yes. I have survived within flammable bombshells, but what next?

From March 16th 1992 to August 17th in the same year, I was among those Koryom Battalion combatants who were all rushed to the Bright Star Campaign (BSC) and Operation Jungle Storm (OJS) to capture Juba city from June 6, 1992 to December 1992[22]. During that time, I witnessed a car accident; a lorry colliding; and lorry crashing with over 40 passengers per lorry on their way to combat zones in militarized operations through Lobonok, Loboju crossing Nile River to western bank, and Kaya River bank, leading to full combat action, when wounded combatants were transported to the dressing place under-trees and in Kajokeji Hospital.

These road head-on collisions are some of the most devastating and potentially fatal types of violent accidents. We battling combatants knew all too well, for fatal cases were brought to Kajokeji Hospital, where I was taken after the transport lorries were destroyed by anti-landmines near the target around the city of Juba. The infectious diseases causing the greatest havoc at that time included schistosomiasis known as bilharzia parasite, malaria parasites, terrifying fevers, and tuberculosis. These diseases affected the battling combatants living in bushes around the cities of Kapoeta, Torit, Magwi, Pageri, Nimule, Yei, Yambio, Maridi, Mundiri, Kaya, Kajokeji, as well as Juba in targeted areas. Tales about the violent deaths at battles fought, fatal accident deaths at roadways and who had

---

22   Madhel Malek Agei was transferred to the Hospital in Kajokeji with wounded combatants under orders from Dr. John Garang de Mabior, C-In-C of the SPLA in August 1992. More than 3,000 wounded combatants were receiving medical treatment under Dr. Nathaniel Atem.

died as a result of it, circulated among us as combatants as we traded our pain and mourning by not saying names of colleagues we lost.

Together with jet air raids, chopper gunship air searches, deadly raids, anti-landmine and anti-personal mines, roadway accidents signaled that death crept around close by. We made injuries and violent accident jokes about the mode of foot, transport, mode of systematized carriages and car collision fatal deaths to hide our horror and panic.

What I saw in Kajokeji Hospital boiled the blood inside me and sent shivers down my spine. It filled me with great shock to see 3,000 combatants hospitalized with multiple injuries, broken limbs, amputated limbs, and damaged spinal columns. I saw death very close to life at that moment. Even today, I get distressed recalling it. It is still fresh in my mind.

My life was similar to a bubble in a stream, similar to the teardrop - it falls in sorrows and disappears in the celebrations. No one knows what the future holds for me. No one knows what is going to happen in the next second. I had never experienced such a heartbreaking sight in my life.

Such accidents were all caused by the carelessness of our car drivers, our lorry drivers and their ignorance and negligence of the basic road rules. I was compelled to think how hazardous lorry collision and lorry crash accident had become for all vehicle drivers, including those driving lorries for combatants in the bushy narrow roads and feeder roads in combat zones.

I want to emphasise that it does not seem culturally acceptable to be enjoying a social happiness while people are in mourning for the tragic accident that happened to a loved one so instantly. Academics have attempted to describe that culture is not static or cast in stone. According to them, culture changes and people begin to ascribe a meaning to culture that most likely is different from what other people may think it is[23].

The blood life compensation, payable in blood life wealth in cattle

23   Mndende, N. (2009, 19 January). Principal turns a beady eye on boy's tradition. In K. van Rooyen, Culture Shock. The Times. Retrieved, May, 19, 2009 from http://www. thetimes.co.za.

equivalent prices, is collected by the surviving members or victimized persons. It is considered by many in the community as comfort and support to the victimized persons and bereaved families to help those surviving to cope with the impact of loss life of a loved one. It is also considered as repentance on the behalf of the guilty and wrong doers. Many view blood life wealth as a way to strengthen forgiveness, reconciliation, healing and to console the bereaved survivors of the family. The problem seems to be that road accident deaths, cultural rituals, mourning and ceremonial grief, are displayed immediately after the burial of a loved one. It is customary for the bereaved Azande of ethnic Bantu families and the bereaved Apuk branch Jieng of ethnic Nilotic families to continue to grieve for a culturally stipulated period of time. The sharp cultural emotional contrast seems to be of core concern to those who still hold traditional mourning practices with high regard.

Aims and Objectives
Aims of the Study
The study aims to understand the perceptions of the people living in rural Apuk communities and to explore their psychological needs in connection to road accidents. This includes how they happen and mourning the dead in modern rural environments as opposed to traditional Apuk settings.

Objectives of the Study
The objectives of the study are/include:
1. To explore the experiences of the rural Apuk people in the occurrence of the road accidents and blood life compensation after road accident fatalities.
2. To understand the road accidents, how they happen and meaning attached to blood wealth compensation payable in cattle equivalent prices in monetary finance.
3. To explore the feelings of people about the cultural effects of road accident deaths on the mourners and how to prevent road accidents.
4. To understand cultural differences in legal compensation claims on

loss blood life, the life of the pedestrians involved in road accidents through customary law hearings and access protection insurance.

Research Questions

The research questions include:

1. What are the experiences of Jieng rural people and perceptions about the blood life compensation after road accident fatality penalties?
2. What are the causes of road traffic accidents and what can be done to prevent or stop them from occurring or minimize occurrences?
3. What is the meaning of the blood wealth compensation penalty to the survivors or grieving and to those guilty families and those who offer support to the bereaved?
4. How do the Azande and Apuk clan people feel about the blood wealth in diverse cultures with different interpretations?

Significance of the Study

There seems to be limited road accident literature that focuses specifically on the changing nature of customary law, blood life compensation through judicial processes after the road accident, and mourning rituals. Contemporary compensation claims on loss of life and burials are approached differently when compared to past traditional blood life compensation, burials and mourning practices. From this perspective, it is imperative to understand how cultural practices evolve parallel to culture, values and traditional beliefs. This includes the way people view road accidents occurrence, grief, bereavement and mourning in this century. South Sudan has yet to come to grips with the varieties of cultural differences, expressions, and those that maintain some form of distinctiveness and group identity. The book hopes to contribute to add to the dynamic nature of cultural practices in the field of blood life wealth compensation after consequences of road accidents, death, and mourning rituals. This book also hopes to break new ground in searching for meaning where road traffic accidents promoting blood life wealth compensation emerge, especially in traditional customs and practices which have not been documented in the formal academic literature. The book will lay a base for future research on the needs of the people living in cities and in different cultural environments, in the process of blood wealth compensation after the road accident fatalities, burial of the dead ones, bereavement and mourning the loss of a loved one.

It is not my purpose in this book to be academic or philosophical about road accidents, compensation involvement in different cultures and relevant concerns, but to write the facts as they were, be they good, unpleasant or difficult.

The title of the book suggests that the journey I travelled in my life-time was extraordinary, difficult, and unpredictable. To have grown up and escaped from death, from the colonial enemy, and witnessed death of my beloved colleagues in horrific collisions. This happened because of the diabolical and barbaric treatment which happened to myself at a young age, which I was subjected to by the Sudanese and Islamic regime. I have fought for the independence of the motherland and finally to have returned alive to my country where I am now investigating roadway accidents involving children, and pedestrians who are road users in the manner I am doing now, was indeed equivalent to coming back to enjoy my normal life in my beloved Apuk Lith home village my country, South Sudan, that was distinct from the old Sudan I left before.

Experiences to be Learnt from this Brief Historical Narration

South Sudanese people should continually be vigilant and not allow their cultural differences, external enemies and unpatriotic seeds or amounts or rudiments to manipulate them.

Division amongst us as a people of this South Sudan can be dangerous and have negative consequences for this nation. The interest of South Sudan culture and its people who are proud about their roots and cultural values as a whole, is of paramount priority. United and vigilant, we as South Sudanese people must never allow ourselves to fall into the situation in which our ancestors found themselves. The dichotomy and illegal separation based on cultural identity or ethnic clan class and subclass, which was introduced by successive Turkish and Arab Islamic colonial arrangements give the impression to be persisting unabated in the minds of a few individual people of beloved South Sudan. Although there is no legal basis for it, in the long term, this will have disastrous and catastrophic consequences to the maintenance of peace and stability of this country. Therefore, it is high time for those who are still suffering from this cultural differences and ethnic clannish scourge to accept the positive judicial change that will popularly promote blood life wealth compensation and will unite all cultures with diverse citizens of this country. These should be the experiences in educations for generations to come.

Chapter Layout

Chapter one of this book presented the motivation for writing this book. It discussed the background of the book, motivation to write this book, the problem statement, investigation aim and objectives, questions and the significance of the book.

CHAPTER TWO

BACKGROUND INFORMATION

Introduction

According to academia, mourning the death of a loved one, whether he or she died by road accident, natural disaster, or violent the solidarity and service which follows is a global human experience. Like any other significant life transitions, following the death of a loved one, the bereaved clansmen and clanswomen need to adjust and go back to normal life. Most cultures have prescribed bereavement, burial and mourning rituals to accelerate adjustment of the bereaved. The current chapter will mainly be on the fatal road accidents as they are understood globally and fulfillment of bereavement and rituals among traditional rural Apuk branch of Rek ethnic Jieng and city communities of South Sudan. A particular focus will be on the changes observed in blood wealth compensations, and the cause or way these accident fatalities on roadways and mourning rituals are currently fulfilled in city and rural communities of South Sudan.

Grief is not comfortable. It does not only demand time but an environment that will allow the person to readjust at his/her own pace. Certain bereavement rituals that have been fulfilled in the past seem to have diminished in many township and city environments[24] around this coun-

---

24   Kilonzo, G. P. & Hogan, N. M. (1999). Traditional African mourning rituals are abridged in response to the AIDS epidemic: Implications for mental health. *Transcultural Psychiatry* 36(3), 259-283.

try. Some communities among ethnic Jieng, Nuer, Azande, Nilo-Hamitic and Afro-Asiatic families have been forced to forgo some of the mourning rituals and adapted Arabic ones from Islamic culture.

For example, the first Arabic speaking indigenous were Muslim Balanda Bviri of ethnic Bantu living in Deim Zubeir slavery camp. But the recent Arabic speaking people are Muslim Falata communities living in Wau townships and newly forming Afro Asiatic classes seen in other living environments. People deal with one death after another within a quick space of time as a result of Ebola, violent conflict, road traffic fatalities and collision crashes. There have been several deaths on anti-landmines and anti-personal mines on public land transport as well as HIV/AIDS and other life-threatening diseases, suicides, traumatic accidents, violent raids, fire-arms and gunshots. This could impact on the effective fulfillment of proper traditional death rituals.

Societies have moved in periods of political, economic, cultural and other forms of evolution for the duration of the past centuries and this still continues in current times.

In the past, many Nilotic and Bantu peoples migrated away from traditional environments in the rural villages mainly for economic reasons. These ethnic classes of people were forced, by the fear of violent slave raiding, to relocate elsewhere - and more were forcefully relocated by the Anglo Egyptian Sudan colonial government to slum settlement townships that were grounded for Arabization and Islamization and that became a home for the majority of indigenous Nilotic and Bantu classes, converted into different 'new groups' of Central Sudanic[25] ethnic classes of peoples[26], and Afro-Asiatic ethnic classes of peoples[27].

---

25   Westermann, Diedrich, 1922a. Die Sprache der Guang. Berlin: Dietrich Reimer.

26   Encyclopedia Britannica, Inc.

27   Evidence against the "early split" scenario shown here is presented in E. Patin et al., "Dispersals and genetic adaptation of Bantu-speaking populations in Africa and North America", Science, Vol. 356, Issue 6337, pp. 543-546 (5 May 2017), doi:10.1126/science. aal1988.

As a result, they found themselves in confused and isolated environments that were somehow not conducive for them to continue with their traditional rural lifestyles and existences. Among these included carrying out of various burial mourning rituals, ceremonies and practices which have a special meaning for people of South Sudan. New lifestyles and or existences were soon adopted, some of the traditional practices were adapted, such as Islamic and Christianity cultures and beliefs and others completely abandoned. For a person who grew up in the rural homesteads, it becomes a shock to realize the different lifestyle and existence that the people who live in the cities around the country have adopted.

This chapter will explore the occurrence of blood life wealth compensation claim which has become part of the road traffic accident death practices fulfilled after a loved one has died in a traffic accident, in a good number of cities and newly created towns.

Roadway Accident Fatalities

Roadway accident fatalities that are leading in the risk factor of death by injury worldwide and now make up a surprisingly significant portion of the global burden of ill health.

Millions of people are reported killed in road traffic crashes on many roadways every year, and millions more are injured, capturing nearly thirty percent to seventy percent of admission beds (orthopedic) in many hospitals[28] in developing countries including South Sudan. If present trends continue, road traffic accident injuries and related fatalities are predicted to increase, becoming the major leading contributor to the global burden of disease and injury[29] in coming years.

---

28   Dinesh Mohan, "Road Safety in Less-Motorized Environments: Future Concern," International Journal of Epidemiology 31, No. 3 (2202): 527-32.

29   Christopher J.L. Murray and Alan D. Lopez, eds., The Global Burden of Disease: A Comprehensive Assessment of Mortality and Disability from Diseases, Injuries, and Risk Factors in 1990 and Projected in 2020 (Boston: Harvard School of Public Health, 1996).

www.ingramcontent.com/pod-product-compliance
Lightning Source LLC
Chambersburg PA
CBHW021850020426
42334CB00013B/266

CRITICAL STUDIES IN ITALIAN AMERICA

series editors: *Nancy C. Carnevale and Laura E. Ruberto*

Joseph Sciorra, ed., *Italian Folk: Vernacular Culture in Italian-American Lives*

Loretta Baldassar and Donna R. Gabaccia, eds., *Intimacy and Italian Migration: Gender and Domestic Lives in a Mobile World*

Simone Cinotto, ed., *Making Italian America: Consumer Culture and the Production of Ethnic Identities*

Luisa Del Giudice, ed., *Sabato Rodia's Towers in Watts: Art, Migrations, Development*

Over one thousand road traffic motor vehicle accident fatalities were reviewed and evaluated[30]. Victims of road traffic accident fatalities comprised motor vehicle passengers, pedestrians, cyclists and motorcycle pillion riders, commonly call *boda boda* riders in South Sudan. The hospital disposition of outpatients and emergency department patients was consistent with road traffic accident severity. For serious road traffic accident fatalities, pedestrians accounted for nearly 20 % to 50% of presentations. Inclusive use of restraints was worryingly low. Not using seatbelts increased the risk of road accident fatalities by five times.

South Sudan bears a large share of the burden among the developing countries, accounting for the highest percentages to nearly eighty-five percent of annual deaths and ninety percent of the disability-adjusted life years lost because of rapid road accident injury[31].

In addition, car road accident injury fatalities affect mainly males which account for seventy percent to eighty percent of accidental deaths. Children are also involved in roadway accidents and other automobile roadway accident-related killings. More than one-half of all automobile accidents kill infants, children and young people up to the age of 35. This happens especially in new township roadways, in new rural roadways, in new road highways, in new city roads, and this burden is creating enormous economic hardship due to the loss of family main source of income. This group are considered to be at their most productive earning

---

30   Juba Teaching Hospital Medical personnel reported partial information about boda boda riders and vehicles accidents between 2007 and 2011, when they were contacted by Madhel Agei. Many medical personnel refused to share information. Few cooperate without disclosing data recorded about outpatients and in-patient affected by accidents in specific period asked. There was no time to reach Torit Hospital at time of writing (2019).

31   One DAILY is roughly equivalent to one healthy year of life lost. For more on the traffic-injury burden, see World Health Organization (WHO) and World Bank, "World Report on Road Traffic Injury Prevent," accessed online at www.who.int, on Feb. 6, 2006.

ages[32]. Each year, almost two hundred children are injured in automobile accidents or crashes, meaning nearly one to three children are harmed every day. Automobile accidents are the leading cause of acquired disability nationwide.

According to the World Health Organization (WHO), in 2015, road injuries were the leading cause of adolescent death among 10–19-year-olds, resulting in about tens of thousands of adolescent deaths, with older adolescent boys aged 15–19 years suffering the greatest burden. Researchers said drivers who are intoxicated from alcohol or drugs can cause accidents with motorcycles *or boda boda* riders and motor vehicles.

Moreover, the disability burden for this age group accounts for 60 percent of all affected by accidents, caused by *boda boda* riders and vehicle users. The costs and effects of these losses are sizeable. Two thirds of all poor families who lost a member of family victim to car collision crash from road death or road traffic death reported a decrease in their standard of living, and 61 percent reported they had to have a loan of money to cover expenses following their loss[33].

The new global survey finds that roadway deaths continued to increase in 2017, reaching an alarming rate[34]. Road collision crash fatalities are now the leading killer of children and young adults, the report of WHO and UNICEF indicates. The risk of road traffic death remains three times higher in third world countries, especially in those poor countries with low-income[35].

Causes of Road Accidents

Distracted driving is a greater threat every year and has been the leading

---

32   Ibid.

33   Babtie Ross Silcok, *Guidelines for Estimating the Costs of Road Crashes in Developing Countries.* (London: U.K. Department for International Development, 2003).

34   World Health Organization (WHO) and United Nations Children Fund (UNICEF) report

35   WHO and UNICEF report

cause of car accidents for the past decade. Drink driving, speeding, reckless driving, rain-water overflow, running through red lights, driving at night, road design, and general defects were identified factors responsible for causes of car accidents.

Motor collision crash victims reports, hospital statistics, and preliminary investigations indicated that speeding, lane indiscipline, reckless driving and driving under the influence of alcohol and other substances are the main causes of motor accidents and/or lorry accident crash collisions.

Substances like drugs and alcohol significantly compromise a driver's responses and reaction time. According to researchers intoxicated drivers do not accurately judge distance or speed and may nod off behind the wheel. The main cause of motor accidents are bad weather conditions. Bad weather can cause bad visibility or cause bad traction for the driver driving the motorcycle *or boda boda*, as well as vehicles on the road surface. This can in turn lead to motors or cars colliding with each other or objects such as trees. Rain, mud, high winds, and bewilder can affect a driver's ability to see ahead, to stop in time, to stay within the lane. For example, flash rain-water overflow can lead to accidents as often it is too late to detect it until it has affected you.

The largest cause of accidents currently, is driver error. These range from following vehicles or motors too closely, falling asleep at the wheel, driving too fast, unsafe overtaking and many other careless and unnecessary mistakes. This is linked to driver error; however, it is more about the driver being distracted by something outside or inside the vehicle. Scores of *boda boda* rider accidents and motor accidents are caused by drivers actually being distracted by another motor accident happening on the road. Cell mobile phone usage, eating, putting on makeup, listening to loud music, talking with passengers, looking into the back seat to check on your children, and looking away from the road are frequent causes of accidents. Whatever makes driver takes his or her eyes off the motor wheel on the road, may likely create a disastrous situation.

Motor and *boda boda* riding accidents are at times caused by bad road design. That is when a part of the road highway and roadway or road traffic control has been poorly placed or designed. These can lead to increased motor accidents in the cities and highways. This can be anything from poorly placed signs blocking driver view of incoming road traffic, or dangerous turnings off intersections of busy roadways or highways. At times, motor accidents caused by poor roadway or highway design will mean that the government or council will then be accused of negligence. At times an accident will be caused by a defect in the vehicle. Such defects can be anything from brake failure to a tire bursting. That defect can cause an accident for the driver driving on the road surface in the area. But at times, these defects will cause several damages in a car accident. For instance, some motors, or cars or *boda boda* will have defective airbags which do not deploy correctly, meaning people involved in motor or car and *boda boda* accidents might suffer worse injuries.

Today, in South Sudan, exposure to potential leading motor accident deaths, road traffic injury and disability caused by automobile accident has dramatically increased largely because of rapid motorization, coupled with poor road conditions. Due in large part to rapid urbanization growth, rapid rural migration growth, rapid population growth. This causes a lack of road safety features in cars as well as crowded roads, poor road maintenance, and lack of traffic police and highway road patrol police enforcement. A good example is that the number of motorcycles grew by approximately 57 percent in 2008, with a linked increase of approximately 62 percent in the number of road traffic deaths, recorded in Juba Teaching Hospital Wards for Senke boda-*boda* riders, in Torit Hospital, and in Wau Teaching Hospital.

Statistical data available in all these hospitals South Sudanese states has not been made public to show people the alarmingly high proportion of road users killed in road traffic accident fatalities. For this reason, I have chosen to focus this book on blood compensation, using the example of a sad story of a boychild, who died in violent collision crash caused by the driver of a Landcruiser, in rural roadway traffic in Pathuon Apuk.

Modes of Transportation

This section focusses on public modes of transport, land transport and road accident fatalities on land transport.

The different three modes of transport are air, water, and land transport. These include rails transport, roads transport, air transport, and water transport. Additional modes of transport also are pipeline transport, cable transport, and space transport.

The Definition of 'Mode of Transportation'

The mode of transport is used to define the different types of transportation systems used to take goods or peoples from one place to another.

Transport modes are the means by which passengers and freight, cargo or goods achieve mobility. They are mobile transport assets and fall into three basic types; namely: land transport (road transport, rail transport, and pipelines transport); water transport (shipping); and air transport (flying).

Prior to every other mode of transportation, individuals traveled on foot, starting from *homo sapiens* to the present people. Can you imagine walking from Jak Holy Shrine Temple of Apuk Malek in southwestern Rek to Apuk Giir or to Twic Bol Nyuol (Twic Mayardit) in the northwestern Rek, up to Malual Rek in northwestern Rek?

Land transport describes transport by road, highways and rural highways; by rail and railways; by pipelines; and feeder road transport.

Road transport refers to the transportation of goods and people from one place to the other on rural roads or roads. A road is a dual carriageway or route connecting two destinations, which has been either surfaced, smoothed or paved to enable transportation by mode of systematized and non-systematized carriages. There are many rewards to road transport in contrast to other modes of transport. For example, the investment demanded in road transport is a smaller amount compared to other modes of transport such as railways transport. The cost of building, operating and maintaining roads is cheaper than that of railway transport.

Road transport is for transporting goods and materials or transporting people. The foremost benefit of road transport is that it can enable door-to-door delivery of hulking goods and can provide a very cost-effective means of cartage, loading and unloading. Sometimes, road transport is the only way for carrying properties and people to and from rural areas which are not catered to by rail, water or air transport. Delivery of goods and chattels between cities, towns and small remote villages is made possible only through rural road transport or rural feeder road transport.

In spite of various merits, road transport also has major drawbacks. For example, there are additional risks of accidents and breakdowns in situation of road transport. Therefore, motorized or automobile transport is not as safe as other modes of transport. Road transport is likewise, quite less systematized compared with other modes. It is irregular and undependable. Rates for road transportation are moreover unstable and unequal, while the speed in road transport is slow and limited, which is a major stumbling block. Transporting properties or hulking goods and chattels on long distances is also unsuitable and expensive.

In modern days, road transport has a serious negative impact on the environment. Building roads needs melting of asphalt or tarmac, or pitch or formulation of concrete, which may harm the connected environment. Since roads have been a fundamental enabler of systematized transportation mode, these vehicles also emit a lot of pollution such as explosive organic compounds, carbon monoxide and countless harmful air pollutants, containing benzene, with adverse respiratory health effects and a severe threat to global warming impact. Road transport of the future aims to address and improve on these issues.

Definition of 'Road Accidents'
A **road accident** may be defined as any accident where at least one road car or motorist (*boda boda* rider) is on a road open to public rotation or movement, and in which at least a person or an animal is injured or lost. Intentional acts such as a victim being shot dead, plane bombings, planned murder, suicides, euthanasia and natural disasters are excluded.

A **car accident** is also described as an undesirable or unfortunate happening that occurs unintentionally and frequently results in harm, injury, damage, fatality, or mishap. It is an unwanted event, which often could have been prevented had conditions leading up to the accident been recognized, and resolved, prior to its occurrence. Most researchers who study accidental injury avoid using the term "accident" and focus on factors that increase risk of severe injury and that reduce injury incidence and severity[36]. This is the main reason for the under-reporting of deaths - because of the very narrow definition of death by *road accident* being used.

An **accident**, also known as a "traffic collision or crash, collision crash", a "motor vehicle **accident**," an "automobile accident, a "car crash" or an "automobile crash", happens when a motor vehicle collides with another motor vehicle, a stationary object, a pedestrian, an animal, road debris, or other stationary obstruction, such as a tree, pole or building.

Road traffic collision crashes or accidents often result in fatality or injury, disability, death, and property damage as well as financial costs to both society and the individuals involved.

Mourning the Dead after Death on Roadway Accidents

Mourning the dead is a universal practice which is mediated by religious practices in cities and cultural practices in different societies. When a death, has occurred, there are certain cultural behaviors and sacrificial rituals to fulfil, such as what to wear, who is to speak to the bereaved, how feelings should be dealt with and what should be done to symbolize the separation of the deceased from the people who are left behind[37]. Customary and specified strict sacrificial rituals exist in every clan and subclan determining for everyone the appropriate traditional behavior in the face of death in South Sudan.

36   Robertson, Leon S. (2015). *Injury Epidemiology: Fourth Edition.* Lulu Books.

37   Parkes, C. M., Laungani, P. & Young, B. (Eds.) (1997). *Death and bereavement across cultures.* London: Routledge.

In many societies in South Sudan and in Africa at large, thorough care is taken to fulfill the burial sacrifice ceremonies in order to avoid causing any offence to the departed also called the ancestors[38], ancestry spirits, or the 'life spirit' or the 'living dead'.

For instance, often there is a burial ritual sacrificial animal, which is meant to be a public or a community symbol that a death has occurred. There are also cleansing ceremonies and sacrificial rituals like *'apeek'*, which is a separation of life spirit of the dead, from evil spirit that caused death, which then returns home to join the surviving clan family members. There is also a memorial service, performed to renew the 'role spirit' of the deceased person, so as to participate invisibility through its life spirit in the family affairs, as well as to complete the process of accepting the status of the deceased among the remaining members of the family, in accordance to custom which is universal in South Sudan.

---

38   Mbiti, J. S. (1975). *Introduction to African Religion*. South Africa; Heinemann International Literature & Textbooks.

CHAPTER THREE

KEY CONCEPTS
RELATED TO BLOOD LIFE

Definition of Concepts

The word *apuk*, 'bloodwealth', 'bloodlife', 'compensation', 'legal', 'justice' 'grief', 'bereavement', 'mourning', 'legal diversity/pluralism', 'violent' and 'customary' are all important considerations, in light of the context of this book.

Although there are differences in the formal definitions, they overlap in meaning and they are often used interchangeably in the literature and in ethnic Nilotic Jieng language[39]. Below I have attempted to set out the most commonly understood definitions.

Definition of *Apuk*

The word *apuk* originated from a punishment or compensation penalty blood fine[40]. According to the ethnic Jieng (Dinka)-English Dictionary, *apuk* is defined as a punishment or a penalty blood fine for killing, or severe wounds inflicted with the full knowledge and intent of the actors.

---

39   Castle, J., & Phillips, W. I. (2003). Grief rituals: aspects that facilitates adjustment to bereavement. *Journal of Loss and Trauma*, 8, 41-71.

40   Agei, Madhel Malek, (2020). Apuk a State in Waiting, Africa World Book Pty Ltd, Australia, Pages 79-98.

Although *apuk* is just one word, it conveys an entire concept. Loosely, it is the method whereby homicides or severe violations committed by clansmen or clanswomen are resolved and ultimately forgiven. The Jieng language definition explains *apuk* as a punishment for killing, or for inflicting severe wounds executed with the full knowledge and understanding of those actions by the clansmen or clanswomen found guilty. It is a compensation payable to the living spirit of the victim, as well as to the family or party of the blood spirit. *Apuk* should also include the living blood of cattle and ritual recitation of prayers through Master of the Fishing Spear.

An *Apuk* perpetrator and his or her clan must pay compensation of collective responsibility to the affected party or person. All clans believe in *apuk* of clan offences payable for lost blood, for blood is life itself and it curses offenders.

According to Madhel Malek Agei, the origin of *apuk* traces 'to realistic peace' based on the use of deity and sacrifice, as well as persuasion by compensation, reparation, reconciliation, and forgiveness.

The term *apuk* itself turned out as a "name" for great nation-state. There is Southern Apuk (Apuk Juwiir) in the southwest and Northeastern Apuk Padoch in the northeast. As well as this, there is the Northern Apuk (Apuk Giir) in the north of Rek branch Jieng of the ethnic Nilotic classes of peoples. *Jieng* is often falsely translated as *Dinka* in foreign languages. The word "Dinka" was coined by foreigners who first travelled to the land of ethnic *Jieng* or *Jaang*.

Apuk as collective responsibility is an expression of the overwhelming solidarity of the entire community. It is the principle of assigning responsibility in a broad sense. The person is allowed to appear in court accompanied by the clan family. If found guilty, the courts determine collective responsibility. The payment of bloodwealth or blood life wealth compensation, known by the term *apuk dhieeth* or *apuk dhiendu,* translated as collective responsibility payment, depends upon the belief and values of that particular clan, affected by the injury or loss. It may be settled in cattle, livestock and/or currency.

The overall bloodwealth in *apuk* price is shared proportionally between those deemed by the courts to have blood relations to thusly take upon collective responsibility for the act. Systems exist traditionally to assess clan bloodwealth compensation payable in collective contribution divided among immediate clan family members responsible for the actor in crimes.

Bloodwealth

Bloodwealth is defined as a certain number of cows, goats, sheep and monetary amount collected by the guilty family member or members to pay for the life lost or injury blood to forgive and reverse curses.

The thirty-one cows paid for *apuk* to the deceased person are called "thirty-one cows of blood" or "spirit body", which is translated as 'blood wealth' in *thuongjang or thongmuonyjam. Wong riem is the singular which is translated as* 'cow of blood' and *hook riem* is the plural which is translated as 'cows of blood', 'blood cows' or 'blood life cows'.

Blood is considered dead however its spirit life does not die instead living on with clan family members. The physical body is believed dead while the ancestor remains in the living world of spirit. Offering sacrifice is the challenge through which living spirits communicate with clan family members on earth. The life spirit of the dead is considered dangerous, especially when family members cannot offer it a slaughtered cow, goat, sheep or white chicken. The invisible evil spirit follows the spirits of ancestors in the world of spirits and may be offered black chicken to be slaughtered at night in the forest or behind the house, (but not under a shrine erected at the middle for the guiding spirit).

Bloodwealth is mainly *apuk riem* and the price as compensation that is issued in cattle and may range from one to more than thirty cows. The person who is injured or killed brings the blood price, and this price connotes some form of bloodwealth *apuk* in compensation payment as agree upon between two parties.

'Blood wealth' is also translated as 'the deceased price' or *apuk ran cithou or apuk ran cinok* in cattle price and in accordance to according to injury or death caused by accident (which maybe a road accident).

Spiritual Wealth

Spiritual wealth is defined as a cultural gift to a Master of the Fishing Spear in cattle, goats, sheep and/or money. Spiritual wealth is a conceived deterrent for other offences that might occur. Spiritual wealth is a fee that will forgive people found guilty of deliberate defamation or damage from offence crimes in sacred blood feuds, divine crimes, and divine disputes.

The Master of the Fishing Spear invokes the clan *jak, jaak, jok, yath*, and *atiep*, which are translated in English as the "clan spirit" to offer a ritual sacrifice of an animal. This is done on behalf of a clan member paying that gift or fee, which has been described as 'spiritual wealth' or 'divine wealth' in the original *thuongjang or thongmuonyjaang* of the Nilotic Jieng family classes of peoples.

Spear Masters or the High Priests of Deities should not have any blood relationship to the victims benefiting from the award of *apuk* and should not be related to the guilty. Libations are poured on the many decorated tethering pegs in surrounding shrines. A white cow or sheep should be sacrificially slaughtered by spiritual priests who shall shed ritual blood. This blood is to be poured down on the soil of the ancestorial land, as an offer to ancestry spirits to wash away sin, evil spirits, and criminal acts. This action is also done to curse or punish devil spirits that falsely cause a person to do wrong or to commit criminal acts.

The purpose of the gift or fee collected by the divine wealth is to reinforce high priest payer, preserve social cohesion and to allow for forgiveness, peace and harmony. This establishes the ability for people to return to normalcy and coexistence again.

Divine Wealth

Divine wealth is defined as an *apuk,* which is translated as compensation to a clan spiritual priest. Divine wealth ranges in accordance with a retaliatory penalty for a specific spiritual crime and the circumstances to a victim, party or family. The divine wealth is an *Apuk Jok* or *Apuk Yath* or *Apuk Atiip,* or ancestry spirit, which can also be translated as 'divine wealth', similar to that of 'spiritual wealth'.

Definition of 'Blood'

The concept of 'blood' does not have one agreed definition but can be understood in multiple ways. Scientists describe blood as a body fluid[41] in human and other animals. Blood is a vital liquid flowing and constantly circulating fluid in the bodies of many types of animals providing nutrients, oxygen and waste removal from those same cells[42]. It is mostly liquid, with numerous cells and nutrients suspended in it, making blood "thicker than water".

Blood has been described as a transport liquid pumped by the heart, or an equivalent, to all parts of the body, after which it is returned to the heart to repeat the process. If blood flow ceases, death will occur within minutes because of the effects of an unfavorable environment on highly susceptible cells. As it contains living cells, blood is alive.

Blood is used in hereditary circles to refers to one's ancestry, origins, and ethnic background as in the word 'bloodline'. Other terms where blood is used in family history sense are blue-blood, royal blood, mixed-blood and blood relative.

However, 'lifeblood' refers to an essential life-giving influence or factor. Broadly, 'lifeblood' may be explained as a nuclear family relationship by birth, identical to that between siblings, differentiated by relationships due to marriage or adoption, blood relative, blood relation by blood etc. 'Blood brothers' refers to a clan relationship, which is to bring about alliance between clans and subclans. There has been oath of blood brotherhood in the past[43].

---

41   Rogers, Kara, Encyclopedia Britannica Editor.

42   "Definition of Blood" Archived from the original on 23 March 2017. Retrieved 4 March 2017

43   Elert G (2012). *"Volume of Blood in a Human"*. *The Physics Factbook*. Archived from the original on 3 November 2012. Retrieved 2012-11-01.

Definition of 'Life and Death'

The definition of life has long been a challenge for scientists and philoso-phers, with many definitions put forward.[44] This is because life is process, not a substance.[45] There are many types of life that exist, from plants, animals, fungi, to protists, and bacteria. In this book, I am exploring environmental knowledge by concentrating on the investigation of life, blood, death, compensation, mourning and sacrifice rituals.

Philosophical definitions of life have also been put forward, with simi-lar difficulties on how to distinguish living things from non-living[46].

Life may be defined as a quality that distinguishes physical bodies that have life processes, such as signaling and self-sufficient processes, from those that do not. Either because such functions have ceased because they have died, or because they never had such functions and are classified as dead, lifeless or spiritless[47].

Personal life can be explained as a course of state of an individual's life, especially when viewed as a sum of personal choices controlling one's personal identity.

Everyday life, daily life, or routine life comprises the ways in which people typically act, think, and feel on a daily basis. Everyday life maybe described as boring, routine, natural, habitual, or normal. Everyday life is a key concept in cultural investigations and is as a specialized focus in the arena of sociology.

Life can be defined as an existence of an individual human being or

44   Emmeche, Claus (1997), *"Defining life, Explaining Emergence,* Neils Bohr Institute. Archived from the original, on 14 March 2012. Retrieved 25 May 2012.

45   Mautner, Michael N. (2000). *Seeding the Universe with Life: Securing our Cosmological Future* (PDF). Washington D.C. ISBN 978-0.476-0033-9.

46   Jeuken M.(1975). *"The biological and philosophical definitions of LIFE".* Acta Biotheretica, 24 (1-2): 14-21. Dio::10.1007/bf01556737.PMID 8110224. S2CID:44573374

47   Baker, Maureen (2010). *Choice and consraints in family life (2 ed.)* Don Mills, Ontario: Oxford University Press. P.1 -ISBN 978-0-19-543159-9.

animal. Life is also defined as a period between the birth and death of a living thing, especially a human being. The real logic or sense of life is to fulfill a purpose in life and accomplish that goal. I am saying so because everyone has a purpose, and he or she is living. There shall be nobody among us who will be here if we all did not have a purpose. Life is carrying eminent influence or authority, according to many people, but its value is generated by us in our minds, and subject to change over time. It must be argued that meaning is essentially, a logic of worth which we may all derive in a different way, from relationships, creativity, accomplishment in a given field, or generosity, among other possibilities. All life characteristics have one fundamental purpose: survival.

Death is the permanent, irreversible cessation of all life functions that sustain a living body[48]. The remains of a previously living creature or animal normally begin to decompose shortly after death.[49] Death is an inevitable, universal process that eventually occurs in all living creatures. Death is the permanent termination of all life or living processes which sustain a physical body, and as such, is the end of its life.

Definition of 'Grief'

Grief is defined as intense emotional response associated with the loss life of a significant person, often precipitated by the death of a loved one[50]. Grief is the individual's personal response to loss life and has emotional[51], physical, behavioral, cognitive, social, cultural and spiritual dimensions[52].

---

48   *"The definition of death"*, Dictionary.com. Retrieved 13 April 2018.

49   "carbonQ1" Reptools.rutgers.edu. Archived from the original, on 24 March 2018. Retrieved 4 March 2018.

50   Rosenblatt, P. C., Walsh, R. P. & Jackson, D. A. (1976). *Grief and mourning in cross-cultural perspective.* New Haven, Connecticut: Human Relations Area Files Press.

51   Hartshone, T. S. (2003). Grief and mourning from and Adlerian perspective. *Journal of Individual Psychology,* 59(2), 145-152.Mbizana, C. (2007). Resilience in bereaved Zulu families.

52   Hartshone, T. S. (2003). Grief and mourning from and Adlerian perspective.

Grief is a normal, internalized reaction to the loss of life of a person[53]. The above definitions could mean that grief is a personal reaction and the reactions may not be visible and may also not suggest that the person is sick or weak.

Definitions of 'Mourning Sacrifice Rituals and Cultural Practices'.

The definitions of mourning sacrifice ritual precisely underline the visibility of expression of the grief in cultural practices. It implies that while grief may not be noticeable, mourning sacrifice rituals are visible to all. Some researchers defined **mourning** as the culturally[54] patterned visible expression of the bereaved practice thoughts and feelings[55]. Others defined **mourning sacrifice rituals** as culturally practiced acts usually performed when a death occurs[56]. Some assert that the mourning sacrifice ritual, is a reflection of the social expressions or act expressive of grief shaped by a given society or a cultural group. Mourning sacrifice rituals are also described as cultural practice symbolizing the social prescription for the way in which we are expected to display grief[57].

Furthermore, there are those who have argued that grief maybe a universal emotion of bereavement but its social expression in mourning is culturally specific. Mourning sacrifice rituals also indicate the process of coping with loss and grief.[58] Psychoanalytical approaches have described

---

53   Mbizana, C. (2007). Resilience in bereaved Zulu families. Unpublished Masters Dissertation, University of Zululand, Zululand, South Africa.

54   Sanders, C. M. (1999). *Grief and the mourning after: dealing with adult bereavement* (2nd edn.). Canada: John Wiley & Sons.

55   Kastenbaum, R. J. (2004). *Death, society and human experience* (5th edn.). Boston: Allyn & Bacon.

56   Rosenblatt, P. C., Walsh, R. P. & Jackson, D. A. (1976). *Grief and mourning in cross-cultural perspective.* New Haven, Connecticut: Human Relations Area Files Press.

57   Cook, A. S., & Oltjenbruns, K. (1989). *Dying and grieving: lifespan and family perspectives.* New York: Holt, Rinehart and Winston.

58   Buglass, E. (2010). *Grief and bereavement theories.* Nursing Standard, 24(41), 44-47.

mourning as both the aware and the unaware practice and paths of action promoting the undoing of psychological ties which binds the mourner to the loved one who has passed away.

Other people realize or understand grief and mourning sacrifice rituals as set processes and procedures. Without the experience of grief, the practice of ritual sacrifice and mourning cannot take place. Sometimes grief is seen as the first stage of mourning, and this makes it difficult to disconnect these processes. A number of cultures do not even have equivalent language for the terms of compensation, bloodwealth, spiritual wealth, divine wealth, blood, blood life, grief, ritual sacrifice and mourning.

For example, the definitions of mourning, sacrifice ritual and cultural practice, discussed in this book demonstrate that they are primarily influenced by the social, economic, and cultural practice context in which the person lives. Thus, mourning rituals are not simply a process of reactions in an individual or just an interaction between the person and his or her environment. Mourning is culturally determined, and it ranges from observational outward signs to achievement or fulfillment of certain cultural rituals. The rituals are social remedies that define whatever people do and how they should behave whenever they have experienced the loss of life of an individual. They are believed to fulfill and to do specific functions, like to assist the people acknowledge the life of death and to cope with the loss of life of a loved one[59].

There has been a growing interest of research in the areas of mourning, sacrifice, rituals, and cultural practice over the recent years[60]. Bereavement represents the experiential state or being in a state of mourning that one

---

59   Romanoff, B. D., & Terenzio, M. (1998). *Rituals and the grieving process.* *Death Studies,* 22, 697-711. Cook, A. S., & Oltjenbruns, K. (1989). *Dying and grieving: lifespan and family perspectives.* New York: Holt, Rinehart and Winston.

60   Opperman, B., & Novello, A. (2006). *The generation of hypotheses with regard to the influence of context on complicated grief,* South African Journal of Psychology, 36(2), 374-390.

endures after realizing a loss. Mourning the dead distinguished as a period during which grief and mourning sacrifice rituals for the loved ones occur.

Compensation

The expression blood life wealth compensation is socially and culturally specific. The objectives for this bloodwealth have been described as the restoration of the social equilibrium through payment of damages. For example, under Jieng homicide law this would be achieved through the payment defined as *Dias,* which is translated as *apuk* of 30 cows per deceased person to the survivals of clan family of that person.[61]

Such blood wealth compensation, which is translated as *Dia* in Arabic language, currently being used in both South Sudan and Sudan, is described as money in monetary currency, cattle, goat, or sheep payable to clan victim according to a scale laid down under individual customary law systems. Blood wealth compensation which is also translated as *apuk* in original Rek language spoken widely by Apuk of ethnic Jieng people.

Collective Responsibility

Collective responsibility[62] is defined as committing a killing injury organized and executed with the knowledge of clan family - or an act intended to kill, crash or injure, on behalf of the community and clan family members. The traditional customary law courts working together with traditional chiefs' courts determine the circumstances of the act of road accident fatality, death or murder and make their judgement. This is done to determine if there is collective responsibility for the act and if so, that the perpetrator should not alone have to pay bloodwealth compensation.

According to Apuk branch of Rek Jieng culture, individuals do not

---

61   Wuol Makec, John., *The Customary Law of the Dinka People of Sudan.* Afroworld Publishing Co. 1988. At 198.

62   Agei, Madhel Malek, Apuk a State in Waiting, Africa World Books Publishing Company, Australia, page 93-98

own property. It is, however, owned collectively by the community. Joint ownership of all property, even in the largest clan families, provides security, a sense of ownership and responsibility for all. Clan families will use their property, like cattle herds, in discharging major obligations such as bride-wealth for marriage and Dias for both bloodwealth and related compensation for wrongs done.

Payment may be in multiples of cows, young girls, or money. Wherever an accidental or criminal act has been committed against another party, it is familiar to charge the accused under the South Sudan Penal Code and if found guilty, to award both punishment under the Code and *Dias* or *Apuk* in Bloodwealth Compensation according to the victim's customary lawcourts.

Society's preference for dealing with road accident fatalities, criminal acts, or murders through traditional means of *apuk* bloodwealth, has been an enduring theme in the legal process since colonization and remains so today in South Sudan. This reflects the strength of feeling on the New Sudan Penal Code, 2003, Section 251, which deals with murder and other crimes of homicide including road accidents. The code containing the provision is quoted as saying that the "Provided that if the nearest relatives of the deceased opt for customary law bloodwealth compensation *Dia*, which described *apuk riem*, the court may award it in lieu of death sentence"[63].

The origin for this lies in the belief, culture, norms, values and practices of the peoples of South Sudan that the purpose of any legal action in respect to crime act or accident fatality is to restore the social equilibrium rather than to punish the wrongdoer. "The principle of a life for a life rarely leads to a permanent peace"[64].

Even if the accused person is tried alone, when guilt has been

---

63   Aleu Akechak Jok, Robert A Leitch & Carrie Vandewint, (March 2004). "A *Study of Customary Law in Contemporary Southern Sudan"*, Pages Unpublished Research Paper, Southern Sudan.

64   P.P.Howell, *A Manual of Nuer Law*, Oxford University Press, 1954, p41

ascertained, the courts determine collective responsibility. The amount of bloodwealth compensation in the Apuk community does not change, however, the whole bloodwealth compensation claim is divided between clan family members deemed by the courts as being in part responsible for the act. The clannish court chief is then required to confirm responsibility, inform the relevant clan family members and organize collection.

The aims for apportioning the whole collective responsibility are key to understanding why customary law courts often provide a more socially acceptable means of dealing with violent crimes, for at least the Azande and Apuk communities in South Sudan. The courts and the community recognize that the clan family member was acting as a representation of their community, and therefore in carrying out a crime the clan family, society, or community bear collective responsibility.

Wherever a criminal act or road accident or any harm has been inflicted, the father or maternal uncle shall claim the bloodwealth compensation from guilty clan family members. Liability for the act may fall on some or all, of the guilty clan family party, the kin group of the guilty party, and the guilty clan or tribe or subclan or subtribe party.

Collective responsibility is a vibrant social and cultural practice and a pure recognition of the solidarity of the clan family, community, or society. It demonstrates responsibility and concern a clan family has for the actions of its members.

Definition of 'Security'

Security can be defined as 'freedom from risk or harm resulting from violence, road accident fatalities, or other intentional acts'[65], or as the 'protection of people and their assets from violence or theft' or violent raids[66]. It relates to a reduction in the harm caused by actions intended

---

65   Humanitarian Practice Network (2010), *'Operational security management in violent environments'*, Good Practice Review 8, revised edition, Overseas Development Institute, p xviii.

66   RedR (2008), *Management of Staff Safety Course Manual*

to harm specific people or groups. Included in this are the consequences of those actions, which indirectly cause harm to other people or groups. Healthy judicial systems and healthy security economies often go together.

Definition of 'Safety' and 'Social Justice'

Safety is connected to, but is broader than, security. For this reason, **Safety** can be defined as the 'protection of people from harm'. For instance, such harm may arise as a consequence of insecurity, poor roadways and economic decline. It may also arise from accidents or other threats posed by the environment or animals.

Social Justice can also be defined, for the purposes of this book, both as 'the quality of being fair or reasonable' and as 'the administration of the law or customary law or local authority in maintaining this fairness'[67] It includes the processes by which disputes or grievances are resolved, as well as the outcomes of those processes.

Definition of 'Legal Diversity' ('Legal Pluralism')

Legal diversity may be defined as a situation where more than one set of customary laws and system exists within a country. There are multiple cultural legal systems functioning and enforcing these different customary laws. Where legal diversity (also called legal pluralism) exists, the law of the state[68] is not the only law that regulates people's lives. Proper customary laws state institutions like traditional chiefs' courts, police, and prisons are not the only institutions applying and enforcing the rules and regulations.

Plural legal systems are particularly prevalent in the former colonial governments or administrations. Where the law of a former colonial authority may exist alongside more traditional legal systems or customary law[69].

---

67   C Soanes, A Stevenson (eds.) (2009), *Oxford Dictionary of English,* second edition, revised (Oxford: Oxford University Press).

68   Adapted from Kyed H (2018), *'Methodological guidance note: Hybrid Justice and Security Systems/Provision in Myanmar'*, unpublished.

69   Griffiths, Anne (November 1996). *"Legal Pluralism in Africa: the Role of Gender*

Customary Law

Customary law can be defined as a legal custom or established pattern of behaviour that can be tangibly verified with a particular social community setting. It is essentially a set of customs, practices and beliefs that are accepted as obligatory rules of conduct by indigenous peoples and local communities. A claim can be carried out in defence of "what has always been done and accepted by law"[70].

A customary law exists anywhere a certain legal practice is observed, and the relevant actors consider it to be law.[71] Customary law is a recognized source of law, within jurisdictions of the civil law tradition, where it may be subordinate to both statutes and regulations. Customary law also deals with compensation for various wrongful actions, such as theft or assault. An example of an area of customary law which has been changed by statute is stock theft.

In addressing custom as a source of law within the civil law tradition, John Henry Merryman notes that, though the attention it is given in scholarly works is great, its importance is "slight and decreased"[72]. One of the striking characteristics of customary law is that it is totally unwritten. Customary laws are not contained in a single document. For instance, the customary law of a particular village can be that only male children are allowed to inherit the estate of their fathers.

Definition of 'Custom'

The Concise Law Dictionary provides this definition of a custom. A "custom is a rule of conduct obligatory to those within its scope, established

---

and Women's Access to Law". PoLAR. 19(2), 93-108

70   Chisholm, Huge, ed. (1911). *"Consuetudinary"*. Encyclopedia, Britannica. Seven (Eleventh ed.). Cambridge University Press. Page 18.

71   Hund

72   Merryman, John Henry (2007). The Civil Law Tradition: An Introduction to the Legal Systems of Europe and Latin America. (3rd ed.). Stanford University Press. Page 24

by long usage. A valid custom has the force of law. Custom to the society is what law is to the State. A valid custom must be of immemorial antiquity, certain, reasonable, obligatory, and not repugnant to statute law, though it may derogate from the common law."

The first customary laws operating in South Sudan were officially adopted and documented by the colonial powers through these conferences. Jieng customary judicial systems were enshrined in the passage of the Civil Justice Ordinance of 1929. The customary trial skills of the traditional courts of the Chiefs Ordinance of 1931 were the second important development because it recognized the legal authority of customary trial skills and court penalties by Chiefs to exercise customary judicial jurisdiction in their traditional clannish ethnicity areas.

This second ordinance 1931 became a novel change in that it lawfully recognized customary Chief's legal authority to exercise customary jurisdiction in own clannish spheres. *Section 7* provided that: *"The Chiefs' Court shall administer the Native law and Customs prevailing in the area over which said Court exercises its jurisdiction provided that such Native law and Custom is not contrary to justice, morality or order."*

Definition of 'Hybridity'

Hybridity defines whenever different customary laws and legal systems overlap, interact, and shape one another. Hybridity may display itself in a multiplicity of ways. For example a mixture of Afro Asianic Arab, Bantustan Balanda and Nilotic Jieng cultural norms and patterns, might inform a cultural dispute resolution process. Azande and Rek clannish institutions might cooperate in or compete over providing security or resolving a dispute. Individuals providing security or justice might derive their legitimacy from a combination of their official position within a Balanda or Zande formal institution as well as their personal background or role within a customary structure.

Definition of 'Inclusivity'

Inclusiveness defines which groups or classes in community or society can access social, political or economic services including security and justice, and whether any specific groups are excluded or disadvantaged. This can relate to age, sex, ethnicity, economic status, physical ability or other variables relating to a person's status or identity.

Definition of 'Legitimacy'

Legitimacy is an acceptance of authority, and consent towards an institution or actor who claims authority. Consent conveys that legitimacy is associated with voluntary or quasi-voluntary compliance, opposed to the imposition of power, and demands exerted through coercion.

Elements of legitimacy that can be assessed include the legitimacy of specific security and justice. It also encompasses the legitimacy of their actions, that is, how security and justice processes are conducted, as well as legitimacy of the outcomes of those processes, whether people accept the outcomes as appropriate.

This definition of legitimacy can be described as 'internal' or 'empirical', as it is based on the actions and perceptions of the people in the research areas, compared to 'external' or 'normative' legitimacy which would be defined by criteria produced by outsiders[73].

Definition of 'Effectiveness'

Effectiveness is defining a degree to which something is successful in producing a desired outcome. Effectiveness may not align with legitimacy when different groups are seeking different objectives. Therefore, different people's perspectives should be considered when assessing effectiveness. The more effective a system is, the more likely it is to be seen as legitimate by those whose objectives correspond with its outcomes. Inversely, the

---

73   Adapted from Kyed H (2018), *'Methodological guidance note: Hybrid Justice and Security Systems/Provision in Myanmar'*, unpublished.

less effective a system is at meeting people's objectives, the less likely they will see it as legitimate[74].

Definition of 'Conflict'

Conflict can be defined as a relationship between at least two parties, for example individuals or groups, who have, or who think they have, incompatible objectives, needs and interests.

Conflict is a widespread phenomenon, and there are many different conflicts, which can or cannot result in violence. South Sudan can quickly list conflicts including, historical, border disputes, tribal and ethnic, regional, intergenerational, religious, class-based, resource-based, political/ideological, and conflict over identity. In conflicts there are often multiple sensitivities of causes; they are almost never simple tugs-of-war between two parties or communities. Many violent conflicts result from a whole collection of sometimes widely differing and even incompatible views, ideas, ideals and sensitivities. Conflicts are over and over again, caused by more than one of these factors.

Likewise, some experts describe violence and conflicts according to different stages, distinguishing, for instance, 'pre-conflict', 'confrontation', 'crisis', 'resolution' and 'post-conflict'.

The majority of lifelong changes in a society are brought about by inquiring and debate on the merits of the changes it experiences. This kind of disagreement or conflict is an integral part of everybody's lives. If conflict is acceptably managed, the parties will develop a common tactic about the speed and dimension of the changes they want. If conflict is badly managed, then the conflict will most likely become violent.

---

74   Ibid

Definition of 'Violence'

Violence 'consists of actions, words, attitudes, structures or systems which create physical, psychological, social or environmental prejudice, and/or which prevent people from achieving their full human potential'.

Visible Violence

Visible violence defines the best-known type of violence mentioned in a media. Visible violence aims to 'intimidate, confine, injure or even to kill people'

There is also 'invisible' violence. This is just as dangerous because it prevents individuals from realizing their potential and is liable to turn violent. Generally, two main categories of invisible violence are recognised: cultural violence and structural violence.

Definition of 'Violent Conflict'

Violent conflict defines a condition in which a violent conflict is most likely to occur. Violent conflict is the same almost everywhere in the world. Below are few examples to note as:

- Petty or negate consultation between two or more sides who disagree.
- Fictitious ideas and beliefs about each other held by the different sides.
- Past, long-time grievances between the different sides, like accidents.
- Imbalanced distribution of power and resources such as food, housing, jobs, and land.

People or ethnic groups involved in violent conflict caused by inequitable distribution of resources, are very unlikely to accept as an outcome any arrangement which leaves their basic human needs unmet. Individuals not only need secure supplies of food, water, shelter, and basic medicine, but also identity and recognition as people or clans, subclans, or ethnic groups.

This is important for mass media professionals to understand as it means that people whose needs are unmet cannot necessarily be seen as unreasonable if they keep up their struggle, even if it seems hopeless or self-defeating.

What this means is that some form of structural change must be on the agenda, to allow those human needs to be met. If there is no agreement on changing these conditions, violent conflict is almost inevitable.

Definition of 'Rural' and 'Urban' Areas

Urban areas can refer to towns, cities, and suburbs. It also includes city itself, as well as the surrounding areas. Rural areas are opposite of urban areas. Urbanization is the transition from a rural to an urban society. Statistically, urbanization reflects an increasing proportion of the population living in settlements defined as urban, primarily through net rural to urban migration. The level of urbanization is the percentage of the total population living in towns and cities, while urbanization is the rate at which it grows.

Mourning Sacrifice Rituals and Practices
Historical Background

There has never been a meaningful and substantial exploration conducted on the practices of sacrifices, rituals, mourning, bloodwealth compensation claims accompanying their processes in the context of South Sudanese communities or societies.

My former texts, which focused on the traditional burial practices of high priest chiefs and Deities of Rek speaking people, asserted that most clans and subclans of Apuk Lith branch of Rek ethnic Jieng speaking peoples are not able to perform or fulfilled their pure customs according to cultural fashions, due to the recent fusions and changed nature of environments in which they lived.

In this book I have focused on the rituals performed after roadway accident fatalities occurrences in the urbanized city dwellers. A particular point of focus was on how widows in transitional societies experience bereavement and the bereavement rituals of loss life and change. The findings of this research showed that bereavement in transitional societies is complicated by factors such as the inability to fulfil or accomplish all the prescribed traditional sacrifices and mourning and rituals, some of them being adapted.

There could be further research conducted on offering animal sacrifices, rituals and mourning in South Sudan; rural comminated religious centres and South Sudan city contexts, however, given the rapid transitional nature of recently urbanized city population, research is crucial to explore the needs of the people living in recently created city or town environments, in dealing with the death of a loved one. The above literature underscores the vast exertion that has been done on bereavement and mourning within the South Sudanese context. However, most explorations conducted so far seem to focus on spousal bereavement, particularly the experiences of widowhood and abandonment within different cultural Jieng and Azande ethnic groups. Even though death has become a common occurrence in South Sudan, most of the explorations focused on the rural areas of South Sudan and few have focused on urbanized city communities. Research on the changing nature of the mourning, sacrifice, rituals, blood life wealth prices after fatal accident deaths and the change in people's living environments seem to have received limited attention.

I have observed that the practice of the burial ceremonies, (including ritual, sacrifice, blood life wealth compensation) and the mourning practices accompanying the death of a loved one after fatal accidents, have been redefined in South Sudan urbanized cities, as compared to the past. One distinct feature that seem to be a common practice and seems to have become popular in the most urbanized cities of South Sudan, referred to as the 'bloodwealth price after death' compensation claim. Immediately after the burial of the dead bodies, friends of the deceased gather to have drinks, mostly alcoholic beverages, usually in a celebratory mood, with loud music and dance. "That would be a way of saying the departed has completed his earthly role, those who remain should forget about him and continue with life"[75].

---

75   Letsosa, R. (2010). *Liturgical aspects of funeral services in reformed churches of*

South Sudanese cultures have their distinct practices, traditional beliefs, values, norms and customs on mourning and grief rituals. The current exploration undertakes to gather information on the direct experiences of the bereaved and those who attend burials at newly created towns and parishes, with specific focus on the phenomena of the 'bloodwealth compensation claim' in monetary equivalent after burial of roadway accident fatalities.

Factors Involving Accident Fatality Mourning and Bloodwealth:
All cultures have rituals that mark the finality of death and prescribe socially supported remembrance, sadness, and mourning behaviours. In a social context sanctioned ceremonies and rituals have been used by cultural ethnic classes as channels for transmitting beliefs and expectations and therefore maintain order within a given culture[76]. According to academia the society moulds its members from early childhood to integrate life and death events into their human experiences[77].

A ritual defines a specific behavioural actions or activity which gives a symbolic cultural expression to certain feelings and thoughts of the actors individually or as a community[78]. It may be a customary behaviour or a past occurrence and may be conducted publicly or privately. The same applies to mourning and animal sacrifice rituals because the mourning are actors, and they symbolize something by accomplishing the animal sacrifice rituals. Rituals can also be described as cultural devices that facilitate

African origin. Verbum et Ecclesia, 31(1), 361-366.

76   Becvar, D. S. (2001). *In the Presence of Grief: Helping Family members to resolve Death, Dying and Bereavement Issues.* New York: The Guilford Press.89

77   Kilonzo, G. P. & Hogan, N. M. (1999). *Traditional African mourning rituals are abridged in response to the AIDS epidemic: Implications for mental health.* Trans-cultural Psychiatry 36(3), 259-283.

78   Rando, T. A. (1988). *Grieving: how to go on living when someone you love dies.* Lexington, Massachusetts: DC Heath.

preservation of social order[79]. The customary factor these definitions of rituals is their symbolic nature and the achievements, comportments or actions to show that they are accomplished, and they are visible. Despite the fact that cultures advocate and practice mourning by conducting animal sacrifice rituals, there are countless differences amid those practices, and they change over time.

The fulfilment of death rituals in South Sudan societies is influenced by the belief in the continuation of life[80] after death. After death, offerings, rituals, and ceremonies will differ depending on culture and degree of adherence in specific ethnic clannish community. Death, on the other hand, maybe described as a transformative process that awards a supernatural spiritual power status of the deceased in ancestry world of spirits. Appropriate burial ceremonies, offering animal sacrifices and rituals ensure that the deceased persons become ancestors in spirit world. It is believed that burial ceremonies and memorial service rites are completed for the determination of ensuring that the deceased persons would be able to join the ancestral spirits world, because in South Sudan tradition, when a person dies, it is believed that his spirit cannot reach the destination to the home or world of the "living dead" before the completion of death rituals.

In South Sudan cultures, when a clan family member dies, the whole community and the bereaved clan family members including the relatives of the deceased person, must fulfil bereavement rituals. There are community open rituals where the community will participate in, such as the burial and the memorial services that would be offered to the mourning clan family, during the process of the preparation of burial. There are also confidential rituals which are mostly undertaken by the clan family and

---

79   Romanoff, B. D., & Terenzio, M. (1998). *Rituals and the grieving process.* Death Studies, 22, 697-711.

80   Mbiti, J. (1969). *African religions and philosophy.* London: Heinemann. Mbiti, J. S. (1975). *Introduction to African religion. South Africa;* Heinemann International Literature & Textbooks.

the immediate relatives of the deceased persons[81]. It shows the traditional significance in accomplishing or fulfilling rituals after a fatal accident and the special meaning that rituals have for South Sudanese communities.

The ancestors are believed to be the mediators between God and the living. The ancestors are also believed to be overlooking, monitoring, and taking care of the living, participating in the active lives of the living. Therefore, practice of the death rituals which is symbolic of the relationship that people have with the ancestors in the world of spirits.

Ritual Changes after Bloodwealth Compensation Claim

Rituals deal with adjustment to offering change in role and status, clan hostilities, violent conflicts, altering and modifying losses and relocation of the deceased person into a new role and function in the clan and subclan. Blood wealth compensation claim reconstructs oaths and bonds between the guilty party and victim's party. According to Traditional Appeal Court Chief Judge; "The victim and homicide clan families will realize that homicide, wrong, and unhappiness will disappear, and their normal feeling will come into harmony with the laws of blood wealth that members of guilty clans or families have donated as their supplications."[82]

This means that the rituals facilitate adjustment and offer controllable changes in role, function and in status of the deceased person. Blood wealth compensation claim is collected from the guilty parties by the relatives of the deceased. According to the cultural practice, if the deceased person is a husband, his wife becomes a widow and there is a specific apron with symbols that she must wear, also accompanied by certain behaviours and actions. Death upsets the social equilibrium of the society, therefore if the death was caused through negligence or killed with intent to kill the deceased, blood life wealth penalty will be claimed from the guilty

---

81   Romanoff, B. D., & Terenzio, M. (1998). *Rituals and the grieving process.* Death Studies, 22, 697-711.

82   Agei, Madhel Malek (2020). *Apuk a State in Waiting,* Africa World Book Company Lt. Australia. Pages

person or guilty clan family members and paid to the family of the victim killed. Certain prescribed rites, like taking oaths, sacrificial animals, and ceremonies, are used to restore the disturbed balance. Rituals of bereavement are most frequently used to facilitate relinquishing of relationships and transition to a new role and reconstructing a bridge of harmonious coexistence relationships between the families.

Community Ceremony after Accidental Death

In South Sudanese societies, ceremonies such as offering animal sacrifice, rituals, mourning, burials, the priest's spiritual prayers, memorial services, and blood wealth compensation payment, serve as a community acknowledgement that a death has occurred and provide an opportunity for the entire community to display of their bereavement[83].

The bereaved clan families show the entire community that they are mourning and pain. This appeals for community support and response. The dress code becomes a symbol of accepting the new social status and they carry a message that the person is now in mourning. Rituals, ceremonies, spiritual prayers and bloodwealth are important because without these healing practices, those mourning may behave in a way that does not position them as in need of support from others and peaceful reconciliation will be in jeopardy.

Healing Cultural Values with Mourning after Accidental Death

Offering animal sacrifices, rituals, mourning after burying the dead and paying blood wealth penalty are understood as the best entry point to smooth or persuasive healing, if death is understood as painful and traumatic[84] for the survivors. A sacrificial ritual in the traditional bereavement

---

83   Cook, A. S., & Oltjenbruns, K. (1989). *Dying and grieving: lifespan and family perspectives.* New York: Holt, Rinehart and Winston, and Romanoff, B. D., & Terenzio, M. (1998). *Rituals and the grieving process.* Death Studies, 22, 697-711.

84   Bento, R. F. (1994). *When the show must go on: Disenfranchised grief in Organisation,* Journal of Managerial Psychology, 9, 35-44.

practice has a deep psychological function and they provide a mouthpiece for expression and control of strong emotions[85]. This suggests the fact that mourning after burying the dead reactions can also be accompanied by strong emotions and running a grieving sacrificial ritual can serve as a mouthpiece of expressing those emotions. While mourning after burying the dead, groups of people join with each other to express words and behaviours symbolic of support and comfort. Neighbours can express their condolences, share what they have to support the mourners to deal with the reality of loss of life. And so, sacrificial rituals and blood wealth penalty claims allow for those supportive interactions to happen which can strengthen family, nuclear family blood ties and collective community responsibilities renewal.

Society Identity

Sacrificial rituals, ceremonies and nature blood life wealth payable after burying the dead ones, furthermore, defines and distinguishes the various clans in South Sudan. They symbolize how people identify with their culture, faith, belief or custom or religion and likewise with the deceased body spirit and life spirit. In Zande branch of Bantu family speaking peoples or Apuk branch of Rek in Jieng clans, subclans and other communities or societies where cultural, faithfulness and symbolic divine spiritual identities are emphasized, they serve to strengthen and reaffirm ethnic clannish group identities. Thus, identity is anchored in a precise social context or in a specific set of cultural relations, social relations, families, next of kin or family member relationships. Hence the identity formation process involves a dialectical together with a linguistic relationship between the individual clan, subclan and the whole society. This indicates that we become who we are because of a precise socialization system.

---

85   Kilonzo, G. P. & Hogan, N. M. (1999). *Traditional African mourning rituals are abridged in response to the AIDS epidemic: Implications for mental health.* Trans-cultural Psychiatry 36(3), 259-283.

Cleansing Mourners after Burying the Dead Ones

In traditional societies of South Sudan, when a family member has died, the family of the deceased is considered as dirtied or contaminated or polluted from connection dealings with the dead. Society members participate in the ceremonies, sacrifices and rituals that aim at removing contaminated or polluted spirit from the mourners and so will be reunited to the society again[86]. Grieving, offering animal sacrifices and rituals after burying the dead are believed to support or assist in the process of cleansing the mourners in this respect.

Mourning Experience in Different Societies

Psychologists have provided insight experiences into the phenomena of grieving, sacrifices, mourning and rituals after burying the dead from the neighbouring societies[87]. They describe the different phases through which grieving is processed, through rituals, to resolve normal and clinical grieving reactions and developed models to enable healing for the mourning, blood wealth compensation penalties, sadness and impact of the death of the loved ones[88].

The hypothesis is that grieving is foreseeable and thus controllable. If the mourning has shown certain symptoms for a stipulated period, then clansman or clanswoman would have successfully dealt with the loss of a loved one[89]. The additional hypothesis is that the expression of

---

86   Ngubane, S. (1977). *Body and mind in Zulu medicine.* London: Academic Press

87   Lindemann, E. (1944). *The symptomatology and management of acute grief.* American Journal of Psychology 101, 141-148.

88   Nwoye, A. (2005). *Memory Healing Processes and Community Intervention in Grief Work in Africa.* Australia and New Zealand Journal of family Therapy, 26(3), 147-154.

89   Neimeyer, R. A., Prigerson, H. G., & Davies, B. (2002). *Mourning and meaning.* American Behavioral Scientist, 46, 235. Retrieved, August, 18, 2010 from http://abs. sagepub.com.

grief, ceremonies, and mourning prayers through high spiritual priest, is universal. Yet, there is a disparity among cultures in the way people resolve their grieving, sacrifices and rituals. According to some in academia, the experience of dying and mourning after burying the dead occurs within a specific social context. On this perspective, it is important to take into consideration the context within which the bereaved clan family members find themselves, such as the socio-cultural, political, economic, and physical contexts. A healing system founded in ecologically sound rituals, sacrifices and ceremonies that assist experiential healing and its target customers are any clan family members of the community burdened by the painful loss of a loved one. South Sudanese people perform rituals, sacrifices and mourning to cope with the impact of the death of a loved one. Performance of mourning, rituals sacrifice after burying dead ones in accident symbolizes how people identify themselves with their culture, religion, divine spirit and also with the deceased body spirit and life spirit.

Accident Fatality and the Beginning of Family Mourning Rituals

Mourning, offering animal sacrifices and rituals reflect the beliefs, divinity spirits and attitudes towards death - and as such, they begin immediately after the family member has been confirmed as dead in a fatal accident. In many societies in South Sudan, when an accident fatality is announced, the clan family is immediately considered as 'polluted' or 'contaminated', which indicates a negative darkness which entails that the clan family is thrown into a state of disequilibrium. Apuk branch Rek of ethnic Nilotic Jieng clans consider a family death to have polluted or contaminated the relatives of the deceased clan person. The term 'pollution' in the context of the death of a family member, was also used by some African researchers to suggest to a state of contamination[90]. In the culture of Rek Apuk in Gogrial East, death is

---

90   Ngubane, S. (1977). *Body and mind in Zulu medicine.* London: Academic Press. Ngubane, S. (2004). Traditional practices on burial systems with special reference to the Zulu people of South Africa. Indilinga-African Journal of Indigenous Knowledge Systems, 3

considered as a graciously intensified shape of contamination or pollution. The clan family of the deceased clan person will be contaminated and anyone who touches the corpse, will similarly be considered as contaminated or polluted.

The phase preceding the clan family burial of the dead is accompanied by certain rituals, which must be performed. These include: the smoke grass fire, which cleanses mourners around the grave who smear it's ash on their face and foot; stepping on grass fire ash if you arrive at late (after fire cleansing), in order to reflect a separation between death evils and guiding spirit of the dead; keeping dead properties far away from reach to avoid further attachment from bad evil spirits; stopping drum bit activities; and protecting the grave from others suspected of possessing evil spirits, from those not cleansed, or from revenge spirits of the dead body or deceased person.

The logic behind all these efforts is to demonstrate openly the intensity of their deep sorrow and remorse.. Among ethnic Apuk group, it is also believed that when a violent accident death occurs in a family, the family members have been symbolically crushed by a dirt divider and need to be emancipated or let go. This imaginary divider surrounding the survivors symbolizes their sorrow and demise. They may not take part in the normal life of the society until they have been purified or cleansed through ritual performance conducted through the Master of the Fishing Spear, with supernatural spiritual powers. There is a mourning interval, which usually takes longer for the family of the deceased. This mourning interval prescribes to the family what acceptable behaviours are and what are not, until the specified end of the mourning interval. Behaviours seen as prohibit in traditional South Sudan societies throughout the mourning interval, include losing one's character, talking loudly or laughing. All things were to be done in restraint.

The predominant role of a married woman whose husband or child have died, is that of the dominant mourner. The mourning rituals day starts with the dominant or foremost mourner occupying a sacred mourning rituals physical universe. This could include being isolated from the community for the interval of mourning, rituals and sacrifices during and throughout the burying process. The dominant mourner will customarily be in the bedroom on a mattress or floor or on the Jieng traditional mat called *aguot or akot* made from hide from sacrificial ox or bull. Because of the scarcity of traditional mats and animal hides in the recent generations, a mattress is commonly used, where dominant mourner will be spending most of the interval. The dominant mourner will be fully attended to for comfort. In case of a child death, the siblings, father, and mother will be allowed to sit closer on the floor, or mat. If this was a husband who died, the widow will fast, and only married women will be allowed to sit with her for comfort. The widow will wear a black garment recently adopted in towns or wear traditional dresses, fastening *nai* around widow body or a mourning attire, which is a dress specifically designed for mourning. In other traditions, the children of the deceased will also wear a small piece of skin cut from a sacrificial animal, on their hand and neck to show that they are observing the interval of mourning. This also functions as a security to guide lives of those children after they lost life of their brother or sister in an accident.

Similar customs have been reported about the experience of widow-hood in many other communities. The end of mourning for the dominant mourner is usually marked by a ritual or a ceremony where mourner will be taking off the designated mourning dress and are symbolically restored back to normal life.

Community Grieving Mourning after Death

There are many written explanations of the process of how the community joins in with the mourners[91]. The message of death of a clan family member is spread by word of mouth (traditionally the case), as well as over the radio recently as fast as possible. The first phase of mourning

---

91   Bopape, M. (1995). *The Bapedi Framework of mourning and bereavement and its implications for helping professions.* Social Work/Maatskaplike Werk, 31(3), 262-266.

rarely begins after relatives and friends encircle the mourner. Members of the community come to 'inquire' about what happened to the family known as *thiec ee thuou in thuongjang.*

There is rarely a mixture of Islamic religion, Christianity religion, and African traditional religions and real traditional practices in greatest of the communities, connecting the way they offer support to the bereaved after death. On hearing of a fatal accident of a community member who could also be a member of a particular house of worship or house of God in the community, the priest or senior or elderly clan family member immediately calls the home of the bereaved to offer condolences and conduct prayers. Such prayers are attended by the whole neighborhood.

Soon after hearing of the fatal accident, clan and subclan elders, priests as well as neighbours and the community at large, flock to the family where tragedy has struck to verify the news and assure the bereaved of their support. Participation of different stakeholders ensures holistic support. Community members provide social services and a workforce towards pitching of the water, providing traditional mats and firewood, cooking, taking care of small children, assisting with buying or bartering essential needs in markets - and other errands, while the priest leaders and elders provide psycho-spiritual sustenance or provision. At a prearranged time, community members gather at the house of the deceased clan's person and varies across forms of tradition, culture, social and beliefs, and religious practices

Parallel practice of community participation is likewise documented in many African countries. The process of a death ritual within the Nilotic ethnic communities has been shown to have similarities. Beginning from the time a death strikes, immediate clan family members and close relatives are usually the first people to arrive, and the entire community would begin to show up few days after, at the house of deceased clan person. The practice of community mourning, rituals, and sacrifices after burial between the Apuk branch of Rek ethnic Jieng of South Sudan have already been highlighted[92]. Furthermore, performance of community mourning rituals in the face of a death of a loved one, and process of community support between the different cultures at a time of death of a community member had been documented across Africa. Some African writers compared the funeral and mourning practices of the Nilotic, Bantu and Nilo-Hamitic Africans in the regions of western and eastern African countries that are said to be more elaborate and lavish in their approach to death[93]. Funerals are among the most important and visible observances in the cultural life.

The Burial after Accident Fatalities

It is true, nearly all cultures dispose away their dead with a ritual or mourning sacrifice, such as burying a dead one to separate the dead from the living. Traditional cultures of the societies of South Sudan are not an exception. There are frequently sacrifices and rituals accompanying the burial, and these vary according to ethnicity, clan, kinship and belief system. For example, corpses are not buried if they have died in a violent conflict caused for defence of Toch, cattle herds society of Apuk, Rek and territory of ethnic Jieng and other Nilotic communities.

In the culture of traditional Apuk in eastern Gogrial, as soon as the death occurs, the corpse is prepared by the dominant mourner, helped by other nuclear family members and close relatives. If a husband dies, the corpse is watched by the dominant mourner, his widow, supported by close married women and clansmen. Burial generally takes place at any time of the day immediately after the death had occurred whether by accident or long sickness. The corpse is buried as soon as possible to avoid decomposing, as there were no mortuaries in the past and there are still no mortuaries in rural homesteads. The climate may be hot and the

---

92   Agei, Madhel Malek (2020). *Apuk a State in Waiting*

93   Adamolekun, K. (2001). *Survivors' motives for extravagant funerals among the Yorubas of Western Nigeria.* Death Studies, 25, 609-619.

corpse may perhaps decompose with a bad smell, so the corpse can be covered with plant-shrub leaves, which is translated as *angier in thuongjang* and emits a strong aromatic smell like mint or perfume. The corpse can be protected from flies through smoking cow's dung, referred to as *tool weer weng or hook in thuongjang*; or smoke goat or sheep's dung, referred to as *tool weer thok* in thuongjang. The situation is different in rural villages compared to the developing cities, with the recent introduction of a new practice of ritual at the mortuary; the corpse will be taken to the mortuary in cities where it will stay for a few days while the family is busy preparing gravesite for the burial. In some big cities or towns, the corpse would be brought from the mortuary into the house of mourner, or to the institution for a watch or a wake before burial.

The occasion of the wake is to help and allow the society groups to say their last goodbyes, even give testimonies about the deceased clan person. Ceremonial offering includes a ritual sacrifice, in the form of killing an animal, which takes place the day before the burial and can be used for preparation of food for the people who are attending the burial. In ethnic Rek branch of Jieng, the skin called *agot in thuongjang* would often be used to wrap the corpse for burial, since there were no coffins in the past. The ritual killing is also performed as a sacrifice or an offering to the ancestors.

Burials in towns and cities of South Sudan are heavily influenced by Christianity, Islamic, and African traditional religions. Several traditional rituals are still observed and practiced even among Christian members, evident in many burial services. As an example, at the breaking of the dawn, on the day of the burial, there is a ritual called *rook cien in thuongjang*, which is the final prayer and viewing of the corpse. As the corpse is carried out of the dominant mourner's house, a final traditional praise-making prayer is done by a nuclear elderly relative. The eulogy function is a means of honouring the deceased and for psychological relief. Eulogy is supposed to evoke a response from the bereaved to cry as it is believed that crying is therapeutic. This also happens at the burial place around the house or city cemetery - and during the burial, where the bereaved dominant mourner would be sitting at one side of the grave, as they are not expected to take part in the singing. The clergy and the community, including church members, usually participate in the burial process. The people attending the funeral will mostly be expected to maintain complete silence at the graveside, except when they would be singing hymns. Women are expected to wear long dresses and cover their heads and men are supposed to wear formal jackets as a sign of respect.

In many cases, burials are usually preceded by a family diviner or divinity spiritual priest, who will go to bless the grave before the burial and perform a traditional ritual. Such a priest will frequently conduct the burial process in cities or towns. After the burial in cities, the people will be invited to go back to the family of the deceased for a meal. All the people and clan family members in rural homesteads must smoke themselves with grass pulled out on thatch houses of dominant mourner, to cleanse bad evil that caused death in the family.

Following the burial, the time of strict mourning for the grieving and mourning family would be observed, which lasts for a few days. The grieving and mourning family would observe the *duong yeth or yeth duong, riak or thuou in thuongjang,* which is translated as 'neck breaking' or 'falling' time in English. There would be total silence at the house of dominant mourner and the deceased, a cooking fire would not be lit, and having fun and celebrations would usually be prohibited, as symbols to commemorate loss and being at a standstill, as a sign of respect for the family of the deceased person. The grieving and mourning may likewise continue to engage in cleansing rituals for purification with special medicine, sacrifice, secret cleansing, libations, using Master of the Spear among Jieng and black medicine among Azande branch of Bantu family during the grieving and mourning after death period, until the end of grieving and mourning period or until death 'fades' away[94].

---

94   Gumede, M. V. (1990). *Traditional Healers: A Medical Doctor's perspective.* Johannesburg: Blackshaws (Pty) (Ltd).

All communities in South Sudan have traditionally used their clans and subclans homestead as a customarily final resting place where their dead would be buried. A clansman or clanswoman may be buried at a yard or a byre of hamlet or homeland. This was made because there was a precise meaning attached to the dead being buried at their hamlet, as a sign of identity. A connection to birthplace is practiced which is woven into the identity for individual clan and subclan members in South Sudan. Every clansman or clanswoman is part of an environment which involves geographical locations, homes, spaces, localities, places and their properties - which have functioned as part of the socialization process at some point and in which, self-identity has developed. To die in the traditional belief is like going back home, where you belong and to continue life as ancestor, body spirit, life spirit and guidance for the family living in the human world on earth. Therefore, the use of word: - *yath, jak, agolong, akuic (singular) in Jieng*, which implies that when a clansman or clanswoman dies, he or she joins the people who died before them, who are the ancestors referred to as *yieths, jaak, agoloong, akuiec* in plural in *thuongjang*. In this matter, one needs a proper burial, where there will be degrees of respect and dignity.

As such one needs a proper burial, with all the elements of respect and dignity. Any respectable Jieng or Azande, Balanda or Bari, Nuer or Pojulu clan person, was buried at hamlet behind or beside their clan family's huts, irrespective of age or gender - except of the head of the family, who was buried alongside the top of the cattle byre or holy shrine tomb place. Recently, especially in South African urban environments, people have moved away from burying their dead in their homesteads due to political and other reasons. Technological advancement and shortage of burial space in metropolitan areas has contributed to popular use of other alternatives to the traditional burial, such as burying in designated areas such as graveyards, or cremation and both forms are gradually gaining popularity among city dwellers.

CHAPTER FOUR

CULTURE, LANGUAGE AND THEIR EXPANSION

Introduction

In this chapter, I will write a little that I know about the general culture, linguistic, history, Azande, Jieng Dinka, and customary practices. This will help me to begin meaningful exploration about blood life wealth penalties. I will provide a brief analysis of Azande and Jieng Dinka cultures, customs, values, norms, religious beliefs, languages, attitudes, and social behaviors to give a foundational conceptual framework within which I can explore the occurrence of blood life wealth compensation claim, which has become part of the road traffic accident death practices. With a focus on rural highway roads in small rural towns in particular. It should be noted that there is a tension between customary law and status law courts hearing as to whether we can speak about customary law system in the singular or only consider pluralism of customary law systems as distinct customary law systems.

Some anthropologists, sociologists, social scientists, and judiciaries present this dilemma in their accounts, interpretations, or books in writing about customary law court hearing sentence systems. The customary law systems of the Jieng and Nuer clans are similar. Their laws have been explored and recorded in greater detail than any other clan. The exploration identified an array of personal factors, social interaction and procedural law system as being primarily under the domain and influence of customary law[95].

Each different clannish group in South Sudan has its own distinct body of customary law and there are approximately over 64 separate clannish groups in South Sudan. In effect there are 64 separate bodies of customary laws. In the interests of simplifying the exploration it is reasonable to classify these customary laws into two generic Azande and Jieng language families.

An Azande driver involved in fatal roadway accident death reflects the customary law of a central authority system. The young Jieng boy child who died in a fatal roadway accident on July 15, 2019, in Jieng Rek Apuk reflects the customary court hearing under a decentralized authority system. Azande and Jieng have a very diverse culture and customary rules.

For this reason, the road accident death between the guilty Azande driver and victim Jieng child who died on July 15, 2019, became a challenge to customary law court hearing sentences. The Apuk law court was to oversee trial fatal road accident death caused by Azande wrongdoing according to the Rek Apuk victim customs, and to bring about reconciliation between the Rek Apuk victim clan family and the Azande guilty clan family.

One of the most obvious aspects of South Sudanese customary law is the absence of distinction between criminal and civil law. Customary laws on the other hand pluralizes their treatment of civil and criminal laws. The objective for this approach has been described as being a strong desire to restore social equilibrium. As an example, under Jieng Dinka homicide law, this would be achieved through the blood life wealth compensation price payment. The plural mixture of civil and criminal procedure does not deny a family or clan family members of victim from exercising their right to pursue civil damages, or alternatively a full-scale prosecutorial action under statutory law.

---

95   Jok, Aleu A., Robert A. Leitch, Carrie Vandewint. (2004). *"A Study of Customary Law in Contemporary Southern Sudan"*. (Not Published). South Sudan. Page13

Central authority systems include the Azande; Shilluk and Anyuak kingdoms, which tend to be based around powerful, centralized hierarchical structures. Decentralized customary legal systems include the Dinka, Nuer, Bari, Balanda Bviri, Balanda and Kherish clans. These systems typically comprise clans, or sub clannish sections where traditional chiefs and sub-chiefs, specialized committees, normally of kinship networks, exercise core social and legal powers[96].

According to the members of the judiciary interviewed, they argued that as soon as the judiciary grows in size, and experience, the influence of statutory law upon society at every level will increase. Inevitably, customary law systems and statutory law will be in regular conflict. Furthermore, history, much in evidence in the literature, adds weight to the argument that customary law and statutory law are by their very nature bound to come in conflict. A system based upon reconciliation must routinely clash with one based upon punishment and deterrence. This is even more likely if the judges who interpret statutory law have a manifestly different cultural viewpoint from those who interpret and execute customary law.

Characteristics of Cultural Practices

The term 'Culture' is used in many different contexts to refer to a category of human behaviour, attitude and pattern. The predominant usage of the term is in the discipline of anthropology, sociology, and social science. The definition is contested, in part due to conflicting theoretical understandings of this concept to extremely diverse human societies[97]. Culture is considered a central concept in anthropology, encompassing the range of phenomena that are transmitted through social learning in human societies. Culture itself may refer to the set of patterns of human activity within a society or social group. It may be a way we act, think, and behave

---

96   Jok, Aleu A., Robert A. Leitch, Carrie Vandewint. (2004). *"A Study of Customary Law in Contemporary Southern Sudan"*. (Not Published). South Sudan. Page13

97   *"Anthropology"*. Oxford Dictionaries UK Dictionary. Oxford University Press. Retrieved October 30, 2016.

based on the shared values of our society. It may be a way we understand symbols, from language to hand gestures. It may be everywhere, and we may continually develop and define our culture on a daily basis.

Culture is an umbrella term which encompasses the collective sum of knowledge, social behavior and norms found in human societies, experience, beliefs, values, attitudes, meanings, orders, arts, laws, customs, religion, notions of time, roles, spatial relations, concepts of the universe, and material objects and possessions obtained by a group of communities or individuals in the course of generations through separate and gathering striving[98]. It refers to the systems of knowledge shared by a large gathering of people. It is capabilities, and habits of the gatherers in these groupings. Culture refers to communication and communication refers to culture. In an extensive sense, it is a cultured or educated behaviour. It is the sum of a learned person, summed experience which is publicly communicated, or more briefly, behaviour through public learning[99]. A culture is a way of life of a collection of society, the behaviours, beliefs, values, and symbols that they accept, generally, without thinking about them, and that are passed along by communication and imitation from one generation to the next[100]. It is symbolic communication. Some of its symbols include a group's skills, knowledge, attitudes, values, and motives. The meanings of the symbols are learned and deliberately perpetuated in a society through its institutions. Culture consists of patterns, explicit and implicitly, of and for behavior acquired and communicated by symbols, constituting the distinctive achievement of human groups, including their embodiments in artifacts. The essential core of culture consists of traditional ideas and

---

98   Tylor, Edward. (1871). Primitive Culture. Vol.1., New York; JP. Putnam's Son.

99   James, Paul; Liam; Scerri, Andy; Steger, Manfred (2015). Urban Sustainability in Theory and Practice; Circles of Sustainability. London; Rotledge. Page 53. ISBN 978-1-138-02772-1. OCLC 942553107. Archived from the original on June 26, 2017. Retrieved May 29, 2017.

100   *"Meaning of Culture"*. Cambridge English Dictionary, Archived. From original on August 15,2015. Retrieved July 26, 2015.

especially their attached values. Culture systems may, on the one hand, be considered as products of action, on the other hand, as conditioning influences upon further action. It is the sum of total of the learned behaviour of a group of people that are generally considered to be the tradition of that people and are transmitted from generation to generation. It is a collective programming of the mind that distinguishes the members of one group or category of people from another.

According to the theory of cultural determinism, the ideas, meanings, beliefs and values that individuals learn as members of society determine human nature. People are what they learn. Determination in culture places no limitations on the capabilities and aptitudes of human beings to do or to be whatever they want. Many anthropologists suggest that there is no universal "right way" of being human. "Right way" is almost always "our way"; that "our way" as members in one society almost never resembles or matches to "our way" in any other society[101]. Proper viewpoint of an informed human being could only be that of tolerance.

The Categories of Culture

Exploring culture is a great working experience from anthropologist. Social scientists, like anthropologists and sociologists, explore culture to understand patterns of human behavior. Although there are unlimited ways that people can express their culture, anthropologists and social scientists have developed two fundamental categories to define belongings produced by a society. First is quantifiable culture. Quantifiable or factual culture is physical belongings that are created by a society.

In South Sudan, we have a strong quantifiable culture based on production of certain items, like dresses or artifacts. As an example, Jieng, Rek and Apuk are proud of their ivory arms wearing, and ostrich feathered helmet culture and Lotuko is proud of its feathered-helmet and spear dance culture. They make ivory arms wearing ornaments, ostrich

---

101   Tylor 1971, 1.

feathered-helmet head dresses, spears. They use ivory ornaments, feathered helmets as symbols of their places in society, wealth, or feelings about the environment. Ivory ornaments, feathered helmets, plus the other belongings that they physically create as South Sudanese Rek, Apuk, Jieng, Azande and Lotuko define their quantifiable culture. Now, quantifiable culture does not mean that it is an object that is bought and sold in market; it can also be something they all make. For instance, pot art is a common thing they all did as women for house uses. It is something that is common enough to unite South Sudanese and therefore part of their quantifiable culture.

The other category is nonquantifiable culture, or the intangible belongings created by a culture. In other words, the parts of culture you cannot touch, feel, taste, or hold. Common examples include social roles, ethics, beliefs, or even language. As a culture, South Sudanese societies believe in agemate or age-group. But you cannot hold agemate, or make it out of pot containers. Agemate is something that does not truly exist; it is an idea that a culture creates about the treatment of people. This is nonquantifiable culture, and it is just as great of an influence on lives of those societies as quantifiable culture is.

Components of Culture

The whole or full culture of an exclusive society is constituted of quite a lot of components, or shares, such as social organisation, customs, religion, language, government, economy and arts.

Social Organization

This is the way that society divides people. In most cultures, there is a ruler who is manager, controller and military or war leader and more powerful than the average person. In many cultures, there may be various several levels of structures of organization based on sex, age, occupation, or even reputation like those who are brave fighters during war time can be levelled as heroes. Social organization is a significant component of culture that defines how the society treats the relationships between different members of that culture.

Customs

Customs or the traditions, values and social norms of a society is the next component. These help a society define their beliefs about right and wrong and create social pressure to obey those beliefs.

Religion

Religion is the most controversial component, which demonstrates morals, and beliefs about spirituality, humanity and reason for existing of a society.

Language

Language is a series of spoken, acted, or written symbols for communication. This is another crucial aspect of how we live our daily lives and connect to people in our society.

Government is the component of structures of culture created by society to maintain order, disciples and adherence to culture. Economy is the rules of buying, selling, trading, and assigning value to belongings. Arts is the material expressions of beauty, emotions, and beliefs. A culture encompasses all of these components to some extent.

As an example, few societies or communities today remain isolated from the development of the modern state system of South Sudan. Communities have lost their legitimacy to perform traditional roles or functions, such belonging as tithing donations, delivering customary justice and defending society territory. These have been replaced by states functions and institutions, such as taxation, judicial law courts, policing and the military intervention. Most of these societies have suffered decline and loss of cultural identity. Cultural membership of a society or community may be understood simplistically as being an identity based on factors such as kinship translated as "clan", ethnicity translated as "race", language, dwelling place, political group, religious beliefs, oral tradition and or cultural practices. Few have adapted to the new political context and transformed their culture and practices in order to survive, whereas some have secured legal rights and protections.

Culture of South Sudan
Introduction

South Sudanese Culture can be defined as symbols, language, beliefs, values, and artifacts that are part of any society. As this definition suggests, South Sudanese people identify themselves with one another on the basis of their African ethnic heritage, African traditional religions and Christian beliefs. These are defining factors that differentiate them from the Arab and Muslim in Northern Sudanese. It is essential to recognize that there is no uniform understanding of the typical South Sudanese experience.

Anthropologists have traditionally categorized the people and clans of South Sudan under distinct groups of the South Sudanese population: (1) Nilotic ethnic classes of people with different clans and subclans, (2) Eastern Sudanic or Central Sudanic[102] or Nilo-Sahara to Kordofanian ethnic classes of people with different clans and subclans[103], (3)Nilo-Hamitic or Afro-Asiatic ethnic classes of people with clans and subclans, and, (4) Azande of Bantu or Western Sudanic ethnic classes of people[104] with different clans and subclans[105].

The Jieng, Jieeng or Jaang (Dinka), a Nilotic people are the largest ethnic group of the people in the Republic of South Sudan[106]. The second is Nuer of Nilotic family classes, Azande of Bantu family classes and Bari family classes of languages. Some communities among the ethnic Nilotic and Bantu family classes have been the recent Arabic speaking people practicing Islamic Muslim culture, living in Wau, Malakal and

---

102   Westermann, Diedrich, 1922a. *Die Sprache der Guang.* Berlin: Dietrich Reimer.

103   Encyclopedia Britannica, Inc.

104   The Chronological Evidence for the Introduction of Domestic Stock in Southern Africa Texas State University. Retrieved December 17, 2007.

105   Evidence against the "early split" scenario shown here is presented in E. Patin et al., "Dispersals and genetic adaptation of Bantu-speaking populations in Africa and North America", Science, Vol. 356, Issue 6337, pp. 543-546 (5 May 2017), doi:10.1126/science. aal1988.

106   Central Intelligent Agency (CIA), 2020.

Juba townships and newly forming Afro Asiatic classes seen in other living environments. They belong to a group of cultures known as the Nilotic people, the Bantu people and the Afro Asiatic people, all of whom live in the Republic of South Sudan.

Attaching the South Sudanese identity to unify to single law of customary court was fully "accepted" by the Jieng Rek Apuk and Azande communities. An open negotiation about blood life wealth penalty, payable in cattle equivalent monetary and the lessons learned from it contribute to discussions about how the various cultures wish to pay blood wealth punishments, and how the South Sudanese national identity can be promoted in the cultural, political and historical context. The expression of the Azande cultural identity; the Jieng Rek Apuk pursuit of its historical identity, cultural identity, nationality identity, clan divinity identity and the behaviour of people of different culture seems to suggest a continuous historical and cultural pillar that need to adopt pluralism of blood life wealth penalty payment, for forgiveness, reconciliation, healing, harmony and peaceful coexistence.

Location of South Sudan

The South Sudanese people inhabit a vast geographical location in northeastern Africa. South Sudan also called Southern Sudan, has rich biodiversity including lush savannas, swamplands and rainforests that are home to many species of wildlife. Prior to 2011, South Sudan part of Sudan, its neighbour to the north.

South Sudan[107], officially known as the Republic of South Sudan[108], is a landlocked country in east- Central Africa[109]. It is bordered by Ethiopia to

---

107   Roach, Peter (2011). Cambridge English Pronouncing and DICTIONARY (18TH ED.). Cambridge University Press. ISBN 978-0-521-5253-2

108   "South Sudan". The World Factbook. CIA. 11 July 2011. Retrieved 14 July 2011.

109   The World Factbook- Central Intelligence Agency. www.cia.gov.Retrieved 12 July 2011.

the east, by Sudan to the north, by Central African Republic to the west, by Democratic Republic of the Congo to the southwest, by Uganda to the south and by Kenya to the southeast. It gained its independence from the Republic of the Sudan in 2011, after 50 years of political struggle, making it the recent sovereign state or country with widespread recognition[110].

This chapter explores the culture of South Sudan encompassing the historical religions, languages, ethnic groups, foods, and other traditions of people of the modern state of South Sudan and inhabitants of the regions in diversity. They share a cultural connection based on their common practice of the Christianity, African traditional religious beliefs and historical experience of struggle from the North Sudan.

In the interests of simplifying the exploration this section will focus primary on two generic ethnic groups of Azande and Jieng language families. This is because I have chosen to focus this book about blood compensation, using the example of a sad story of a boychild from Apuk Rek clan family, who died in violent collision crash caused by the driver from Azande family who was driving a Landcruiser in rural roadway traffic in Pathuon Apuk Rek, eastern Gogrial region.

Azande History Culture, Name, Language and their Expansionism

This section is about the blood life wealth penalty fine payable after the occurrence of death, injury, defamation, and damage cause by negligence, accident, or killing. I will attempt to address the challenges facing the Jieng Rek and Azande family members, customary law court judges, cultural history, blood life wealth penalty payable in cattle for compensation of life lost to forgive and reverse curse of guilty clan family.

Before people can clearly understand *apuk riem*, clan crimes or offences, clan spirit forgiveness, blood wealth for forgiveness, and repentance, they should understand the offence, the wrongdoer, and particularly the effects of the crime on the relatives of pedestrian victim, loved ones, and

---

their clan. *Apuk reim* blood life wealth compensation helps Jieng Dinka family members of child killed in road accident collision crash, to ease the reconciliation processes with the Azande family members of guilty driver. Family of guilty Azande driver family of victim child Jieng Rek family can then forgive and restore peace and harmony between two diverse family cultures.

I will write the little I know about the history, culture, language, origin, custom, divinity spiritual reconciliation, spirit forgiveness, beliefs and ritual sacrifices. The implications of traditionalism, divinity penalties, and clan spirit roles will also be a discussion. I welcome those having an interest to write on the subject and look forward to more research being done regarding the vast issues besetting the region. I attempted to discuss the following issues:

The origin of the culture, language, Azande, Bantu, history, people, names and Zande itself. What skills that Azande kingdom has brought about and adopted by the indigenous groups they conquered, occupied and integrate.

The identity of the Azande, Bantu, Zande people of South Sudan, and its clans, how Bantu or Azande expands to South Sudan.

The Azande political, economic, cultural and social organization.

Azande Bantu Geographical location, boundaries, demarcation and definitions or meaning of the word 'Bantu', 'Azande', 'Zande', 'Pa-zande', 'Zandi'.

The difference between Azande, Zande, Pa-Zande, Pa-Dio, Zandi, Sande, Zandeh, Kizande and Bazande according to the Azande themselves.

It is important to mention that all these issues will not be fully discussed in this book.

It is my assumption that the remaining aspects of compensation punishment after the death of the loved one killed in road accident collision crash would have been tackled by other Azande clan writers.

Little has been written about blood wealth compensation. The little that there is, is even scattered across the few documents or in fragment of written books not purposely about blood life wealth penalty, payable in cow(s), which is translated as *hook apuk riem* in *Thuongjang*. I call *hook apuk riem* or *weng apuk riem* as 'blood wealth'. The word '*apuk riem or hook apuk riem or Weng or Wong apuk riem*'[111] translates 'blood life wealth compensation penalty price payable in cow or cows to victim family by guilty family or party for committing a crime to kill the loved one. But rather on other topics in which the word 'hook apuk riem' Jieng Dinka people as you might expect, never surface. Even what you do find as a purported detailed account of the compensation punishment is sometimes an account of legal compensation punishment hearing sentence event written entirely by outsiders who have had infrequent interactions with and *apuk riem* Jieng Dinka customary law[112] study of the traditional law court hearing in the Jieng-Dinka communities.

The practice of the 'blood life wealth' penalty, payable in monetary or money equivalent after death of victim in accident is a new phenomenon in the Jieng culture. But the Azande people use only blood wealth compensation penalty, payable in monetary finance acceptable in the Azande customary rule, which is different to the Jieng customary using cattle, collective responsibility and spiritual priest prayers, sacrifices, ritual ceremonies and so on.

Due to the fact that there is nothing substantial out there for researchers interested in blood life penalty in this largest and hugely influential Jieng clan in the Republic of South Sudan compel me to take my time

---

111   The word *apuk* means compensation. *Riem or riim* means blood shed as a result of injury inflicted. According Jieng, blood is life, sacred and this must be compensated with living blood, substituted in cow, goat, sheep. *The word hook* (plural) means cows, or *weng* (singular) means cow. *Hook* are cows or cattle totaling two cows or five cows to thirty cows. Thirty cows or thirty-one cows are blood life wealth compensation punishment payable for death homicide crime, but slight injury to severe injuries can go beyond five cows which will be determined by the customary law court

112   Wuol Makec, John., *The Customary Law of the Dinka People of Sudan*. Afroworld Publishing Co. 1988. Page 220

and jot down something to go along the way in promoting knowledge and information about the blood life wealth penalty Jieng Dinka society.

It is my hope that the Azande refers to as *Juur* Non-Jieng people, translates as *Nyam-Nyam Lwalla* warriors (Azande warriors), who have hardly any knowledge about the Jieng people including Azande people themselves and others, would be the ones to benefit most from this undertaking case. The word "Jur" is a Jieng artificial name for "alien" or "non-Jieng"[113]. The word "Nyam-Nyam Lwalla" warrior is a Jieng artificial name for great brown Azande king warrior believe to be a great eater warrior or great Azande warrior eater in war time. However, it is to be noted though that majority of the Jieng and Azande people, both within the country and in the Diaspora, are as ignorance of themselves as the next foreigner striving to learn about the *apuk riem* prices defining blood life wealth compensation penalty, payable for committing homicide crimes. The reason being that many of Jieeng and Azandes either grew up outside the country as a result of the long civil war that has profoundly affected the people or were exclusively raised within their respective clan enclaves, shut off from other sections of the Jieng and Azande Communities.

The expectations of the overwhelming majority of returnees are perforce manifestly different from the cultural norms of those who remained behind and whose culture has been little affected by external influences during the past decades of years

The Azande Historical Cultural, Linguistic and their Expansion
Today, it is widely acknowledged that the history of African Bantu culture, and their languages originated from West Africa[114]. The Bantu are an ancient group of people from Africa, whose origins are unclear. Some of

---

113   Beswick, Stephanie (2004). *Sudan's Blood Memory: The Legacy of War, Ethnicity, and Slavery in South Sudan*. Boydell & Brewer. p. 245. ISBN 1-58046-151-4.; online at Google Books

114   The Chronological Evidence for the Introduction of Domestic Stock in Southern Africa Texas State University. Retrieved December 17, 2007.

the people from West Africa traversed from the Congo or Niger Delta Basin[115] to become the main inhabitants of South Sudan. They migrated slowly, such as in small groups and in the process of traveling they became known no longer as West Africans, but rather the Bantu and later the Azande, which translates as "The People."

The eastward Bantu occupation begun with the introduction of crop farming and iron age technology they newly acquired from Nubia culture or Atlantic cultures which made weaponry, conquest and supremacy possible. So, the people moved southwards. The Azande of Bantu people probably brought with them the technology of iron ore smelting. As they moved southwards, eastwards, and northwestwards, they were searching for locations with iron ore resources and hardwood forests. They needed the hardwood to make charcoal to fuel the smelting furnaces. The Azande migrations split into eastern and northwestern streams, partly triggered by the desire by rivals to control the iron ore mines and hardwood decoration in the east, southwest and northwest in Bahr Al-Ghazal areas.

They used agricultural techniques and plants and warfare techniques that destroyed natural population control and exploded the population and necessitated an enlargement of occupation or settlement, which led to the expansion of Bantu Azande tribes or clans and subclans to far beyond tropical rainforests and savanna lands to the colonization of the whole western plateau of South Sudan in Africa. They utilized relatively advanced technologies of the Iron Age compared to the indigenous Nilotic Jaang Rek and Sudanic Balanda people they displaced. They also led to profound changes in savanna valley regions they entered.

There are no written records, no major buildings, or any large established settlements or culture. This was due to fact that the entire sub-continent was a war zone and has been left depleted and destroyed. Cultures were destroyed in the war, nations-states were destroyed in the war, people and populations were destroyed in these conquests.

---

115   http://www.mnsu.edu/emuseum/cultural/oldworld/africa/bantu.html,

Their greater numbers led to independent Azande kingdoms that writers are still looking for to find anyway. It had also led to the expansion of Nilo-Sahara of Nilotic kingdom cultures, which they changed to chieftaincy cultures, to the cultures of colonizers. They also led to profound changes in edible plants, edible roots, and edible fruit trees in savanna areas they entered, such as the area presently known as the neighboring homesteads for southwestern and northwestern Jaang Rek clans. The key evidence for this expansion movement is linguistic; a great many of the cultural languages spoken across Equatorial region[116] are remarkably similar to each other, suggesting the common culture origin of their original proto-Bantu of language speaking people, who spread from an original nucleus, located in the regions of Cameroon and Nigeria across much of tropical rainforest savanna Africa[117]. In the process, the Proto-Bantu cultural language speaking incomers and colonizers displaced or absorbed predating wild animal hunter, wild food gatherer and pastoralists that they combatted[118]. Linguistic study suggests that the cultural expansion ensued across the Congo rainforest region towards east to west of South Sudan[119] along the Congo river divided borderlines.

In the beginning, archaeologists assumed that they could find archaeological similarities in the ancient cultures of the region that the Bantu speakers were held to have crossed; but linguists, classifying the cultures,

116   Clark, John Desmond; Brandt, Steven A. (1984). From Hunters to Farmers: The Causes and Consequences of Food Production in Africa. University of California Press. p. 33. ISBN 978-0-520-04574-3.

117   Adler, Philip J.; Pouwels, Randall L. (2007). World Civilizations: Since 1500. Cengage Learning. p. 169. ISBN 978-0-495-50262-3.

118   Berniell-Lee, Gemma; Calafell, Francesc; Bosch, Elena; et al. (2006). "Genetic and Demographic Implications of the Bantu Expansion: Insights from Human Paternal Lineages". Molecular Biology and Evolution. 26 (7): 1581–9. doi:10.1093/molbev/msp069. PMID 19369595.

119   Pollard, Elizabeth; Rosenberg, Clifford; Tignor, Robert (2011). Worlds Together, Worlds Apart: A History of the World: From the Beginnings of Humankind to the Present. New York: Norton. p. 289. ISBN 978-0-3939-1847-2.

languages and constructing an ancestral record of relationships, believed they could reconstruct substantive culture and language factors. They believed that the cultural expansionism was caused by the development of agriculture, the making of pots, and the use of iron weaponries and farming tools, which permitted new ecological zones to be exploited.

The hypothesized cultural expansion of Bantu classes and subclasses pushed out or assimilated the hunter-forager proto-Azande clans, who had formerly inhabited western South Sudan. In western Equatoria and Bahr Al-Ghazal, culture of Bantu Azande classes and subclasses of speaking language people may have adopted livestock husbandry from other unrelated indigenous Nilotic-speaking people they combatted and conquered. Cattle Herding cultural practices reached the far west several centuries before Azande branch of Bantu family speaking language migrants did. Archaeological, linguistic, genetic, and environmental evidence all support the conclusion that the Azande culture expanded through territorial conquests and occupations was a momentous human migration in history of culture in South Sudan.

The word 'Bantu' and 'Azande' of Culture in South Sudan

This section focusses on ethnic word Bantu and Azande or Zande of culture practice by Azande classes and subclasses in South Sudan.

History of Azande of Bantu Language Family Speaking People

Some historians think history of Africa began with the Bantu people, a group of African Bantu language family speakers that originally lived in the indentation of western Africa[120].

---

120   Blench, Roger, The Benue-Congo languages: a proposed internal classification. "No comprehensive reconstruction has yet been done for the phylum as a whole, and it is sometimes suggested (e.g. by Dixon 1997) that Niger-Congo is merely a typological and not a genetic unity. This view is not held by any specialists in the phylum, and reasons for thinking Niger-Congo is a true genetic unity will be given in this chapter. It is, however, true that the subclassification of the phylum has been continuously modified

Bantu people is used as a general label for the 300 to 600 ethnic groups include Azande people who speak Bantu languages in Africa. They inhabit a geographical area stretching to east north, south and northwest, from Central Africa across the African Great Lakes region down to Southern Africa. Bantu is a major branch of the language family spoken by most populations in Africa.

The geographical origin of the Bantu great expansion is somewhat open to debate. Two main scenarios are suggested, an early expansion to Central Africa, and a single origin of the dispersal radiating from there, or an early separation into an eastward reaching clannish Nilotic clans, northwest-wards and a southward wave of dispersal[121]. Pastoralist Azande of Bantu families occupied land they conquered. When they met hostile Nilotic ethnic clans, they used iron weapons, which they developed around 400 A.D. Waves of Iron Age of Bantu immigrants originating in the vicinity of adjoining regions of Cameroon and Nigeria[122], spread across the broad Equatoria and Bahr al-ghazal peninsula, easily displacing the indigenous Stone Age inhabitants of South Sudan. By the movement within the years of AD 500-1800 century, stable patterns of settlement had emerged.

Beginning from the twelfth century onward, the processes of state formation amongst Bantu people increased in frequency. This was probably due to denser population, which led to more specialized divisions of labor, including military power, while making emigration more difficult;

---

in recent years and cannot be presented as an agreed scheme. The factors which have delayed reconstruction are the large number of languages, the inaccessibility of much of the data, and the paucity of able researchers committed to this field. Emphasis will be placed on three characteristics of Niger-Congo; noun-class systems, verbal extensions, and basic lexicon." See also: Bendor-Samuel, J. ed. 1989. The Niger–Congo Languages. Lanham: University Press of America.

121   Vansina, J. (1995). *"New Linguistic Evidence and the Bantu Expansion,"* Journal of African History. 36 (2): 173–195. doi:10.1017/S0021853700034101. JSTOR 182309.

122   Williamson, K. 1971. The Benue–Congo languages and Ijo. Current Trends in Linguistics, 7. ed. T. Sebeok 245–306. The Hague: Mouton.

to technological developments in economic activity; and to new techniques in the political-spiritual ritualization of royalty as the source of national strength and health[123].

A Series of Azande Kingdoms covered the southwestern portion of the South Sudan plateau while Nilotic ethnic Jaang Rek speaking people inhabited the east, south and north of western Sudd wetlands, on the west of Nile Valley regions. The "Sudanic" family of 'Eastern Sudanic', is now classified as Nilo-Saharan of Nilotic ethnic groups. After the Bantu Azande expansion, many of the great kingdoms were ruled by Bantu people and Nilotic people, who tended to be highly resourceful and adaptable. The Azande kingdom conquests swept across much of Equatoria areas and western Bahr Al-Ghazal, leading to the extinction or absorption of much of the indigenous populations there. This was one of the largest human conquests in our history.

When the Azande met hostile Nilo-Saharan, mainly Nilotic and Sudanic groups there, they used iron weapons they developed around 400AD. They interacted with the Atlantic coast groups and Central Africa, in regions that by the 15th century was a centralized and well-organized Kingdom of Bantu family branches of people. It is a part of three countries now. When they reached their destination, Azande kingdom warriors married the pre-existing people there, who were the Nilotic Jaang or Jieeng and Sudanic Balanda clannish people[124]. During their transition from nomads to settlers, they adapted farming and keeping livestock. But those who wished to remain hunters and gatherers were forced off the farming land and into the rainforests and river banks to remain as fishermen.

The Word 'Bantu'

The word Bantu for the language families and its speakers is an artificial

---

123   Roland Oliver, et al. *"Africa South of the Equator,"* in Africa Since 1800. Cambridge, UK: Cambridge University Press, 2005, pp. 21-25.

124   Toyin Falola, Aribidesi Adisa Usman, *Movements, borders, and identities in Africa,* (University Rochester Press: 2009), pp.4-5.

saying based on the reassembled "Proto 'Ntu'" word for "people" or "humans"[125] , as it was first used by Wilhelm Bleek on the word "Ba-ntu or Bantu"[126]. He assumed that a vast number of language families showing distribution of light brown Bantu ethnic groups and medium brown Bantu ethnic groups found in western, central, southern, and eastern Africa, shared common cultural characteristics that they must be part of a single language families[127]. Wilhelm Bleek coined the name Bantu primarily to represent the word for "people" in loosely reconstructed root Proto-Ntu, from the plural noun group prefix 'ba' labelling "people", and the stem form for 'ntu' or 'tu' for "some (entity), any" single for "person", abantu or bantu for "people", into "thing" or "things". There is no traditional native term for the group indigenous word for the group to mention is not there, to the same degree populations belong to the languages by cultural identity but did not have an idea for the largest ethno-linguistic phylum. Wilhelm Bleek coined the word Bantu because he was inspired by the anthropological observation of ethnic groups identifying themselves as "people" or "the true people"[128].

---

125   *The Chronological Evidence for the Introduction of Domestic Stock in Southern Africa* Archived March 25, 2009, at the Wayback Machine.

126   *The Chronological Evidence for the Introduction of Domestic Stock in Southern Africa* Texas State University. Retrieved December 17, 2007.

127   Raymond G. Gordon, Jr. (ed.), 2005. *Ethnologue: Languages of the World,* Fifteenth edition. (Dallas, Tex.) online edition: Language Family Trees.www.ethnologue. org. Retrieved December 17, 2007.

128   Total population cannot be established with any accuracy due to the unavailability of precise census data from Sub-Saharan Africa. A number just above 200 million was cited in the early 2000s (see Niger-Congo languages: subgroups and numbers of speakers for a 2007 compilation of data from SIL Ethnologue, citing 210 million). Population estimates for West-Central Africa were recognized as significantly too low by the United Nations Department of Economic and Social Affairs in 2015 ("World Population Prospects: The 2016 Revision – Key Findings and Advance Tables" (PDF). United Nations Department of Economic and Social Affairs, Population Division. July 2016. Retrieved 26 June 2017.). Population growth in Central-West Africa as of 2015 is estimated at between 2.5% and 2.8% p.a., for an annual increase of the Bantu population

The Word 'Azande'

The word "Azande" means "people" in many Azande or Zande languages. They identify themselves as "Azande people" or "Zande people", living in the tropical savanna rainforests in Cameroon and northeastern Congo River basins. There were a centralized and well-organized kingdom ruled by Azande kings and protected by Azande warriors, hunters, and farmers in this region, but became widespread to central Equatoria, western Equatoria, western Bahr Al-Ghazal and beyond eastward, to southwest and northwest of Nilotic regions.

The Azande warriors abducted subgroups and captured the indigenous Nilotic ethnic groups taken into the slavery. Azande kingdom nations owned slaves integrated into Azande warriors. Azande names spread all over the areas reflect the presence of large numbers of Azande, and indicate how Azande expansionism changed the landscape and culture of the indigenous, which they had conquered, captured, domesticated and driven to enslavement jails, like Rum Ateny who was captured from southwestern Jaang Rek.

Jaang Rek had first contacts with Azande pioneers they described as Lueel warriors, or Nyam-Nyam warriors in the battles where they realized that those Azande warriors of from the kingdoms posed a threat to local populations. As an example, Rum Atany planned intensive warfare similar to what he had seen and experienced from military training he had participated together with Azande warriors, which is translated in Jieng language as Lueel warriors or Luella warriors. Jaang Rek repulsed back Azande warriors from advancing to their territory through many battles in wars they fought with them. They repulsed aggressive Azande king warriors, defended their homelands, to compete and to stand up with the Lueel warriors or Azande warriors[129].

---

by about 8 to 10 million.

129   Philip J. Adler, Randall L. Pouwels, World Civilizations: To 1700 Volume 1 of World Civilizations, (Cengage Learning: 2007), p.169.

This hypothesis has repeatedly been framed as a mass-migration, but I must say that it was actually a cultural diffusion and not the movement of any specific populations that could be defined as an enormous group simply on the basis of common language traits.

The Azande cultures had brought new warring weaponries, new crops and farming skills or methods to western, and southwestern regions, and taught new cultures in South Sudan. The farming and military cultures used by these people enable them to move every few years. Those new farming or agriculture cultural practices are called slash and burn. A scrap or patch of the forest is cut down and burned. The ashes are mixed into the soil creating a fertile garden area. However, the land loses its fertility quickly and is abandoned for another land conquests in a new territory. When they moved, they shared their skills with the people they encountered and conquered, adapted their cultures to suit each new environment, and learned new values, cultures and customs of the conquered, as they moved ahead.

They followed the Congo River branches northwards and eastward to Sue River basins through the rain forests. Coming to occupy the central highlands of indigenous at the Bahr Al-Ghazal River basins, Sue River basins and Busseri River basins. In a breathtaking rainforest at a river basin it is equally safe for the Azande kingdom to think on how the king fighting military forces could be able to defend the kingdom nations against the many enemy armies. There they farmed the riverbanks; the only place that received enough sunlight to support agriculture. As they moved towards the western Sudd wetlands of the western Nile Valley, they adapted cultural practice of herding goats and sheep to raising cattle. From there a final eastwards migration took place into the Balanda homeland resulting in some ethnic and linguistic mixing. The final movement into the southwestern ethnic Jaang Rek homelands resulted in the displacement of the southwestern Nilotic aboriginal people.

The Name 'Azande'

The name Azande or Zande means 'people' or 'Azande people' in the language of Azande origin, because the word 'Azande' originated from the union of Bandia and Vungara ethnic clans in Cameroon. The word "Nyam Nyam" translates the name "Azande" or "Zande", which is an artificial word coined in Jaang Rek language to describe "Azande people" or "Zande people" as great eaters. They believe that Nyam-Nyam are great warriors who are great human flesh eaters at war times.

The word "Lwalla" or "Lueel" defines or describes Azande or Zande with medium brown colour and light brown colour respectively.

Also, the name Azande or Zande means 'Nyam- Nyam' in the language of Jaang Rek origins, hypothetically portraying cannibalistic propensities. Jaang Rek describes Azande clansman or clanswoman as a great eater or a great human flesh eater, which they translated as 'Nyam-Nyam'. Similarly, the name or word "light brown Azande" or "medium brown Azande" is translated as "Lueel" or "Lwalla" in language of Jaang Rek origin. They also describe Nyam-Nyam Azande describe by colors. The name or word "Lueel warrior" or "Lwalla warrior" defines a "light brown Azande warrior" or a "medium brown Azande warrior" according to their colours. They assumed that light brown Azande warriors are great fighters who would fight the battle and eat human flesh like lions whenever they kill a Jaang warrior[130]. They assumed that light brown Azande warriors (Azande-Lwalla warriors) have lion hair, which they usually see on their bodies, head, and eyes together with their wide

---

130   Eating human flesh was seen in practice in Monrovia City streets during Liberia civil war in 1990. Tribes used human flesh parts which they cut off from people killed in the war between Charles Taylor and President Samuel Kanyon Doe as a deterrent. This indicated that "Nyam-Nyam Warriors" may have been a great human flesh eater in Azande clans as branch of Bantu clans. The tribes deterred their enemies by killing people and cutting out their parts and put human flesh parts into their mouths while moving openly in the streets of Monrovia. Human hearts and livers were used as medicines for soliciting ministerial positions in governments in some countries. This is closer to what Jaang Rek language describes as human flesh eaters.

mouths, large noises, grey-red eyes, huge body buildings, big arms and so on[131].

Azande people were nomadic predators during the waves of Iron Age expansion era, when Jaang Rek people identified them as the Lwalla Azandes of Bantu ethnic groups. This had occurred against a backdrop of centuries at wars with Nilotic they conquered which gave them name Nyam-Nyam.

Nilotic and Zande clan warriors were frequently attacking each other in rainforest hunting for wild games, which halted Zandes of kingdom warrior expansionism to the north, eastward and along the Sue Rivers to the eastern river banks and borders of Nilotic clans of Jieng Rek clans some centuries ago.

According to the early-split state of affairs, the northwards (and eastwards) dispersal had reached the central rain forest by around 1500 BC, and the Savannas by around 500 BC, but around 1,000 BC[132], the eastward dispersal reached the Congo River Basins, Sue River basins, Bahr Al-Ghazal river, expanding further from there, as the rich environment supported a dense population. Possible movements by small groups to the southeast from the Congo River Basins could have been more rapid, with initial settlements widely dispersed and some people crossed near the Sue River basin to become the main inhabitants of Western Equatoria region, western Bahr Al-Ghazal region and central Equatoria region, Bahr Al-Ghazal River Basins, Busseri River Basins and Tonj River Basins and

---

131   Elder persons interviewed about the word "Nyam-Nyam Warrior" did not hesitate to say that Lueel warriors were the same Nyam -Nyam Warriors who were raiding villages. After people returned from hiding, they found out that those people killed by Lueel warriors had their private parts cut off by Lueel warriors who raided the camps. Other elders mentioned that the Nyam- Nyam warriors were so fearful because of their appearance. Nyam- Nyam warriors are lions but they changed to be human in the day or as they want. They finished killing and eating my great grandparents. My grandfather said this and I saw them with big mouths and red eyes like cats.

132   Newman (1995), Ehret (1998), Shillington

near other rivers, due to comparatively harsh farming conditions in areas farther from water. Such culture of expansionism has been identified as containing remnants of the culture of "Bantu people who stayed home", as the bulk of Bantu Azande language speakers migrated away from the region[133]. They moved around slowly, like in small groups and in the process of going around they became known no longer as Congolese Bantu people, but rather the Azande warriors, which interprets as "The Azande People" or "Zande people."

There are quite a lot of suggestions as to why the Zande clans moved; one being that the population simply became too large and thusly forced some to move and practice agriculture; another is that they were searching for fertile land. When the Azande clans met hostile clans they used iron weapons, which they developed during the Atlantic trade interacted with and transformed these earlier aspects of slavery at around 400 AD. Powerful leaders of Azande kingdoms would control the slave industry and deal with the Europeans in order to further their wealth and status with foreigners. When they reached their destination, some of the Azande clans married the pre-existing people there; who became known as the Western Sudanic, now called Central Sudanic, and the Eastern Sudanic, now called Nilo-Saharan or Nile Sudanic people in South Sudan. In names of migration, genetic examination shows a significant grouping and subgrouping of genetic traits by region, suggesting admixture from local populations. During their transition from nomads to settlers they adapted farming and keeping livestock culture, but those who wished to remain hunters and gatherers were forced off the farming land.

Powerful kings of Azande people and their powerful Azande warriors would control the slave enterprises and deal with the slave buyers, slave agents and slave business coordinators in order to further their wealth and

---

133   Evidence against the "early split" scenario shown here is presented in E. Patin et al., "Dispersals and genetic adaptation of Bantu-speaking populations in Africa and North America", Science, Vol. 356, Issue 6337, pp. 543-546 (5 May 2017), doi:10.1126/science. Aal 1988.

status with foreigners. For example, Azande warriors reached southwestern Nilotic Rek in Apuk village and kidnapped Rum Ateny and trained as soldier to fight the enemies.

They utilized relatively advanced technologies for the Iron Age compared to the Nilotic speaking people. They displaced people in the life-threatening west of southwest Rek clans. They took some children and women as slaves, displaced herders and captured Rum they took to the king of Azande clan warriors. They probably brought with them the technology of iron smelting. As they moved southward, eastward and northward, they were searching for locations with iron ore resources and hardwood forests.

They utilized relatively advanced technologies for the Iron Age compared to the Dinka Rek people they displaced. They also led to profound changes in edible plants, edible roots, and edible fruit trees in savanna areas they entered. The final movement into the western Equatoria, central Equatoria and western Bahr Al-Ghazal in South Sudan regions resulted in the displacement of the aboriginal Moro, Balanda Door, Bongo, and Kerish people, resulting in some ethnic and linguistic mixing.

Zande Language, People and Location

The knowledge of minimum of the distinct languages of Africa, including South Sudan, is stagnant very short. There are known to be in extra of 1,500 distinct languages. Numerous efforts to classify them have been inadequate because of the greatest complexity of the languages and because of a confusion involving language, "race," and economy. For instance, there was once a phony interpretation of pastoralism as interconnected to cultures whose members spoke "Hamitic" languages and were descendants of ancient Egyptians[134]. One of the further recent efforts to classify all the African languages, prepared by the linguist Joseph Greenberg, is based on the standards of linguistic analysis, and not on geographic, ethnic, or other nonlinguistic standards.

---

134   Encyclopedia Britannica, Inc.

In South Sudan today, there are approximately 64 indigenous language families classified under the Nilo-Saharan Language, mainly Nilotic and Sudanic groups which represent divisions of Eastern Sudanic or Nile Sudanic and Western Sudanic.

The Nilo-Saharan language family classification as it is known today, was only gradually recognized as a linguistic unit. It is perhaps the most controversial because of inadequate research and the family is the most scattered. In early classifications of the languages, one of the principal standards used to distinguish different groupings was the languages' use of prefixes to classify nouns, or the lack thereof.

The most original point in that classification is the Bantu family classification language which linguistically incorporates all the Azande clan subgroups of Bantu languages found dispersed from Cameroon, Kongo River basins, to southeast -central along Sue River basins through Bahr Al-Ghazal river covered portion of western South Sudan[135].

Azande Language Family Classification

The Azande clans speak Zande language family, which they call: Pa-Zande language family, meaning Pa-Dio, Zandi, Azande, Sande, Zandeh, Kizande and Bazande language family classification spoken by more than 1.1 million spears[136].

Zande language family is commonly used to represent the real Azande language family and sub-clan languages comprising Adio, Barambu, Apambia or Bakpo, Geme, Kpatiri, Nzakara and a number of indigenous clans spreading languages over a vast area from northeastern to

135   Williamson, Kay; Blench, Roger (2000). *"Niger-Congo"*. In Bernd Heine; Derek Nurse (eds.). *African Languages: An Introduction*. Cambridge University Press. pp. 11–12.

136   Zande in: Lewis, M. Paul (ed.), 2009. *Ethnologue: Languages of the World*, Sixteenth edition. Dallas, Tex: SIL International. Simons, Gary F.; Fennig, Charles D., eds. (2018). *"Zande"*. *Ethnologue: Languages of the World* (21st ed.). Dallas, Texas: SIL International. Retrieved 2018-06-29.

south-central regions across the Sue River basins to south, east, to north-west and west of South Sudan. The Congolese Azande speaking clans live along the Uele River; Isiro, Dungu, Kisangani and Duruma. The Central African Azande speaking clans live in the rainforest areas of Rafaï, Bangasu and Obo. And the Azande speaking clans of South Sudan live in Equatoria to the west towards southeast and northwest to Deim Zubeir, and Wau of Bahr Al-Ghazal areas[137].

After the early expansion toward east west, and a single origin of the dispersal radiating from there; the Azande speaking clans occupied much of the Equatoria and Bahr Al-Ghazal regions to the west because they were following the Congo Nile River Divide line through the tropical rain forests along the river's headwater flowing riverbanks. There they farmed the river-banks, which was the only place that received enough sunlight to support agriculture. As they moved eastward into the savannas to South Sudan forests, they adapted their techniques for herding goats and sheep to raising cattle. Passing through what is now National Park and hardwood thick forests, they learned to cultivate new crops. Some such crops were the banana, pineapple and yam, which came from travelers of Atlantic coast of Central Africa.

They created iron and copper weapons and adornments, practiced free trade with their neighbors to the east bank of the river, who are inhabitants of the west bank of the river. Other Related Nilo-Saharan languages were spoken, such as Bari, Lotuko, Acholi. Jie, Murle, Mondari, Pojulo, Zande, Moro, Balanda Door, Balanda Bviri, Avukaya, Makaraka, Mangayat, Morokodo, Moru, Mandari, Mundu, Ndogo, Ngulgule, Nyangwara, as well as the Azande languanges such as Pa-Dio, Sande, Kizande, and Bazande languages. Passing through what is now Bahr Al-Ghazal River basins and Tonj River basins in western Sudd wetlands and central-western Jieng Rek, they learned to cultivate new crops.

Azande Traditional Beliefs

Many Azande before practiced a traditional African religion. This has been

---

137   Zande, Encyclopedia Britannica.

replaced to a large extent by Christianity. Many Azande now participate in faithfulness in the Catholic belief. Some Azande clan traditional beliefs include Azande witch doctor or medicine man or shame and magic. The Azande witch doctor or witchcraft or mangu, is believed to be an inherited ingredient in the belly which hints a moderately independent life, and has power to accomplish bad magic on adversaries of a person. As they thought that Azande witch doctor or witchcraft is inherited, a postmortem of a suspected witch clansman would also show that a certain living Zande clansman, connected to the dead, was or was not a witch clansman.

A medicine man, shame or mangu is believed to be passed down from parent to child of the same sex; and from father to son or from mother to daughter down the line. So, if a Zande clansman were to be confirmed to possess mangu or shame ingredient, this conclusion would extend to that Zande clansman's, sons, brothers, and so on[138]. According to the Zande, mangu or witch clansmen can occasionally be ignorant of their magic powers, and can unintentionally strike other people to whom the witch or sorceress wishes no evil. Because mangu clansman is believed at all times to be present, there are numerous rituals linked to protection from and stopping of mangu clansman that are done almost daily. After a little out of the ordinary occurs, customarily something unfortunate, to a person, the Azande clan people may blame mangu or medicine man, just as Jang Dinka Rek clan people might blame "misfortune" or "unluckiness".

According to anthropologists, the psychic aspect of witchcraft or mangu or Azande witch doctor is the soul of witchcraft clansman. It often leaves the physical body of the witch clansman at night, when the victim is asleep, and is directed by the witch into the body of the victim. When victim moves, it shines with a bright light that can be seen by anyone during the nighttime. However, during the day it can be seen only by

---

138   Stein, Rebecca L.; Stein, Philip L. (2016). The Anthropology of Religion, Magic, and Witchcraft (3rd ed.). London: Routledge. p. 214. ISBN 9780205718115. OCLC 928384577.

Azande clan traditional spiritual experts[139].

Oracles are a technique of controlling the source of the believed Azande black magic witchcraft clansmen, and were for a long time the crucial legal power and the main controlling factor in how clansman would respond to the dangers. The Azande use three different types of oracles. The most powerful oracle is the "benge" poison oracle, which is used solely by Azande clansmen. The decisions of the oracle are all the time accepted and no clan person questions it. A smaller famous except more freely accessible is the termite oracle. Azande-Lueel clanswomen, clansmen, and children are all allowed to consult this oracle. The smallest expensive except also smallest reliable oracle is the rubbing-board oracle. The rubbing board oracle is described in Culture Sketches as "a device resembling a Ouija board, made of two small pieces of wood easily carried to be consulted anywhere, and at any time"[140].

139   Stein, Rebecca L.; Stein, Philip L. (2016). *The Anthropology of Religion, Magic, and Witchcraft* (3rd ed.). London: Routledge. p. 214. ISBN 9780205718115. OCLC 928384577.

140   Singer, André (1981). *"Witchcraft Among the Azande"*. johnryle.com. Retrieved 2018-01-09.

CHAPTER FIVE

JIENG-DINKA GROUPS AND HISTORY OF CULTURE, IDENTITY AND LANGUAGE FAMILY IN SOUTH SUDAN

Jieng Dinka History, Location, Language Family, Religion and Culture

I will attempt to address the challenges facing the Jieng Rek and Azande family members, customary law court judges, cultural history, blood life wealth penalty payable in cattle for compensation of life lost to forgive and reverse curse of guilty clan family.

Before people can clearly understand *apuk riem*, clan crimes or offences, clan spirit forgiveness, blood wealth for forgiveness, and repentance, they should understand the offence, the wrongdoer, and particularly the effects of the crime. *Apuk reim* blood life wealth compensation have been shown to help members of a Jieng Dinka family related to a child killed in a road crash, reconcile with the Azande family members of a guilty driver. The family of the guilty Azande driver can be forgiven, restoring peace and harmony between two diverse family cultures.

I will write the little I know about the history, culture, language, origin, custom, divinity spiritual reconciliation, spirit forgiveness, beliefs and ritual sacrifices. The implications of traditionalism, divinity penalties, and clan spirit roles will also be a discussion. I welcome those having an interest to write on the subject and look forward to more research being done regarding the vast issues besetting the region. I attempted to discuss the following issues:

a. The origin of the culture, Jieng, Dinka, history, people, names and Dinka itself. How they identify themselves and expand will be included.

b. The identity of the Jieng people of the Republic of South Sudan, and its clans.

c. The Jieng political, economic, cultural and social organization.

d. Jieng Dinka Geographical location, boundaries, demarcation and definitions or meaning of the word 'Muonyjieng', 'Muonyjeeng', 'Muonyjang', 'Muonyjaang'.

e. The difference between Muonyjang, Muonyjaang and Jieeng according to the Jieng themselves.

It is important to mention that all these issues will not be fully discussed in this book.

That little there, is so scattered across the few documents or in fragment of written books not purposely about 'blood life wealth penalty', payable in cow(s) translates as *hook apuk riem* in *Thuongjang*. H*ook apuk riem* or *weng apuk riem* defines 'blood wealth penalty'. The word '*apuk riem or hook apuk riem or weng/wong apuk riem*'[141] translates 'blood life wealth compensation penalty, payable in cow or cows to victim family by guilty family or party for committing a crime to kill the loved one. The Jieng language definition explains *apuk riem* as a punishment or penalty

---

141   The word *apuk* means compensation. *Riem or riim* means blood shed as a result of injury inflicted. According Jieng, blood is life, sacred and this must be compensated with living blood, substituted in cow, goat, sheep. *The word hook* (plural) means cows, or *weng* (singular) means cow. *Hook* are cows or cattle totaling two cows or five cows to thirty cows. Thirty cows or thirty-one cows are blood life wealth compensation punishment payable for death homicide crime, but slight injury to severe injuries can go beyond five cows which will be determined by the customary law court

blood fine of customary court for killing, or for inflicting serious wounds executed with the full knowledge and understanding of those actions by the clansmen or clanswomen found guilty.

There has been little study on the topics fully addressing the word 'hook apuk riem' Jieng Dinka people. Whatever you do find as a purported detailed account of the compensation punishment is the result of the account from legal compensation punishment hearing sentence of event written entirely by outsiders who have had little knowledge about it or have not heard anything about *apuk riem* Jieng Dinka customary law[142] and less on the traditional law court hearing in the Jieng-Dinka communities.

The practice of the 'blood life wealth' penalty, payable in monetary or money equivalent after the death of victim in accident is a new phenomenon in the Jieng culture. Cultural transformation made Jieng Dinka living in townships to adopt new system of blood wealth compensation penalty, payable in monetary finance acceptable in the Azande culture and various non-Jieng cultures in South Sudan.

It is certain that there is nothing substantial out there for researchers interested in blood life penalty practices by the largest and hugely influential Jieng clan in the Republic of South Sudan. It is my belief that the contents of this book this will promote knowledge and information about pluralism of blood life wealth penalty Jieng (Dinka) society of the Republic of South Sudan.

As a Jieng, or Jang-Muonyjang myself, and someone who is greatly fascinated by this proud clan, I thought that I am better placed to get the word out, both to the native people of Jieng-Muonyjang and Non-Jieng-Muonyjang people referred to as '*juur*' in plural or 'Jur' in singular in *Thuongjang or Thuongmuonyjang or Thongjieeng or Thongmuonyjaang*. Most importantly, it is my hope that the *Juur* Non-Jieng people who have little knowledge about the pluralism of blood life wealth penalty Jieng people,

---

142   Wuol Makec, John., *The Customary Law of the Dinka People of Sudan*. Afroworld Publishing Co. 1988. Page 220

will be the people to benefit most from this endeavor. "Jur" is a Jieng word for "alien" or "non-Jieng"[143]. However, it is to be noted that majority of the Jieng people, both within the country and in the Diaspora, are as ignorant of themselves as the next outsiders. The reason for this is many of the Jieeng people either grew up outside the country as a result of the long civil war, or were exclusively raised within their respective clan enclaves, shut off from other sections of the Jieng society.

The expectations of the overwhelming majority of returnees are manifestly different from the cultural norms of those who remained behind and whose culture has been little affected by external influences during the past decades of years.

History of Jieng Dinka

Oral historical tradition is the inspirational reference that has been seriously acting as clan custodians. Oral traditions say that the Dinka also known as Jieng originated from the Gezira island in the Sudan. The earliest historical records come from Anglo-Egyptian Sudan sources, which describe the land upstream towards the south as "wretched"[144]. In medieval eras, this region was ruled by the kingdom of Alodia; a Christian, multi-ethnic empire dominated by Nubians[145]. Living in its Southern periphery and interacting with the Nubians, the Jieng (Dinka) absorbed a sizable amount of the Nubian vocabulary[146]. From the 13th century,

143   Beswick, Stephanie (2004). *Sudan's Blood Memory: The Legacy of War, Ethnicity, and Slavery in South Sudan.* Boydell & Brewer. p. 245. ISBN 1-58046-151-4.; online at Google Books

144   S. O. Y. Keita (1993). *"Studies and Comments on Ancient Egyptian Biological Relationships".* History in Africa (JSTOR) 20: 129- 154. Retrieved 2015-04-11.

145   Werner, Werner. (2013). *Das Christentum in Nubien. Geschichte und Gestalt einer afrikanischen Kirche (Christianity in Nubia. History and shape of an African Church)* in Germany Lmt.ISBN. 978-3-643-12196-7

146   Beswick, Stephanie (2004). *Sudan's Blood Memory: The Legacy of War, Ethnicity, and Slavery in South Sudan.* Boydell & Brewer. Page 21. ISBN 1-58046-151-4.; online at Google Books

with the disintegration of Alodia kingdom, the Jieng began to migrate out of the Gezira island fleeing slave raids, and other military conflicts as well as drought[147].

The Jieng history begins with cultural heroes of the clans-people such as the spear masters, or spiritualists or deities. Thus, oral history is the grandfather compass or array that the people of Jieng clan and subclan nationalities use to tell their social, political, and cultural time of day. It is a compass they use to find themselves on the human geography. It tells them where they are, who they and where they come from.

The river lakes Nilotes is part of the territories of the Ancient Kush King, Meroe Alodia kingdom and the Jieng nation of Nilotic descendants which is older than Ancient Egypt or Sudan. It was recognized in 1893[148] as home to numerous ancient civilizations, such as the Kingdom of Kush, Meroe and Alodia. Most of them flourished and simultaneously evolved systems of kingship along the Nile valley[149]. The early history is interweaved with the history of ancient Sudan and ancient Kush. It is possible that the Jaang nation-states descend from a people whose original language, habitat and migrations through many centuries can no longer be traced. Therefore, the Apuk clan state developed mostly in seclusion. When determining how to respond to the unique cultural, historical, and divinity challenges it faced. One of these challenges was confronting the fundamental aspects of reality that are the grounds and influences of its history, culture, and nationality.

This would mean the uprooting and complete destruction of the systematic and ruthless mental murder sustained through and by the

---

147   Beswick, Stephanie (2004). *Sudan's Blood Memory: The Legacy of War, Ethnicity, and Slavery in South Sudan.* Boydell & Brewer. Page 29-31. ISBN 1-58046-151-4.; online at Google Books

148   Abbas Abbas, Mekki. *The Sudan question: the dispute over the Anglo-Egyptian condominium,* 1884- 1951 (1952)

149   Warburg, Gabriel. *Sudan Under Wingate: Administration in the Anglo-Egyptian Sudan (1899-1916)* (1971)

formation of historical denial which brainwashed and indoctrinated generations into thinking that the historical identity nation Jieng does not exist.

The number of Jieeng speakers is about 4,500,000 in the early 21st century. The Jieeng form many independent groups of 1,000 to 30,000 persons. Those groups are organized on a regional, linguistic, and cultural basis into clusters, of which the best known are the Agaar, Aliab, Bor, Padaang, Rek, Twic, and Malual[150].

Linguists have divided the Jieeng language family into the Padaang language family of the northern group. The Rek, Agaar, and Bor constitute the Western, Southern and Eastern groups respectively. The Padaang language family group has 12 sub-languages, whereas the three other languages have four to five sub-languages each. The Jieeng languages, like all other languages in general, have grammatical, lexical and phonological differences.

Dinka also called Jieng or Jieeng people live in the savanna country surrounding the central swamps of the Nile.

This section discusses about Jieng, Jieeng, Jang, Jaang or Muonyjeng, Muonyjeeng or Muonyjang or Muonyjaang Dinka people, who are living in the Republic of South Sudan occupying vast territories on both western and eastern White Nile River and its tributaries, from Renk in the northeast to Boor or Bor in the south and from Boor in the East to Aweil in the west, as well as from the north to the south of the western White Nile.

Dinka falls into five main language families namely:

1. **The Southeastern Bor Jieng-Dinka language family:** This Boor/Bor Jieng group is comprises of Boor Athooc, Boor Gok, Twic East, Nyarweng and Hol;

2. **The South Central Jieng or Jaang-Dinka group:** This Jaang or Jieeng Agaar group is comprises of Aliab, Agaar, Chiec, Ghok, and Atuot;

3. **The Northeastern Padaang Jieng-Dinka group:** This Padaang Jieng group is comprises of Padaang, Luach, Abiliang, Thoi, Dongjol, Ngok Lual-yak, Rut and Ageer.

---

150   www.britannica.com

4. **The Northwestern Ruweng Jieng-Dinka group: This** Ruweng Jieng group is comprises of Ruweng Panaruu, Aloor, Paweny and Ngok Abyei.

5. **The Southwestern Rek Jang or Jaang-Dinka group:** This Rek Jang or Jaang group is comprises of Abiem, Aguok, Apuk (north, north-east, & south), Awan, Lau, Luac, Malual, Paliet, Palioupiny, Nyang, Abuok, Leer, Luanykoth, and Twic.

Some linguists have described four major language varieties, which they classified as: Eastern Jieng language, which is Boor based; Northern Jieng language called Padaang language, which is Dongjol based; Southern Jieng language, which is Agaar based; and Western Jieng or Jang language, which is Rek based.

But, Luacjang to the east of Tonj and Twic to the north of Gogrial have slight language varieties, different from Rek language.

It is argued that the four major languages above are the varieties in which translations of the Bible or some primers have been written. Insignificant variations do exist in each major group. The differences that exist between the major groups, although greater than those in the major group, do not challenge the harmony and union of an exploration that covers the 'blood wealth', payable in the cause of death of the loved ones, injuries, defamation, murder, homicide, crime, and damage according to the culture of victims of Jieng Rek community.

There is no recorded history as to when and from where the Jieng or Jang Dinka people originated from to their present geographical location. Jieng and Nuer are closely connected through manifestation, the language and customary code of conduct or traditional laws. The Jieng and Nuer practice a complex of twin straining that entertain and think of descended from a common ancestral language. How closely Nuer with its varieties is connected to Jieng with its varieties has not yet been determined with firmness at this moment.

The Jieng and the Nuer construct or constitute one subdivision of

Western Nilotic ethnic language family[151]. Burun is the second subdivision of language family. The Shilluk, Anyuak, Jurchol, Acholi of South Sudan, the Luo of Kenya, and the Lango and Alur of Uganda construct the third subdivision of language family. They are all branches of Nilo-Saharan family classification, which is the most controversial, because of inadequate research, and the language family widely scattered[152].

Western Nilotic is itself a sub-branch of Nilotic which, in turn, is a branch of the Eastern Sudanic division of the Chari-Nile subfamily of the Nilo-Saharan language family[153].

The Jieng Dinka language *Thuongjang* has the largest number of all the more than 60 African languages spoken in the South Sudan. Jieng Dinka is classified as an Eastern Sudanic language of the Nilo-Saharan phylum[154].

Nilo-Saharan phylum is tightly connected to Nuer, which together with Jieng constitutes a sub-group of the Western Nilotic languages. Jieng language is spoken in the central part of South Sudan, along the White Nile and its tributaries. The area extends from Renk in the Upper Nile region to Boor in Jonglei region, and from Rumbeek in Lakes region to Aweil in the Western part of Bahr Al-Ghazal region.

Jieng Geographical Location
The Jieng (Dinka) is an ethnic group of several related peoples living in the Republic of South Sudan along both sides of the White Nile River. They are inhabiting the Bahr Al-Ghazal region of the White Nile basin, Jonglei and parts of southern Kordofan and Upper Nile regions. They

---

151   Seligman, C.G.; Seligman, Brenda Z. (1965). *Pagan Tribes of the Nilotic Sudan.* London: Routledge &Kegan Paul.

152   Ehret, Christopher (1983). Mack, John; Robertshaw, Peter (eds.). *Culture History in the Southern Sudan.* Nairobi, Kenya: British Institute in Eastern Africa. pp. 19–48. ISBN 9781872566047.

153   Gerrit Dimmendaal (2008) *"Language Ecology and Linguistic Diversity on the African Continent",* Language and Linguistics Compass 2/5:841.

154   Greenberg, Joseph H. (1963) *The Languages of Africa.* Indiana University Press

cover a wide geographical location along the streams flowing towards western Sudd wetlands and various Nile river tributaries, concentrated in the Upper Nile region in southeast Sudan and across into southwest Ethiopia. They are largely agro-pastoral people, relying on cattle herding at riverbank cattle camps during the dry season, beginning January to April annually, and growing millet translated as *awuou in thuongjang* and other varieties of grains, which is translated as *rap in thuongjang* languages in fixed settlements during the rainy season, beginning from May to July, but the months of August, September, October and November to December are used for harvest per year. They Jieng Dinka number around 4.5 million people, making 18% of the population of the entire country, and constitute the largest ethnic clan and subclan in South Sudan.

Jieng (Dinka) History

Ancient symbols, ornaments, human paintings, animal drawing and cattle pictures in Egypt give reason to connect the Jieng Dinka with the introduction of domesticated cattle south of the Sahara. The Jieng ways of burying noble families who have died along with living sheep, seen in Egypt, are other factors to believe they were there or have something in common. Around 3000 BC, herders who also fished and tilled settled in the largest swamp area in the world, the area of South Sudan where the flood plain of the White Nile is also fed by the Rivers Bor, Bahr Al-Ghazal, Aweil and Renk.

The Jieng Dinka are one of three groups that gradually developed from the original settlers. Jieng Dinka society spread out over the area in recent centuries, perhaps as the oldest recorded Nilo-Saharan language of Nilotic languages dating to about the AD 9th century. The Jieng people defended their area against the wave of Iron Age of invading Bantu and Azande king warriors in the earlier AD 500- 1000 and repulsed attempts of great kingdoms of Azande king warriors to conquer them to settle or occupy their territories. They also fought with Ottoman Turks in the mid-1800s and resisted slave merchants to convert them to Islam. Otherwise, they have remained separate, independent, and lived in isolation.

Jieng (Dinka) Identity

South Sudan's identity is found in its diverse cultures and nationalities. Identity should remain a security factor, for if it is not then subsequent work would not be grounded. This way people can see how the question of compensation, land ownership, citizenship, free-movement, the social organisation and political parties, and unity of people, all hinge on a clear definition of identity. History is South Sudan's clarifier and its memory. Every struggle that forgets its history is doomed to repeat it. The dilemma of our culture lies in the non-existence of social justice services and the lack of social equalities[155].

The Jieng (Dinkas) are one of the branches of the River Lake Nilotes. While circulated for centuries as "Dinka", they identify themselves as *Jieng, Jieeng, Jang, Jaang* in *thuongjang*, translates "peoples". Muonyjang, Muonyjaang, Muonyjieng or Moinjeeng. In Thuongjang this translates as "Peoples of the peoples". The Jieng clans have their symbol of identity within the nationalities in twelve subdivisions of Jieng (Dinka) clan and subclan: Atuot, Aliab, Bor, Chiec, Agaar, Gok, Rek, Twic or Tuic East, Twic West, Luachjang, Malual, and Ngok. Malual and Rek are the largest groups, each numbering over a million people. The name Jieeng or Jaang or Jieng in thuongjang means "peoples". It is written using the Latin alphabet with a few additions.

Jieng or Jang definition of clan or subclan, or tribe is autonomy, state or nation or country. According to Jieng, country refers to *wut, gol,* and all are semi-autonomous or independent from each other and can unite for individual interests, political issues, security reasons, wars and natural disasters.

They still live close to the hot and humid native land of the river-Lake Nilotes. The branches of the river lake Nilotes of South Sudan Luo includes people throughout central Uganda and neighboring sections of Zaire and the lake area of western Kenya.

---

155   Agei, Madhel Malek (2020). *Apuk a State in Waiting,*

Jieeng or Jaang (Dinkas) are the largest ethnic branch of the estimated 64 indigenous ethnic groups, belonging to a group of cultures known as the Nilo-Saharan Language, largely Nilotic ethnic divisions of Eastern Sudanic or Nile Sudanic or river lake Nilotes, all of whom live in the Republic of South Sudan.

The word "Dinka" has wrongly represented true identity of Jieeng or Jaang as they know it. The clansmen who were named 'Dinkas' by visitors were native clans among the first ancient people. Early travelers asked clansman to say the name of community living in this location. Instead of saying Jieng or Jang or Jaang or Mounyjieeng or Jieeng or Muonyjang, the name which they supposed everybody already knew, the clansman gave the name of his chief. Any foreign explorer who visited the river lakes Nilotes, will ask a village clansman what the name of the clan was. He or she would say: "We are the people of Ding Kak", a very common name among them. The explorer simply wrote down *Din* and *Ka*. Thusly, the word *Dinka* circulated widely around the world as the name of a proud people living around the lakes and rivers in the region.

The Jieng-Dinka groups retain the traditional pastoral life of the Nilotes, but have added agriculture in some areas, growing grains, peanuts, beans, corn (maize) and other crops. Clanswomen do most of the agriculture, but men clear forest for the gardening sites. There are usually two plantings per year. Some are fishers. Their culture incorporated strategies for dealing with the annual cycle of one long dry season and one long rainy season.

The Jieeng seasonal migrations are determined by the local climate, their agro-pastoral lifestyle responding to the periodic flooding and dryness of the area in which they live. They begin moving to wetland *toic* between January and February rain begins to rain and moving out from wetland *toic* around April to May at the onset of the rainy season to their "permanent settlements" of mud and thatch housing above flood level, where they plant their crops of groundnut, millet and other grain products.

The boys tend goats and sheep while the men are responsible for the cattle. The cattle are central to the Jieng-Dinka culture and worldview. A man will identify with one special ox, will name it and compose songs and dances about the ox. He calls himself by the name of the ox, which is given to him at his initiation to adulthood. The ox will be referred to by many reference names, allusions to the direct name, which is actually its colour.

The Jieng expect an individual to be generous to others in order to achieve status in the society. Jieng base their life on values of honor and dignity. They discuss and solve problems in public forums.

Rainy season settlements usually contain other permanent structures such as cattle byres translates as *luak in thuongjang* and granaries translates as *jong in thuongjang*. During dry season period, beginning about December–January, everyone except the aged, ill, and nursing mothers migrate to semi-permanent dwellings in the toic for cattle grazing. The cultivation of sorghum, millet, groundnut, and other crops begins in the highlands in the early month of May of rainy season and the harvest of crops begins in August when the heavy rains are stopped or reduced between September and November in the year. Cattle are driven to the toic in September and November when the rainfall drops off; allowed to graze on harvested stalks of the crops

Jieng Language

The Jieng (Dinkas) peoples speak a language, which is known by numerous names: Dinka, Thuongjang, Thongjieng, Thongjieeng, Thongmuonyjaang, and Thongmonyjang language family. These are a series of spoken languages connected together, which are grouped by linguists into five broad language families. These five formal languages are called by linguists as: - Northeastern, Northwestern, Southeastern, Southwestern and South Central. These titles encompass all the known languages of Jieng -Dinka speech.

They number around 4.5 million people according to the 2008 Sudan census, constituting about 18 % of the population[156] of the entire country, and the largest ethnic clan in South Sudan. Jieng Dinka as they called themselves as Muonyjang (singular), and Jieng, Jieeng, Jaang, Muonyjaang, or Muonyjieeng (plural) make up one of the branches of the River Lake Nilotes, mainly sedentary agro-pastoral peoples of the Nile Valley and African Great Lakes region who speak Nilotic languages, including the Nuer and Luo[157] and others like Jurchol, Shilluk, Anyuak, Acholi and so on. *Thuongjang* is one of the Nilotic languages of the Eastern Sudanic language family.

Jieeng are sometimes noted for their height, believed to be the tallest in Africa. The Jieng clans and subclans of associations of nationalities, nearly a dozen in all, derive themselves from the *Raan de Jieng* or *Kooch de Jieng*. That is, Jieng clansmen and clanswomen or Jieng states or nations or countries.[158] The Jieng or Kooch de Jieng clans are original stem from where other clans separated off during migration eras. These clans settled in the eastern Nile from north to east.

The Jang Rek clans are derived from the Raan Muonyjang or Raan Jang or Raan Muonyjeeng or Kooch Jang or Kooch Muonyjeeng or Jang Rek nationalities. The Jieng Rek clan is the original stem from which other clans branched off during migration periods. These clans separated and settled in the western Nile territory in the middle of the Bahr Al-Ghazall Region.

Ongoing research and analysis entail continual revision of the formal classification of Jieng or Jang speech forms.

Each subclan identifies its own clan speech by that name of clan and around thirty-seven sublanguages have been identified among the five language groupings. For example, Jieng Twic or Tuic East has its own

---

156   Ancient Historical Society Virtual Museum, 2010

157   Seligman, C.G.; Seligman, Brenda Z. (1965). *Pagan Tribes of the Nilotic Sudan.* London: Routledge &Kegan Paul.

158   Nebel, Arthur, *The Dinka Dictionary,* Published by Veronica Father, Wau, 1954

language, and it is an independent clan in Jieng, and Luac-jang West has its own language, and it is an independent clan in Jaang communities.

Classifying Twic East under Bor is totally wrong, it is a separate language. Moreover, classifying Luac-jang West under Rek is totally wrong too, it is a separate language from Rek languages.

Some linguists refer to these technically distinct languages as one language. The Jieng-Dinka languages are written in Latin script.

Jieng Customs

The Jieng or Jaang (Dinka) group or clan or clan is as a coalition, or a union of lineages that are bound by blood and other people or families who had attached themselves either by marriage or otherwise. The clans or groups identify with a particular lineage originally derived from one of the main chiefly or kingly or *beny*, who are dominant or governing or prevailing and said to have the land or birth homeland of the group. They claim a single ancestor and base their right or birth right to political and religious superiority or dominance on some particular important myth about their descent.

The second category of clans, the members of which had no special hereditary religious functions, is called collectively *kiic* or commoners. They vary considerably in size and area of distribution. The 'commoner' clans were scarcely regarded as *wut kiic* or *dhieth kiic* but as disunited families with no sense of a wider agnatic or paternal relationship.

The commoner clans in the midst of the Jieng or Jaang-Dinka are also translated as *koc tong*, meaning people of the war spear, or pursuers in connection to the predominantly clans who were *koc bith in thuong-jang*, translates as people of the supreme master of the fishing spear and war leader, or high chief priest, or Deity. This distinction, on the other hand, is one of culture, not of function. In the past Jieng-Dinka culture, Master of Fishing Spear or High Priest Chief is believed to possess super-natural powers associated with truth-telling, justice, wealth, knowledge, and prophetic vision. These people are responsible for health, good life, prosperity, peace, reconciliation, life guidance, rainmaking and all kinds of protection for their society.

The Jaang or Jieeng falsely known as "Dinka" are proud, hospitable, friendly and ethnocentric. They also demonstrate a high moral standard, code of behaviour, feeding mannerism and sense of personal dignity refers to as *dheeng puou or dheeng puou* and integrity. They deal with others on the basis of reciprocity. The Jieeng people are least touched by modernization; their pride and ethnocentrism must be important factors in their conservatism and resistance to change[159]. Jieng (Dinka) culture is centred on cattle. It is the medium of exchange whether in marriage, payment of debts and blood wealth compensation or payable blood price, or for sacrifices to the spirits and on major occasions and rites, ceremonies, burials or rituals.

Jieng Naming

A Jieng or Jang (Dinka) male is likely to be given an ox by his father, uncle or whoever is responsible for him. If a color of his 'ox name' is *Makuei, Madok, Mayen, Mabior or Malith,* a boy child will be named after it. Another Jieng Dinka names also derive from colour of their cattle and a girl child may be named as *Ayen, Yar,* or *Akeer.* The name of a boy could also be named after the colour of the best ox or cow, for instance: *mayom, mayen, malith, or marial* or cow like *ayen, ayom, or ayar* that was given in marriage by the father. Like other Nilotic ethnic groups, the Jieng-Dinka people have special names for twins: *Ngor, Angeer, Chan, Bol, Madit, Deng, Amuor, Achan, Atoc, Adit* or so indicating being a twin.

These people normally identify themselves Jieng from Upper Nile or identify themselves Muonyjang from Bahr Al-Ghazal. The Nuer identify them 'Jiang'; Shilluk identify them 'Jango', Azande, Balanda and Kerish identify them 'Ziengge', Arabs, Bari, Kuku, Kakwa or other people in

---

159   Acuil Deng, (4 February 20120. *Pioocku Thuongjang:* Let's Learn Dinka (not published)

Equatoria identify them 'Jiengge'; all names stemming from Jieng or Jieeng.

The Jieng-Dinka culture is the only system practicing combined identity colours in Africa. They have large vocabulary for cattle, their colours and take great interest and pride in the art of making different conformations to which their horns can be trained to grow. It has been estimated that they have more than 400 names of different colors to refer to cattle alone, their movements, their diseases, and their variety in color and form. The minute discussing, debating, dialoguing on whatever or in a dance, a Jieng usually throws up his arms in imitation of the shape of the horns of ox, or a cow in general.

Jieng Marriage

A marriage is obligatory among the Jieeng or Jaang (Dinka) communities. A male is always expected to raise a family and can marry as many wives as possible. Polygamy is the ideal for the Jieeng-Dinka, though many men may have only one wife. The Jieeng Dinka must marry outside their clan (exogamy), which promotes more cohesion across the broader Jieeng Dinka groups of clans and subclans. Kinship clans or groups are connected and associated with named descent clans identified by a symbol or an emblem, and wives leave their descent clan to become part of their husbands and lineage clan.

A "bride wealth price" is paid by the family of groom to finalize the marriage alliance between the two clan families. Levirate marriage provides support for widows and their children. All children of co-wives are raised together and have a wide family identity. Co-wives cook for all children, though each wife has a responsibility for her own children.

Relatives marry to the ghost of a male or female who died in infancy, adolescence or adulthood. Therefore, there are so many 'ghost fathers' existing among the Jieeng (Dinka) communities or peoples in South Sudan.

The bride price differs from one Jieng Dinka clan subdivision to the other. It ranges from some a few tens in Upper Nile and Bahr Al-Ghazal to a few hundred in Bahr Al-Ghazal and small section in Upper Nile. Small section in Bahr Al-Ghazal raises bridge price relatively higher to two hundred or more. In the same way the bride price is raised by the family of groom contribution. Bride price contributed in cattle numbers is distributed accordingly between uncle to uncle, brother to brother, and so on in the clan of Bride.

Daughters of Chief families fetch more cattle in the same way son of family of chieftaincy is expected to pay more cattle for his wife. A girl holding a degree has raised bride wealth prices to fetch over two hundred cows or equivalent. This is a factor which is most likely to positively promote enrolment of girls in schools amongst Jieeng communities in the country. Like other Nilotic ethnic communities, sex is only for social reproduction among the Jieeng (Dinka) communities. Thus, fornication is prohibited; adulterer is despised and heavily fined, sometimes this may be source of clannish conflict and clannish fighting. Incest is commonly unthinkable and indeed abhorred.

The Jieng people did not live in villages, but traveled in clan family divisions and subdivisions living in temporary homesteads with their cattle, before the coming of the British colonial administrations. The homesteads could be in gatherings of one or two all the way up to hundred families. Small towns grew up all round British administrative centers. Each village of one or more extended clan families is led by an influential leader chosen because of his merit or what he does to community.

Girls learn to cook, but boys do not. Cooking is done outdoors in pots over a stone hearth. Clansmen depend upon clanswomen for a number of aspects of their life, but similarly the division of work assigns certain functions to the clansmen, such as fishing and herding, and the periodic hunting.

Traditional homes were made of mud walls with thatched conical grassroots, which could last for a number of years. Only clanswomen and children sleep inside the house, while the clansmen sleep in mud-roofed cattle pens, runs or coops. The homesteads were located to enable movement in a range allowing all-year-round access to grass and water. Permanent villages are now built on higher ground above the flood plain of the Nile but with good water for irrigation. The clanswomen and older clansmen tend crops on this high ground while younger clansmen move up and down with the rise and fall of the river.

The Jieng Dinka Adulthood Initiation in South Sudan

Initiation into adulthood takes different styles and ceremonies. After initiation to adulthood, the social spheres of the genders overlap very little. They invariably remove the four (4) lower canines as a sign of maturity. A girl's physiological evolution and attainment of puberty is marked by celebration, commonly by clanswomen, to demonstrate readiness for marriage. Some Jieng-Dinka clan divisions and subdivisions or sections scratch or lacerate the face to mark graduation into adulthood and age-group. In some, clanswomen of particular status have their faces scratched or lacerated.

The basic food is a heavy millet porridge, eaten with milk or with a vegetable and spice sauce. Milk itself, in various forms, is also a primary food. Linguistic evidence also indicates that the custom of milking cattle was also directly from Cushitic cultures in the area[160].

Jieng Dinka Social and Political System

The Jieng -Dinka is an alliance or association of clans and subclans, which practices a divided system of political leaderships and hierarchical structures[161]. It is a political federation of sub-nationalities. Each clan division and subdivision or section is a separate political entity with established clan-based rights to well defined territories. The concept of state and

---

160   J. D. Fage, A history of Africa, Routledge, 2002, p.29

161   *Dictionary of the social sciences,* Calhoun, Craig J., 1952, Oxford University Press. New York: Oxford University Press. 2002.

hence political institutions, structure and so authority exists on a separate clan national identity, but Jieng clans unite or come together for security protection or security threats. Each Jieng Dinka division is an autonomous or an independent political entity in itself, under *wut* which translates as "a nation", "a state' or "a country".

Chieftaincy is ritualized in the lineage of a clan. It is hereditary and holds the title of *beny baai or beny bith for one person only. In plural, bany baai*, which translates into traditional chiefs or *bany biith* translating masters of the fishing spear or bany translating both traditional chiefs and masters of the fishing spear. This translates into different possessions like chief, divine priest chief, knowledgeable, skillful or military officer. There has always been the dual control title for military leaders and ritual priest chiefs. The title always has an attribute attached to indicate the office, for example, *beny ring or beny rim* (or riem) *beny baai, beny deng, beny yath, beny wut, beny diaar, beny bith, beny tong, beny rap, beny aciek* and bany *baai*, means chieftainship of the clan people[162].

The word *ring* (or *rem* or *riem*) refers to the supernatural powers of the chief or his spirit powers and is also referred to as *jak* or *jok*, *yath* or *yieth*. *Bith*, on the other hand, refers to the sacred fishing-spear (un-barbed or un-serrated) as a symbol of power of clan divinity master of spear and clan spiritual powers.

The word ring (or rem) probably refers to the supernatural power of the chief. Bith, on the other hand, is the sacred fishing-spear, which is unbarber or un-serrated spear, as a symbol of spiritual powers. The spiritual leaders or masters of the fishing spear chief, medicine women/men, and others exert great influence. Except in few cases, the spiritual leaders more often reject secular authority. Jieng Dinka chiefs exercised authority by persuasion not through any known instruments of coercion and force.

Spirituality and Beliefs

The sphere of the living and the dead (ghosts) interact. Tradition permits

162   Agei, Madhel Malek (2018). *Apuk a State in Waiting*

addressing God and the spirits of the dead or departed ancestors and relatives either directly or through a medium in a special offering place called shrine refers to as *horrou* in thuongjang, which is erected in the middle or the Holy Shrine translates as *yik*, situated in every Jieng Dinka homestead. Holy Shrine or Holy Shrine Temple is translated as *yik*, supervises by master of the fishing spear or by the Supreme Deity who is a descendant from clan with divine spirits or supernatural spiritual powers.

Jieng Dinka Cultural Arts and Material Culture

The most important cultural asset of the Jieng Dinka is the cattle camp, where all social activities; traits and behaviours including courage, bravery, heroism, generosity, *dheeng* and respect for social norms are cultivated. Jieng Dinka literature remains orally expressed and communicated in songs, poems, and folklore.

The different Jieng Dinka sections have evolved their different articles of arts, music and folklore. There are many different types of dance formations and songs. The common art is that of war: spear and stick. The Jieng-Dinka start practicing stick and spear contesting or sparring with great dexterity from their youth.

The Jieng clansmen and clanswomen have recently adopted wearing few clothes commonly available in their small marketplaces around their own village. Adult clansmen may be totally naked or stark-naked except for beads around the neck or wrist. The clanswomen commonly wear only goatskin skirts, but unmarried adolescent girls will normally be stark-naked. Clothes are becoming more common among Jieng clans in this modern time. Many Jieng clansmen will be seen in the long stylized Muslim robe or short coat. Jieng clans own little material possessions of any nice, caring, or thoughtful or variety.

Private grooming and decoration are valued. The Jieng peoples rub their bodies with oil made from boiling lulu tree nuts, and cow milk butter. They cut decorative designs into their skin. They remove some teeth for beauty and wear dung ash to repel mosquitoes. Clansmen dye their hair red with cow urine, or with ash acaca tree ash while clanswomen shave their hair and eyebrows, but leave a knot of hair on top of the head.

The most important influence before was exercised by "divine spiritual high priests" or "high chief deities" or "master of the fishing spears" or "spear masters." These are highly respected clan elite class who provided health through mystical spiritual powers. Their role has been reduced due to changes brought about by Christianity and the modernization culture. Jieng is an egalitarian society that belief in human equality with no class system[163]. All people, wealthy or poor, are expected to contribute to the common good.

The art forms include poetry and song. Certain types of songs for different types of activities of life, are songs for festive occasions, field work, preparation for war and initiation ceremonies. Historical identity and social identity are communicated, conserved and treated from beginning to end through songs. They sing praise songs to their ancestors and the living. Songs are even used ritually in competition to resolve a quarrel in a legal sense. Clanswomen make pottery and weave baskets and mats. Clansmen are blacksmiths, wooden craft, hide design, making all sorts of implements.

Jieng Cultural and Religious Beliefs

The Jieng-Dinka believe in a universal single God, whom they call Nhialic. They believe Nhialic is the creator and source of life but is distant from human affairs. Humans contact Nhialic through spiritual intermediaries and entities called *yath, jak* or *jok* which can be manipulated by various rituals. Nhialic is the creator god of the sky and rain, and the ruler of all the spirits. High priests with supernatural spiritual powers took to worshipping gods and built temples, holy shrines and tombs for them. They remained the official centres of worship for Jieng clan divinities

---

163   Dictionary of the social sciences, Calhoun, Craig J., 1952, Oxford University Press. New York: Oxford University Press. 2002.

until foreign religions such as Christianity entered the arena. Influential Jieng clans with spiritual powers did not decline in power or succumb to Christian domination. Rather, the traditional master of spears inserted themselves and remain as key social, political and military authorities and believed themselves as idols of culture and religion for the Jieng people concerned.

Christian missionaries came and converted some members of the clans. Religious experience is locked into the culture, and the culture is locked into identity. Where one varies, so too does the other.

These rituals are administered by divine spiritual masters, or deities and healers. They believe that the life spirits and body spirits of the dead or departed become part of the spiritual sphere of this life or life spirit. They have rejected attempts to convert them to Islam. But have been open to Christian missionaries. Evangelical sources report that 2% of the Jieng Dinka are Evangelical believers.

The breakaway Christian churches often include drumming and dancing in their services, a practice since adopted by the established churches in an attempt to avoid losing members. Another issue has been how Islam and Christianity have chosen to incorporate the traditional practice of polygamy. Christianity has officially disallowed it, while Islam has allowed men to have up to four wives; however, breakaway Christian churches often have placed no limits on the practice.

Cattle have a religious significance. They are the first choice as an animal of sacrifice, though sheep may be sacrificed as a substitute on occasion. Sacrifices may be made to yath and jak, since Nhialic is too distant for direct contact with humans. The family and general social relations are primary values in the Dinka religious thought.

The typical lifestyle of pastoral Jieng (Dinkas) is exposed in their religious beliefs and practices. They have one God, Nhialic, who speaks through spirits that take temporary possession of clansmen and clanswomen in order to speak through them. The sacrificing of oxen by the "masters of the fishing spear" is a key component of Jieng religious practice. Age is an important factor in Jieng culture, with young clansmen and clanswomen being inducted into adulthood through an initiation ordeal which includes marking the forehead with a sharp object among others. Furthermore, at some stage in this ceremony, they acquire a second cow-colour name. The Jieng, Jieeng, Jang, Jaang or Muonyjang-Dinka derive religious power from nature and the world around them, which is so different from Christianity and Islamic religion.

Jieng Culture, Belief and Traditional Curse

Certain curse sacrifice rituals that have been practiced in the past seem to have diminished in many South Sudan urban environments. Some communities have been forced to forgo some of the cursing and blessing sacrifice rituals and adapted others like Christian and or Islamic denominations in their living environments. People deal with one death after another within a short space of time as a result of roadway accident fatalities, *boda boda* rider fatalities, revenge killings, war, snake bite, malaria and also other life-threatening diseases, suicides and traumatic road accidents and this could impact on the effective practices of proper traditional curse and blessing sacrifice rituals.

Azande and Jieng Rek communities have gone through a period of political, economic, cultural and other forms of transition during the past centuries and this still continues in contemporary times. In the past, Azande people migrated from traditional environments in the early expansion to Central Africa, and a single origin of the dispersal radiating from there, or separating into an eastward reaching clannish Nilotic territories they conquered and occupied briefly, mainly for economic reasons. Small break away Azande kings relocated themselves to present Azande clannish ethnic kingdoms based on ethnicity, security sharing and that became a residential home for the majority of Azande people.

As a result, they found themselves fighting with neighbouring Jieng in separate environments that were contested by Azande king warriors and Jieng warriors because of water resources, Azande slave raids, iron ore, hardwood forests, ivory hunting around what has now become Bahr Al-Ghazal region in the west. Jieng repulsed back violent invasion forces of king Azande warriors. They also prevented king Azande warriors to capture more domestic slave workers, concubines, and military recruitments that led to the kidnap of the jailed Rum Ateny who escaped and returned as effective military leader for Jieng Rek in southwest. Rum Ateny who was captured and taken to military training in captivity by predators in Azande kingdom with whom he wrestled all day and night. He escaped experience great fighter, introduced Azande warfare skills and built confident in Jieng Rek of Apuk that took fierce fight with Azande raiders to continue with their traditional lifestyles. Among these included practices of various curse and blessing sacrifice rituals.

CHAPTER SIX

JIENG SPIRITUAL BELIEFS

Introduction

In beginning this exploration, I will focus on fatal road accident occurrence in this chapter with understanding spirituality, beliefs, life, ritual sacrifices, mourning, and death cosmology, involving core value understandings, spiritual beliefs, rituals, expectations and customs164. I am going to write a little about religious divinity spirit or divine spiritual power as a reputable master of the fishing spear within the context of divine clan divinity spirits or divine priest chief.

I am going to have a brief Jieng examination of historical justice of the customary court practices that sanctioned cattle be transferred to clan spirits and ancestral spirits that pardoned people for the wrongs, and sins of crimes to kill in roadways. This will give a foundational conceptual framework within which I can study 'spiritual wealth cattle' 'divine wealth cattle', 'blood wealth cattle', 'collective responsibility and obligation laws' for fatality and homicide crime penalty, payable in money or non-money to the victimized clan family.

Spirituality is the fundamental culture of the divine connection that the people have as a diverse group. It is just as varied from Azande Nilo-Hamitic or Bantu to Nilotic Muonyjang Rek, to Padaang Jieng to Agar

---

164   Parkes et al., (1997).

Jieng to Bor Jieng, to the Afro-Asiatic and variety of Nilo-Saharan in South Sudan.

Divine clans traditionally have ritual chiefs, known as the "masters of the fishing spear" or *beny bith in Thuongjang*, who have two separate lines of authority. They control of both the priesthood (*beny bith*) and lead the fighters in times of war. They have powers providing divine unity, reconciliation, peace, body spirits, human life, clan spiritual prayers, sacrifices, mediation, invocations, and leadership. This goes all the way back to the development era of the ancient dynasties[165].

Nilotic people in South Sudan do not have centralized political authority. They are an alliance of many independent nations or *wut* united as a result of any security threats, socioeconomic interests, symbols of divinities and the religious spirituality. Symbols which are the identities of the clan divinities are non-human. The spiritual being worshipped have multiple names such as *Yath or Yieth, Jok or Jak or Jaak, Agoloong or Agolong, Atiip or Atiep are* all associated with the gods of ancestors. Throughout the clan's history, Nhialic has been a central aspect of identity, a symbol of power, authority, unity and the interconnected clans and subclans of nationalities.

Powerful clan spirits are important symbols of identification and a significant factor regarding historical identification, social cohesion and managing clan security and control.

Spiritual Belief

Like any other traditional religious belief in Africa, South Sudanese spiritual belief deals with human death, life, misfortunes, knowledge, the problem of the unknown, righteousness, justice, evil and injustice.[166]

---

165   Agei, Madhel Malek. (February 18, 2020). *Apuk a State in Waiting.* African World Books Publishers, Australia. PAGE

166   Hiebert, Paul G., Shaw, Daniel and Tienou, Tite, *Understanding Folk Religion, A Christian Response to Popular Beliefs and Practices.* Grand Rapids, MI: Baker Books, 1999. Page 74

The spiritual beliefs and traditional socio-cultural and political institutions differ from Azande of Bantu, Bari, Moro, Acholi, Nuer, Jieng or Balanda according to ethnic groups. Moreover, South Sudan beliefs are clannish beliefs, which cannot be proliferated, spread or circulated to various clannish ethnicity. There is no changeover or switch from one customary belief and spiritual beliefs to another, since belief is part of the clannish life. Furthermore, spiritual beliefs are not like 'Script' beliefs. They are also not invented into set of dogmas. Every clan family member grows assimilating whatever ideas and practices are held in his family and society.

Although there are a number of unique clans, subclans and spiritual practices, for the purpose of this study I will concur with the hypothesis of validating the exploration of traditional spiritual beliefs in South Sudan as a whole.

The principal emphasis is on the common native origin of indigenous clans and subclans, and the similarities of the major characteristics of their culture and spiritual beliefs. Some writers argue that Africans including people of South Sudan, retain certain common traits as well as similar cultural and religious beliefs or spiritual beliefs and practices. In this background, the concept of God the names given to God, for example, are common over the whole country, South Sudan. One finds that God goes by the same or similar names over wide areas. Moreover, many translations of the names for God suggest that God is the Creator, Almighty in Heaven. Since the real cohesive factor of belief in South Sudan is the "living God", and without this factor all things would fall to pieces[167].

As an example, like all clans of the South Sudan, the Jieng people call the God, Creator, translates as *aciek, acing ee koc cak in Thuongjan*, which they can express names in their own language, Divinity ee *Nhialic*, Creator is God, *Nhialic is one; Nhialic ee tok*. The Christians call it as

---

167   Oborji, Francis Anekwe. *"In Dialogue with African Traditional Religion: New Horizons"*. Mission Studies, Vol. 19, Issue 1, 2002, p. 13-35.

'God', the Muslims call it as 'Allah'[168], the Jews by several names, and the list is so long. Nonetheless, divinity is also a widespread term for multiple conceptions that differ significantly from one another. The powers of divine clan spirits and the clan divinities are distinct from one another, although most simply say *ee Nhialic*, "it is Divinity"[169], in southwestern Apuk. Multiple gods cause no problem in the context of clan language and life. Nevertheless, it is impossible to completely avoid the problems when statements bearing upon the subject are translated into other languages.

The Jieng Rek Apuk have a circular temple of deities and of course, Nhialic[170] who controls the destiny of every human, plant and animal on Earth. *Atiep* or *Atiip*, *Jok* or *Jaak* or *Jak*, *Yath* or *Yieth*, and *agolong* or *agoloong* are all associated with the gods of ancestors. Throughout the clan's history, Nhialic has been a central aspect of identity, a symbol of power, authority and unity. There is no concept of a clansperson as an atheist in antiquity. There is only the concept of the antique native spirituality; *yath dhieeth.*

The name Yahweh, the god of the later Israelites, may indicate connections with *yath* or *yieth* or *yanhwah, yanhda, yanhwei, yath dhieeth, yanh dhieeth* etc. These are the gods of the ancestors of the southwestern Jieng Apuk clans and Subclans of nationalities[171].

The name Yahweh, the god of the later Israelites, may indicate connections with *yath* or *yieth* or *yanhwah, yanhda, yanhwei, yath dhieeth, yanh dhieeth* etc. These are the gods of the ancestors of the southwestern Apuk clans.

---

168   Lienhard, Godfrey, *"Divinity and Experience: The Religion of the Dinka"*, Oxford University Press (1961)

169   Ibid

170   Ibid

171   Agei, Madhel Malek. (February 18, 2020). *Apuk a State in Waiting*, Africa World Books publishers Ltd. Australia. Page

Important Characteristics of Spiritual Beliefs

My first book provides supportive visions of understandings of concep-
tualized South Sudanese spiritual belief or religious belief in some ways.
The diversity of clans and sub-clans or clan faiths do share some common
characteristics.

Once again, I will refer to Madhel Agei summary with emphasis on
those important characteristics of belief in God as key aspect that separated
from the original ancestors and contributions[172]:

1. A belief in a supreme deity above a host of lesser gods, or semi-divine
    figures.
2. A belief in the superior spiritual powers of the divine priest 'the master
    of the fishing spear' who is tasked to give life, make prayers, invoca-
    tions, and to make sacrifices for the cure of the sick.
3. A belief in the power and mediation of lineage spirits.
4. An idea of sacrifice and libation to ensure divine protection, rainmak-
    ing, peace-making and generosity.
5. A need to undergo rituals of passage to move on from different stages
    of life, such as childhood to adulthood, and from life to death.
6. A divine clan divinity spirit interpretation of life, sacred flesh, blood
    spirits, life spirit, body spirit, power blood life to curse offenders,
    predators, evil, devil, wrongdoer etc.
7. A divine wealth ritual sacrifice prayer to reconcile clan spirits and
    ancestors for a cursed clan family or person to restore life in the clan
    or person for spiritual crimes, divine disputes, devil offences, oaths,
    fatal homicides, bewitching, wrongdoings, and evil eyes.
8. A dignify respect for cultural hero, the 'High Priest Deity' or the
    'Powerful Clan Spirit People' embodied in a traditional education,
    initiation rite, social and political life.
9. A sense of the nuclear family, demonstrated in collective responsibility

---

172   Agei, Madhel Malek (February 18, 2020). *Apuk a State in Waiting*, Africa
World Books Pty. Ltd. Australia. Page

to an action clan family member, divinity identity and the body of ancestors.

10. A sense of community life expressed by participation in the life of the community in which the individual is introduced by various initiation rites[173].

Many clan religions have creation stories that speak of the structure for the self-identification of these clans in a universal context. The role of humanity is by and large seen as a harmonizing connection between nature and the supernatural forces.

Symbol of clan divinities is a vital form of communication, a core value and a cultural symbol of a people and their identity.

South Sudan people believe in one God who is the Creator of humanity and the universe. Spiritual beliefs and myths also speak of an estrangement between God and humanity. Some idea in this myth is that individual sorrow for the crime of actions in life is interpreted as the work of evil spirits, witches, sorcerers, the evil eye, broken taboos, perjured oaths, or even the deities, ancestors or ancestral spirits. Individuals are the architects of their misfortune and withdrawal of God from humanity's immediate surroundings. Spiritual belief has therefore, the characteristic of trying to re-capture this primordial relationship with God. This is principally possible to achieve by using approaches, which are not always directly to good God, against whom humanity has sinned, by causing withdrawal of God from the created universe, but through the mediation of the High Priest Deities, and the ancestors. Likewise, in spiritual belief, misfortune is generally interpreted as the work of evil spirits, or witches, or sorcerers, or evil eye, broken taboos, perjured oaths, or even the deities or ancestors. However, it is believed that when good spirits, like the Supreme Being, the deities and ancestors inflict some physical evil, they do so as a

---

173   Oborji, Francis Anekwe. *"In Dialogue with African Traditional Religion: New Horizons"*. Mission Studies, Vol. 19, Issue 1, 2002. Page 16-17.

premonitory, corrective or punitive measure. They are believed to be for the overall good of the individual and the society.

Sacrifice Blood in Spiritual Belief

People of South Sudan who obey these cultural religious beliefs or spiritual beliefs seek to avoid evil fatality, or after they deal with it to evoke the original condition. Sacrifice blood is one famous case of a ritual used to control or cope effectively with evil or evil fatality when it occurs. Sacrifices involve the shedding of blood of human beings, animals or birds174. Sacrifices can atone for a fatal offense or accident fatality, seek the favor and assistance of a god divinity or affirm an oath. They can be made to God, the High Priest Deities, or the divine clan divinity spirits.

In religious belief, after blood is shed in making a sacrifice, it means that the purpose of the sacrifice must be a serious one. This is because, in South Sudan traditional society, life is closely associated with blood. So, after blood is shed in making a sacrifice, it means a human or animal life is being return back to God, who is true Creator, the ultimate source of all life. That kind of blood sacrifices can be made when lives of communities are in danger. The life of one person or animal is sacrificed in the belief that this will save the lives of many people or communities.

As an example: Spear masters and elders Apuk Rek community decided to let Rum Ateny be captured by the Azande king predators as they reasoned that the Azande Lwalla would slay him (Rum Ateny) as a stranger and pour his blood on the soil as a sacrificial beast so that it would pour down on the land of ancestors and clan spirits. That blood sacrifice would wash away sorrowful crimes, killings, sins, evil spirits and devils from the Apuk homeland for the benefit of the entire ancestry world of spirits in southwestern Jieng Rek territories. They believed that Rum's blood, flesh, life spirit and body spirit could curse the predatory Lwalla, Azande

---

174   Mbiti, J. (1969). *African religions and philosophy*. London: Heinemann. Mbiti, J. S. (1975). *Introduction to African religion*. South Africa; Heinemann International Literature & Textbooks.

king raiders, forever.[175] They meant to use Rum as a ritual blood victim. This way the clan spirits and independent spirits would curse away his killers. It was the occasion for forgiveness of offence for the divine spirits to repulse the recurring abduction, torturing and massacring of the local people. They seemingly thought this might have been brought about by the curses of angry gods, wrongdoings, evil spirits, disobedience to divine spirits, or ancestors that had turned up in the homestead. Some believed a curse been left there by a witch.

Thus, the destruction of one becomes the protection of many. Offerings accompanied with sacrifice blood, a ritual killing or offering demonstrate that immolation is an essential factor in spiritual belief. In this sort of sacrifice blood, impressive is always completed to the offering to show that is or sin or evil act has been removed from human use and given over to God. In addition, in some cases, it is what is said in prayer at the ritual sacrifice that gives the clue as to the sort or kind and purpose of a particular sacrifice. "Sacrifice is primarily a ritual prayer. It allows work to achieve communion with God through mediation of the offering."[176]

A Continuous Life Sequence in Spiritual Belief

A continuous life is perceived as a sequence, and there is no heaven or world to come in belief or religious belief. Rituals invoke the religious spiritual powers of divinities to work on behalf of human beings and to put right broken relationships. After people died, they aspire to join the ranks of their ancestors and to use their increased religious spiritual powers to work on behalf of their families and clans. Oborji argues that life is viewed as a communion with the created order, the universe, the spirits, ancestors, one's family and the community, but also with the Creator God. The final aspiration of every person is to reach the spirit land of

175   Agei, Madhel Malek. (February 18, 2020). *Apuk a State in Waiting.* Africa WORLD Books Pages

176   Oborji, Francis Anekwe. *"In Dialogue with African Traditional Religion: New Horizons".* Mission Studies, Vol. 19, Issue 1, 2002. Pages 13-- 35.

one's ancestors and to be venerated by one's descendants as an ancestor.

Spiritual belief is in itself not a redemptive or prophetic religious faith. Particularly stipulation redemption is to be considered from the point of interpretation to shed blood sacrifice of individual person or freely decided, for the eschatological salvation of people. Religious faith is not supposed to achieve such salvation of people. Rather, the role of faith is to enlist the help of God, the deities and the ancestors and to harness the forces below human beings to strengthen the life of women and men on earth[177]. The Perennial Dictionary of World Religions concurs with this assessment. It states, "African religions tend not to be concerned with personal salvation or dogmas about God. They are instead religions of structure, in which self-realization arises through participation in the socio-cosmic web of relationships first laid down by God and the primal beings. God and the spirits are primarily worshiped because they, together with man, maintain the divinely established order."[178]

Customary Beliefs and Ritual sacrifice

South Sudan cultures have their practices, traditional beliefs, values, norms and customs surrounding fatality death and achievement of bereavement, burial and ritual sacrifices in mourning the death of belove one. There is a graceful nature in how ethnic Jieng Apuk, Rek, Atuot, Agaar and Padaang family language people treat fatality deaths. Bloodwealth seems to be strange to Azande of the Bantu family speaking people of South Sudan. The current exploration undertakes to gather information on the direct experiences of the bereaved and those who attend burials at newly created towns and parishes on the phenomena of the 'bloodwealth' compensation penalty payable in monetary equivalent after burial of roadway accident fatalities.

---

177   Ibid. Pages 29.

178   Crim, Keith, Gen. Ed. *The Perennial Dictionary of World Religions.* San Francisco: Harper and Row Publishers, 1989. Page 6.

The cattle herding Nilotic peoples of South Sudan are remarkable for the intensity of devotion to God, Creator, Almighty, Heaven Creator, refers to as *Nhialic, aciek, acang-cakoc in Thuongjang* language. It is customary to offer brief morning prayer and evening prayer, in which Creator God, Heavenly Creator God is thanked for the gift of another day of life, and his help is invoked for the tasks of the next day. Spontaneous prayers are always before any special activity like a hunt or transacting journey is started.

The particular dwelling place of God are Heavens, from which He looks down on the "black ants" who humbly worship Him. The question whether god existences or not is unthinkable among the Nuer and Jieng (Dinka).[179] For example, Jieng communities are concerned with their ancestors: clan spirits (*yieth* in plural, *yath* in singular), and independent spirits (*jak or jaak* in plural, *jok* in singular) than with god in their practical life[180].

There is a crucial ethical and practical contrast between these sets of spirits. The ancestors and clan spirits are partial and protective, while independent spirits are "free" and largely destructive. Thus, the destructiveness of *jak* is not continually negative: it could be a resort to a vital evil to enforce, reinforce or sanction a virtue to fatal crime doing. A spirit could likewise be called upon to mediate between man and another good spirit or evil spirit. Spirits usually have particular characteristics that distinct or display themselves through human experience. A few of them are known to inflict specific types of pain, death, injury, accident fatality or illness. A few are known to have certain likes and dislikes. As soon as they "fall upon" a clansman or clanswoman and possess him, they can be identified by the aberrational behavior they induce in him. The community Jieng

---

179   Crim, Keith, Gen. Ed. *The Perennial Dictionary of World Religions*. San Francisco: Harper and Row Publishers, 1989. Page 6.

180   Deng, Francis M. *"The cow and the Thing Called "What": Dinka Cultural Perspectives on Wealth and Poverty"*. Journal of International Affairs; Fall 98, Vol. 52, Issue 1. Page 122-123.

Rek Apuk have a circular temple of deities and of course, Nhialic[181] who controls the destiny of every human, plant and animal on Earth. *Atiep* or *Atiip*, *Jok* or *Jaak* or *Jak*, *Yath* or *Yieth*, and *agolong* or *agoloong* are all associated with the gods of ancestors. Throughout the clan's history, Nhialic has been a central aspect of identity, a symbol of power, authority and unity. There is no concept of a clansperson as an atheist in antiquity. There is only the concept of the antique native spirituality; *yath dhieeth*.

Rituals involving blood sacrifice are often used to appease the spirits and to gain or achieve relative control over human experience, Lienhardt shows how sacrifice provides a victory over death by placing its control in human hands. More generally, he argues that ritual can provide a means for humans to express control over, and hence shape, their experience. This control, as he says, is generally understood, to effect not physical circumstance, but what he calls the moral realm[182].

Divine master Peace Making Between Two Families After Fatality

I have chosen to focus this book about blood compensation, using the case of a sad story of a boychild of Jieng Apuk, who died in violent collision crash caused by the driver of an Azande of Bantu family languages, in rural roadway traffic in Pathuon Apuk in Gogrial region. The primary responsibility in the customary court law was to oversee trial accident fatality death caused by wrongdoing and negligence in traffic rule according to the victim boy customs and to bring about reconciliations, repenting, forgiveness and harmony between the victim boy Apuk clan family and the guilty driver Azande clan family. Apuk customary court law was tasked to investigate road accident fatality death, tried them, and guilty driver Azande clan family member was given the sentences ranging from 'blood life wealth cattle' and 'divine blood life wealth cattle' apuk compensation

---

181   Lienhardt, Godfrey, *"Divinity and Experience: The Religion of the Dinka"*, Oxford University Press (1988)

182   Lambek, Michael Ed. *A Reader In the Anthropology of Religion*. Oxford, UK: Blackwell Publishing Ltd. 2002. Page 330

and fines in cattle, money, and imprisonment for weeks, months, and years, if compensation penalty is not paid.

Similar to Apuk Rek in southwestern Nile Valley, the Apuk clan is an association of sub-clans with independent authority. The main aim of the association was to protect life and have a domain of their own identity of which they could be proud of cultural eagle identity, eagle that fights. Apuk clans permit the dual control of war leader and divine spiritual master or high priest chief of deity. The role of the divine spiritual master is akin to that of the master of the fishing spear in the Rek and other Jieng of Nilotic ethnic groups, mainly Nilo-Saharans in the sub-Sahara. His duty is to give life. He is 'the holder of life' and his life is bound together with the vitality of his society he is chosen to serves. Some of the main functions of priest chief are[183:]

a. Prayers and invocations.
b. Sacrifices for the cure of the sick and rainmaking.
c. In war, he is the guide of his people, as well as the mediator and peacemaker.

There is blood ritual sacrifice ceremony which presents an example of a peace-making ceremony between driver of Azande clan family and boychild of Apuk clan family, after a road accident fatality death had taken place on July 15, 2019, in Luonyaker Apuk in eastern Gogrial region.

Practically, the two clan families sat about 18 yards to 30 yards apart in customary court hearing sentencing. His kin represented the killer family clansman. 'The blood life wealth cattle' penalty, payable in compensation to the family of the victim clansman, were placed between the two clan families, with a small ritual sacrificial bull blood. The clansman who directs the ritual sacrifice blood ceremony should be a divine spiritual master or a high diviner, or a prophet or a high priest of Deity who have the supreme

---

183   Agei, Madhel Malek. (February 18, 2020). *Apuk a State in Waiting*, Africa World Books Pty, Australia. Page

gift of communicating with the clan spirits of the dead by reciting ritual ceremonial prayers, invoking ritual sacrificial bull blood.

The kin of the guilty killer clansman seized the forelegs of the ritual sacrificial bull blood, and those of the family clansman who was killed seized the hind legs. Together they turned the ritual sacrificial bull blood on its back and each thrust a 'spear divine wealth cattle' and 'blood wealth cattle' into chest bull blood. The bull blood was then cut in half to pour blood on soil and "the entrails were taken out and scattered over the two clan families, and each clan family went off separately to divide its meat. After this, the divine spiritual master went to the spot where the ritual sacrificial bull blood had been slaughtered where blood dropped on soil and placed a 'spear divine wealth cattle and blood wealth cattle' in reconciliation and forgiveness. Thereafter he took some of the remains and threw them over the two families of clan nationalities (Azande and Apuk clans of nationalities) who by this time had resumed their places.

The families then advanced in three pairs, three from each side, and holding 'the spear blood wealth cattle' fatality death between them in both hands bit into it, following this with spitting to the left, to the right, to the air up and downwards upon their own chests. They are said every now and then to spit upon each other. Ashes were then sprinkled over the knees of the families, and this was the end of the ritual. There is no speech and no form of words to be spoken. It is believed that, after the conclusion of this ritual ceremony, anyone who reopened the feud would die[21].

I will here refer readers of this book to summary quotes of Malek Agei[184]:

- *"I always make sure I have passed my spirituality message clearly that whenever, by your survival (existence) and functioning, clan victim and homicide families bring revenge dispute and unhappiness, and cause their own clansmen's desires to be exercised in opposition to the desire of the*

184   Agei, Madhel Malek. (February 18, 2020). *Apuk a State in Waiting.* Africa World Book Pty. Australia. Page

blood wealth spirits of thirty cows for apuk of clan victim and one cow for oath in blood sacrifice by the use of Priest Chief that ritually prays, then you, the victim and homicide clans must be destroyed by body spirits, jak, yath, life spirits and divinity spirits."

- *"Since I am the Priest Chief of the Appeal Court for clan offence sentencing, I warned those victim and homicide clans to never be permitted to come into a continuation of revenge dispute again."*

- *The victim and homicide clan families will realize that homicide, wrong, and unhappiness will disappear, and their normal feeling will come into harmony with the laws of blood wealth that members of guilty clans or families have donated as their supplications."*

- *"They will then understand why evil exists, and why wars, hatred and misery continue to blight the lives and happiness of clan peoples. Why, as some say, do clan spirit permit all these things to exist, flourish, and apparently contradict the truth Clan Divinity is good, and the fountainhead of all goodness?"*

- *"The use of the deity and spiritual master practices derives from ritual prayers that the laws of apuk penalty must rule according to the customary justice system in all the apparent harshness, suffering, and want of forgiveness. The belief of the customs overshadows the victim and finally makes the corrupted and wicked clansman become one of purity and goodness. The law of apuk penalty terms of compensation is necessary to preserve and bring about the reconciliation, forgiveness and harmony between the guilt and the ancestors and spirits, which is absolutely necessary."*

Lienhardt concludes that the biting of the spear symbolized an oath to abide by the settlement. He interprets the spitting, scattering with entrails, and dusting with ashes as forms of purification and blessing.

In the Parum family of clan divinity powers, family possesses very essential ritual sacrifice spears with specific names attached to them as follows:

1. Spear Oath service, translates as *alol ee kueeng or alol ee meel tier ku*

meel jony in Thuongjang. This means that: Oath Services for Truth and only as the Truth and Divinity is my witness, presided over in the society by Divine Spiritual Master, Malek Agei, heir son etc.

2. Spear homicide penalty for *apuk* 'blood wealth cattle' and *apuk* 'divine wealth cattle' or Spiritual wealth cattle providing reconciliation and forgiveness between the victim clan family and guilty clan family and concerned members of the two clan families, *Tong tem ee tier apuk ku kueeng ku adoor dhieth ci teir looi ee kam keen*,

3. Spear blood life, translates blessing blood by cutting or slitting animal throat to let blood life drops on soil of ancestors and clan divinity spirits in the process of ritual sacrifice ceremonies. Spear blood life or lifeblood means *tony ee wei, tong ee wei weng ku wei raan, tong ee koc-kooc, tong teem riem piny teen atiip etc.* This can be translated as 'spear blood life' for blessing life human beings and life animals.

4. Spear house spirit power or Spear housing spirit Power, known as "Fishing Spear". I call it 'Spear power house' or 'Spear housing power 'or 'Sacred Fishing Spear'. The clansman using fishing spear is referred to as "Master of the Fishing Spear", translates as *beny bith*. The divine spiritual master duty is to fulfil the ritual sacrifice animal blood prayers, and libation to ensure divine protection, rainmaking, peace-making and generosity.

The sacred spear is the most powerful instrument uses by the clan divinity members possessing supernatural spiritual power in a manner acceptable to the society serve by the user. Sacred spear power shows signs of sharing and thanks to God. It is asked during the sacrifice prayers for forgiveness to continue giving life, to guide life, and to protect the people from evil, evil spirits and sickness.

The spear for offering beasts of ritual sacrifices to clan spirits, *atiip, jak, agoloong* and divinity for peace-making, rainmaking, guardianship and oath taking, are believed to have powers that forward the intended invocation through to guide the body spirit, life spirit and living spirit of the heir from evils wanting to intrude to take away those powers from strong spiritual descendants.

During ritual sacrifice blood animal, praying dialogues and offering prayers, the master of the fishing spear asks clan divinities, clan spirits, *yath*, and ancestry *atiip* to come nearer to the people for spirit forgiveness. This is done to help them and not to harm them. That is the way the believers have come to dialogue with the divinities and spirits. They believe the creator is close and can listen, see, and order punishment for wrongdoing or disobeying a God. The spear master is there to guide and pray for people in times of crisis, natural disasters, military campaigns, hunting/fishing, and for forgiveness and peace-making for all the people or societies.

Ritual of Fatal Accident Death

All cultures have rituals that mark the finality of violent fatality death, whether slow death or painful death, and prescribe socially supported remembrance, sadness and mourning behaviors. In a social context sanctioned ceremonies and rituals have been used by cultural ethnic classes as channels for transmitting ethnic class beliefs and expectations and therefore maintain order within a given culture[185]. According to academia the society molds its members from early childhood to integrate life and death events into their human experiences[186].

A ritual defines a specific behavioral actions or activity which gives a symbolic cultural expression to certain feelings and thoughts of the actors individually or as a community[187]. It may be a customarily pedestrian

---

185   Becvar, D. S. (2001). *In the Presence of Grief: Helping Family members to resolve Death,* Dying and Bereavement Issues. New York: The Guilford Press, 89 .

186   Kilonzo, G. P. & Hogan, N. M. (1999). *Traditional African mourning rituals are abridged in response to the AIDS epidemic: Implications for mental health.* Trans-cultural Psychiatry 36(3), 259-283.

187   Rando, T. A. (1988). *Grieving: how to go on living when someone you love dies.* Lexington, Massachusetts: DC Heath.

behaviour or a past occurrence and may be accomplished publicly or confidentially. The same applies to mourning and sacrifices of animal blood rituals because the mourning are actors and they symbolize something by accomplishing the sacrifices of animal blood rituals. Animal blood rituals can also be described as cultural devices that facilitate preservation of social order[188]. The customary factor these definitions of rituals is their symbolic nature and the achievements, comportments or actions to show that they are accomplished and they are visible. Despite the fact that cultures advocate and practice mourning animal sacrifice rituals, there is a countless difference amid those practices and they change with phase.

The fulfillment of death rituals in South Sudan societies is influenced by the belief in the continuation of life[189]. After fatality death, offering beast rituals and ceremonies will differ depending on culture and degree of adherence in specific ethnic clannish community. Appropriate burial ceremonies, offering animal sacrifices and rituals ensure that the deceased persons become ancestors in spirit world. It is believed that burial ceremonies and memorial service rites are accomplished for the determination of ensuring that the deceased persons would be able to join the ancestral spirits world, because in South Sudan tradition, when a person dies, it is believed that his spirit cannot reach the destination to the home or world of the "living dead" before the accomplishment of death rituals.

In South Sudan cultures, when a clan family member dies, the whole community and the bereaved clan family members including the relatives of the deceased person have to fulfill bereavement rituals. There are also confidential rituals which are mostly accomplished through the clan family and the immediate relatives of the deceased persons[190]. It shows

---

188   Romanoff, B. D., & Terenzio, M. (1998). *Rituals and the grieving process.* Death Studies, 22, 697-711.

189   Mbiti, J. (1969). *African religions and philosophy.* London: Heinemann. Mbiti, J. S. (1975). *Introduction to African religion. South Africa;* Heinemann International Literature & Textbooks.

190   Romanoff, B. D., & Terenzio, M. (1998). *Rituals and the grieving process.*

the traditional significance in accomplishing or fulfilling rituals after fatal accident and the special meaning that rituals have for South Sudanese communities.

The ancestors are believed to be the mediators between God and the living. The ancestors are also believed to be overlooking, monitoring and taking care of the living, participating in the active lives of the living. Therefore, practice of the death rituals which is symbolic of the relationship that people have with the ancestors in the world of spirits.

A Reconciliation Peacemaking Between Offended Families

The *apuk* penalty rule can culturally be achieved through the 'payable blood life wealth cattle', 'payable divine wealth cattle', reconciliation and repentance for forgiveness to bring back peace and harmony from sorrow regarding fatality crimes of actions in life.

The English definition of the law of *apuk* is referred to as compensation, where a clansman or clanswoman becomes penitent in earnest[191]. Through traditional persuasions, the spirit forgives these wrongdoers or sinners of their crimes and makes a new life possible. In the event of reconciliation following a fatal killing, a ritual sacrifice beast ceremony should not take place until true repentance and forgiveness have taken place in the hearts of victimized clan family and guilty killer clan family who were involved in fatalities. This goes far beyond ritual of the designated offering said divine master to slit throat animal sacrifice to pour blood on soil for purity ceremony and to repent in order to restore peace and harmony. A judicial court hearing sentencing blood life wealth compensation penalty, payable in cattle or equivalent and a commitment not to seek further retribution can take place but the Zande have mixed cultural practices readily with other smaller clans in the region and their customs, practices

---

Death Studies, 22, 697-711.

191   Lufti, G. A., *The Future of English Law in the Sudan*. The Sudanese Judgment and Precedents Encyclopedia. Sudan Judiciary, Khartoum. At 2.

and customary laws reflect the heterogeneous nature of their communities. Lacking cattle, their currency in customary law is principally money, which they use in 'blood life wealth' penalty, payable in monetary money equivalent. The Zande are agriculturalists with a history of conflict with the Jaang Rek (Dinka), at what time they have attempted to raise cattle herds. Zande people have a reputation for practicing 'witchcraft' and other forms of mysticism.

Traditional Burial Rites in South Sudan

A great number of cultures dispose of their dead with a ritual sacrifice like burying the dead ones in order to separate the dead from the living. South Sudan cultures are traditionally not an exception. There are as a rule, a number of ritual sacrifices which go together with the burial and these vary according to ethnicity, clan, kinship and belief system.

In traditional Jieng culture, when the man dies, the body is prepared by the chief mourner helped by other married women. Burial ordinarily takes place on the day after the death. The body was buried as soon as possible in order to avoid decomposing since there were no mortuaries in the past and still today in the rural villages and in newly created small townships and primary health care centers (PHCCs).

Environment is usually hot and humid and the body might quickly decompose with a bad smell. The body will be covered with branches of leaves which are branches of water lily leaves that emit a strong aromatic smell repelling fly away. Contrary to the current practice where the mortuary ritual took over, the corpse will be taken to the mortuary available in some hospitals in cities where it will stay for a few days while the family is busy preparing for the burial. The corpse would be brought back from the mortuary into the house on the eve of the burial for friends, and colleagues to support and allow the community members to say their last goodbyes, even give evidence and be a witness about the deceased. Ritual sacrificial killing in the form of slaughtering an animal which will also take place before the burial, may be for provision of food for the people who are attending the burial. The skin would often be used to wrap the corpse for burial since there were no coffins in the past. The ritual killing is also performed as a sacrifice or an offering to the ancestors[192].

The most symbolic action describes by Lienhardt is that the Jieng people of South Sudan do not talk much about death, and are not always practicing open burial or funeral ceremonies to make any attention to others. For example, rural highway road accident fatalities always result in loss of life, damage and long-term severe injuries, caused by the careless-ness of our drivers and their ignorance and negligence of their car accident rules. Fatality victims suffer from soft-tissue injuries, other road accident fatalities have led to many deaths after two to five years suffering from long-term severe injuries. When a clansman or clanswoman dies later his or her decorations, body dresses and ornaments are removed according to tradition. Deceased head is shaved and his or her body is washed and then anointed with oil. A skin or hide shield is put on the floor of the grave, and deceased body is placed upon it. She or he is laid on her or his side with the head facing to the west, her or his knees are flexed and her/his hand is positioned under her/his head, in the position of sleep. His/her exposed ear is covered with a skin so that dirt will not enter in it. The burial group straighten up, facing away from the grave, and pushes dirt into it with their hands. They then wash off their knees over the grave, and a clan family member place a mat over the grave.

After three days, the clan family of the deceased person bring a small sheep to the grave. They take straw thatch grass from the hut of dead clan-sperson, throw it near the grave and set it on fire. According to Lienhardt description, the smoke blows over the *tol* people, people attending *tol or nyoor koc gup*[193]. The people tol, or koc tol, and the senior member of the

---

192   Mbiti, J. (1969). *African religions and philosophy.* London: Heinemann

193   People attending *tol or koc nyoor ke kup in Thuongjang* Jieng (Dinka): can be described as people cleansing out evil, devil eye and curse invisible, which are all the cause of recurrence death. They should be kept out or washed away on the living family members through smoke fire and ash. Assumption is that evil, bewitching, curse, divinity

clan family, or divine master of the fishing spear if he has been called in, walks round the *tol* people beating the living sheep on the ground. Divine master finally holds the bleating sheep over the fire a little, and then makes an incision in its belly and takes out the entrails. Their contents area sprinkled over the people attending *tol,* and the carcass is thrown away for the vultures. This "smoking" of the people is called *atol (tol-smoke)*, and the kid is the *nyong atol.* The Jieng (Dinka) say that the offering is to please the deceased and a sheep is chosen because it has a special relationship to Divinity spirits *like jak, Atiep, agolong, aciek, akuic.* After another day a sheep or goat or cow is sacrificed. This is called *the alok lok chiin* "the hand wash". Sometime later a whole bull is sacrificed, and prayers are offered and invocations made by a divine master of the fishing-spear. This final sacrifice, called *apek*, propitiates the deceased, who without it would be likely to injure his people and kill their cattle[194]. A similar practice could be conducted where special traditional rituals of cutting chicken will be used to cleanse the tools that were used to dig the grave which should be put on the grave and those who carried out the burial.

Burials in South Sudan today are heavily influenced by Christian

---

punishment for sin or sins committed unaware may have been the cause of death in the family. Car accident may have been made possible by ancestry spirits, *yath, atiip, jok, agoloong, or curse* because of disobedient from one of the family members. Fire, smoke and ash are believed to be the most powerful tool to clean the sin or curse away, immediately. If not done so or failure to show up in the cleansing smoke fire or step on ash after coming late *tol or nyoor kuc gup*, divinity spirit is looking at you and time is there to punish you in many ways. Example, frequent sickness, disappearance of livestock from the family, injuries, other bad luck happening to family members etc can be seen as punishment because one person had failed to cleanse on fire or to step at ash at the time the death occurred and people attended cleansing *tol* fire or smoke fire and ash. This cleansing through smoke fire and ash must be done closer to grave. *Tol* is done at 5:00 AM to 5:30 AM, before other people have woken up or started moving around and avoiding not to be seen by evil eye person moving around in the areas.

194   Lambek, Michael Ed. *A Reader In the Anthropology of Religion.* Oxford, UK: Blackwell Publishing Ltd. 2002. Page 334.

and traditional religious beliefs. A number of traditional rituals are still observed to be practiced even among Christian members and several of them are evident in many burial services. As an example, at the breaking of the dawn, on the day of the burial just after the house or homestead, there is a prayer for the final viewing of the corpse. As soon as the corpse is carried out of the house or homestead, a traditional praise-making is sometimes done by a close elderly relative. The tribute or eulogy serves as a means of honouring the beloved deceased one and also for psychological relief. The clergy and the community including church members usually participate in the burial process. The people attending the burial will mostly be expected to maintain complete silence at the graveside except when they would be singing hymns. Women are expected to wear long dresses and cover their heads and men are supposed to wear formal jackets as a sign of respect.

Burials are usually preceded by a family diviner or divine master who will go to the grave before the burial and perform a traditional ritual. The clergy will be mostly conducting the funeral process. After the burial, the community will be invited to go back to the family of the deceased for a meal.

The bereaved family would observe the symbols to commemorate loss still sticking around such as complete silence at the home of the deceased, parties and celebrations would normally be prohibited as a sign of respect for the family of the deceased. The bereaved would also continue to engage in cleansing rituals for purification with special medicine, using Black medicine and Black magic during the mourning period in Azande or Zande community for example, until the end of mourning or death 'fades' away[195]. Contrary to the Western cultures where it is presumed that life will continue after the burial, people get on with their normal lives.

People of South Sudan have traditionally used their homestead as a final

---

195   Ngubane, S. (1977). *Body and mind in Zulu medicine*. London: Academic Press.

resting place where their dead would be buried. This is more popular in this country so much polarized by clannish attachment today, but may die out in the near future. As an example, a man would be buried in a middle of a shrine in the yard of the homestead, especially if a man comes from clan divinity spiritual powers. This was done because there was a specific meaning attached to the dead being buried at their home. This concept as place identity, divinity identity, hereditary identity and historical identity. There is often an attachment to place, which has become woven into the individual's personal identity and or birthplace identity.

Some divine masters argue that to die in the traditional belief is a fulfilment of a mission accomplished in life and you have now been called by ancestors to join and going home where you belong. It also is to carry the message to ancestry world with the spirits that created earth. Hence it implies that when a person dies, he/she joins the people who died before them. As such one needs a proper burial, where there will be origins, foundations and factors of respect and dignity. Any respectable Jieng person has been buried at home at the back or sides of their family's huts or sides of their family's cattle camps, or gender except of the head of the clan divinity family who was buried alongside the top of the cattle camps. People in South Sudan urban environments have recently moved away from burying their dead in their homesteads due to political and other reasons. Shortage of burial space in metropolitan area and recent advancements of technology have contributed to widespread use of other alternatives to traditional burial like burying in designated areas, commonly called graveyards. Another disposing form for the dead in urban environments which is gradually gaining popularity is cremation practices by the Asian community[196].

In urban townships, the observation has been that there would be more or less a period between five to six days before the day of the burial.

---

196   Mbizana, C. (2007). *Resilience in bereaved Zulu families.* Unpublished Masters Dissertation, University of Zululand, Zululand, South Africa.

Contrasting it to the rural burials Ngubane highlighted that urban burials involve a lot of coordination in preparation of many different institutions: the local authorities, the florist, the medical examiner (who is a medical personnel who investigates the cause of death and issues a death certificate), the clergy and the bureaucratic urban system[197]. In addition to this, the deceased gets to be moved away from home to the mortuary where he would stay and the body washed and prepared and only come home on the day before the burial for the final viewing. All of these come with a cost!

Lienhardt believes that the mourners fill the grave facing away from it so that they will not have to witness the final internment. The suffering of the small sheep of smoke represents that the suffering of the mourners is transferred on to the animal. The Jieng Dinka believe that the dead will haunt those who do not perform the burial rites.

The Jieng do not expect that the sacrifices will automatically achieve some specific result. When they perform a sacrifice for a sick person, they will often seek medical attention as well. Jieng often explain that when a desired result is not attained, the Divinity or ancestry spirit refused or there was an error in understanding the power behind illness of a family member or troubles. Ritual sacrifices are not made just on behalf of the clan family member undergoing a difficulty or facing a special need, but on behalf of the whole society or community. Lienhardt summarizes the rites of ritual sacrifice in this way, "In victimizing a bull or an ox the Jieng-Dinka are aware of using or manipulating something physically more powerful than themselves; and through the identification of the victim with the divinities they also control something spiritually more powerful."[198]

---

197   Ngubane, S. (2004). *Traditional practices on burial systems with special reference to the Zulu people of South Africa.* Indilinga-African Journal of Indigenous Knowledge Systems, 3(2), 171-177.97

198   Lambek, Michael Ed. *A Reader In the Anthropology of Religion.* Oxford, UK: Blackwell Publishing Ltd. 2002. Page 377.

CHAPTER 7

'APUK RIEM' WEALTH
IN CATTLE EQUIVALENT

Introduction

The current chapter covers norms and cultural practices of Rek Apuk societies and will mainly be on the performance of customary law blood wealth, funeral sacrifice, bereavement, and mourning rituals among traditional rural and modern urban South Sudan communities. A particular focus will be on the changes observed in the customary legal system, blood wealth 'apuk', burial rites, purification, and mourning rituals of Rek Apuk community.

Grief is not a joke. It does not only demand time but an environment that will allow the person to readjust at his or her own pace. Certain practices, such as allowing fire smoke to flow over people during bereavement rituals, seems to have diminished in Luonyaker townships and in other Apuk Giir urban environments. Some Apuk communities in Amuk, Buoyar (Buoi-yar), Adoor, Biong, Nyarmong, Abior and Apol communities have been forced to forgo some of the mourning rituals and adapted others in their living environments.

In the past, many Rek Apuk people migrated from traditional environments in the rural villages mainly for economic reasons. New lifestyles were adopted, and some of the traditional practices were demonstrated while others were completely forgotten. For a person who comes from rural areas, and regularly sees traditional practices, they may be shocked at the different lifestyle of those who live in the urbanized city environments.

Azande and Rek Apuk Branches

Across history, the Rek Apuk and Azande or Zande lacked understanding for Azande matters of Bantu branches and Rek Apuk of Nilotic branches. The Azande Bantu speakers originated from West Africa[199] and spread beyond the geographic region of Western Equatoria, and the regions of the Democratic Republic of the Congo (DRC) and Central African Republic (CAR), bordering South Sudan. The key evidence for this expansion is linguistic.

Linguistic study suggests that the expansion ensued in two directions[200]: the first went across the Congo rainforest region towards east to South Sudan, and the second, and possibly others, went south along the African coast into Gabon, the Congo River Basins, and or inland along the many north and south flowing rivers of the Congo River system.

They spread across to Bahr Al-Ghazal down to Equatoria. In the great Azande expansion, a rapid dissemination during the wave of Iron Age[201], they moved across the river basins, and moved south along the western Nile basins towards Rek Apuk ethnic communities. This hypothesis has repeatedly been framed as a mass-migration. I must say that it was actually a cultural diffusion and not the movement of any specific populations. There is a strong history of conflict with other tribes, particularly the Dinka, when they have attempted to farm cattle.

---

199   *The Chronological Evidence for the Introduction of Domestic Stock in Southern Africa* Texas State University. Retrieved December 17, 2007.

200   Pollard, Elizabeth; Rosenberg, Clifford; Tignor, Robert (2011). *Worlds Together, Worlds Apart: A History of the World: From the Beginnings of Humankind to the Present.* New York: Norton. p. 289. ISBN 978-0-3939-1847-2.

201   Philip J. Adler, Randall L. Pouwels, *World Civilizations: To 1700 Volume 1 of World Civilizations,* (Cengage Learning: 2007), p.169.

The Azande people brought warring weapons, new crops and farming skills or methods to South Sudan as well as taught new ideas, and principles of administration to the Kingdom nations. They introduced crop farming and Iron Age technology newly acquired which made weaponry, conquest, and supremacy possible. The new crop farming increased the population. This in turn lead to a demand for an expansion of territorial claim, which at first, led to settlements. As a subsequent result, Bantu-Zande and Rek Apuk have remained in a condition of war, fear, pain, and suffering. Due to Rek Apuk pastoralist conquests caused by the development of agriculture, making pots, and the use of iron, new ecological zones were exploited, and easily displaced the Indigenous Stone Age inhabitants.

The Zande are agriculturalists have a history of conflict with other clans, particularly the Rek Apuk ethnic groups, when they have attempted to farm cattle. They have a reputation for practicing 'witchcraft' and other forms of mysticism. They searched for territories with iron ore, gold, copper, precious stones, animal hides, ivory, steel, metal goods, resources, and hardwood forests. They looked for hardwood to make charcoal to fuel the melting incinerators, boilers, kilns, or blast furnace.

Many Rek Apuk people were forcefully captured, abducted, and forced into becoming concubines, slave soldiers, domestic slave workers, administrators, farmers, slave traders by agents and warriors in Lueel-Azande kingdoms. Soon after Rek Apuk people were captured, they were considered property by their owners, were assimilated into their new cultural identity, and often were separated from their family, forever by all accounts.

The hypothesized Proto-Bantu incomers and colonizers assimilated into the hunter-foragers, becoming proto-Azande in the process. They combatted, conquered, and pushed out others around the Equatoria and Bahr Al-Ghazal areas[202].

---

202   Berniell-Lee, Gemma; Calafell, Francesc; Bosch, Elena; et al. (2006). *"Genetic and Demographic Implications of the Bantu Expansion: Insights from Human Paternal Lineages"*. Molecular Biology and Evolution. 26 (7): 1581–9. doi:10.1093/molbev/msp069. PMID 19369595.

The Azande or Zandes might have adopted a culture of agricultural practices with a history of conflict with other clans. Particularly, the Rek Apuk, when they have attempted to practice or keep livestock from other unrelated Cushitic-and Rek Apuk speaking people they combatted. Powerful Azande kings and their Azande warriors would control the slave enterprises and deal with the slave buyers, slave agents and slave business coordinators in order to further their wealth and status with foreigners. Their greater numbers might even have led to small independent kingdoms that writers are still looking to find. It had also led to the expansion of Sudanic kingdoms, which then changed to the colonizers of the indigenous cultures in South Sudan. This was one of the largest human conquests in our history.

The Zande have mixed more readily with other smaller clans and subclans of nationalities. They have abandoned cattle keeping and practice agriculture crops farming system.

Mourning the Dead after Burial

The Rek Apuk Lith of the Jieng ethnic language speaking people, have established specific traditional customary rules and regulations, whereas Azande speaking people have fewer regulations about customary law bloodwealth compensation claims. These practices come out of custom, cultural priorities and the meaning of the blood wealth benefitting survival.

In a successful fatal accident claim the bereavement award is due payable by the negligent party even if there is no loss of income or benefits for the dependents. Using bloodwealth compensation reduces the impact costs of punishment on the community. It can prevent further lives being lost from the family as well as helping to maintain main sources of financial income when individuals are at the most productive age. This is done by preventing the costs of lengthy imprisonment or captivity.

Reconciliation and Punishment Bloodwealth 'Apuk Riem'

What customary law blood life wealth compensation in cattle equivalent currency impact can do is to promote peace, security, and reconciliation. It is important to consider the:

a. Fatal roadway hit collision crash occurrences for children who sustain road traffic injuries.
b. Risk factors that increase the risk for vulnerable road users include riding or walking in mixed traffic, cycling on pavements or footpaths, and not wearing reflective clothing.
c. Teenage drivers who are at increased risk because of their age and risk-taking behaviour, including drinking and driving, speeding, distractions while driving, and fatigue.
d. Risk factors for road traffic injuries which include poor supervision, poor vehicle design; the road environment as it relates to volume of traffic; poor land use and road network planning.
e. Lack of playgrounds, sidewalks, and bicycle lanes; and
f. lack of safe and efficient public transport risk factors for Azande speaking people.

The question personalized by investigating personnel engaging local communities was to ask: 'What can we do to protect our wives, husbands, sisters, brothers, mothers, sons, daughters from the hit collision crash violence that affects our communities?'

The Beginning of Family Mourning at Home

Madhel Malek Agei explains that in most South Sudan societies, when a death is confirmed or announced, the family is immediately regarded as 'devastated' 'crushed' or 'polluted' or 'contaminated'. Apuk consider a family death to have contaminated or devastated the relatives of the deceased. The term 'pollution' or 'devastation' in the context of the death of a family member was also used by Agei in his book (2020). The family of the deceased will be devastated or contaminated and anyone who touches the corpse will also be regarded as such.

The period preceding the burial will be accompanied by certain rituals that will be performed. These include the smearing of the mother, with ash to reflect a gloomy atmosphere, stopping drum dances from the playing ground and switching off radios and television sets. The underlying principle behind all these efforts is to demonstrate openly the intensity of their deep sorrow and remorse. Again, the underlying principle would be to symbolize death to the whole community.

Among the Jieng ethnic group, it is traditionally believed that when a death occurs in a family or a community, the family members have been symbolically 'crushed' by an angry divinity spirit, or ancestor, a curse or an evil eye. The person is demonized and need to be released. This imaginary Divinity spirit surrounding the survivors symbolizes their bereavement. As a result, they may not take part in the normal life of the society until they have been purified through performance of a ritual prayer. There is a mourning or bereavement or grieving period which usually takes longer for the family of the deceased. This mourning period prescribes to the family what acceptable behaviors are and what are not until the stipulated end of the mourning period.

There was a very unusual situation where the Apuk communities have an evil eye or devil person painted as a social pariah. This person is demonized in the burial rites and then offers animal sacrifices and grief during the mourning ceremonial celebrations.

The married couple whose child had fatally died is designated as the chief mourner. The beginning of the mourning period will include the chief mourners occupying a sacred mourning physical space. This could also mean being isolated from the community for the period of mourning. The chief mourners will usually be in the main bedroom on a mattress or floor or on the traditional mat called 'akot' or 'aguot' or 'yaak' (recently, because of the scarcity of traditional mats, a mattress will be used which will be unmounted from the stand) where parents or couples spend most of their time. The bereaved couples will wear a black garment, or a mourning attire called 'nai', which is a dress specifically designed for cultural mourning. Body decorations are removed completely. In other traditions, the siblings of the deceased child will also wear a small black badge to show that they are observing the period of mourning.

In South Sudan culture, the stipulated time for couples to be in mourning is usually a year. During that time, the bereaved couples and other bereaved family members stay at home and are not allowed any social contact or even drum game participation. They do not participate in any social activities or public gatherings like weddings, funerals, parties, and ritual sacrifice offering ceremonial services as they are believed to be contaminated or devastated.

Similar descriptions have also been recorded by Madhel Malek Agei and various academia about the widowhood experiences among the Nuer, Balanda, Azande, Rek Apuk on the Jieng framework of mourning and Agei on the experiences of Apuk Lith widows and the practice of religious and cultural rituals. The end of mourning for the widow or bereaved mother of the child deceased is usually marked by a ritual or a ceremony where she will be taking off the black garment or traditional rope or 'nai' and symbolically restored back to normal life in the society.

Apuk Lith Community Mourning

I will explain the process where the Apuk community will join in with the mourners[203]. The message of the death of a family member is usually spread by word of mouth as well as over the radio or newspaper as fast as possible. In Apuk community culture, the first stage of mourning usually begins when relatives and friends surround the widow or widower, or the mother or father or couples immediately after the death of family member. Members of the Apuk Lith community come to 'inquire' about what happened to the family known as 'riak bai' in Apuk language or 'devastation' in the family.

---

203   Dlukulu, P. M. (2010). *Black Urban Widows: Their experiences of and coping with bereavement in a transitional society.* Unpublished Doctoral Thesis, University of Pretoria, Pretoria: South Africa.

There is usually a mixture of Christian religious and cultural practices in most of the communities regarding the way they offer comfort and support to the bereaved. Many investigations recorded that on hearing of a death of a community member, who could also be a member of a particular church in the community, the clergy, imam, or Divine master or elderly leader immediately calls the home of the bereaved to offer condolences and conduct prayers. Such prayers are attended by the whole neighborhood. Madhel Agei and exploratory investigations also recorded that grief among the Catholic Church members or Anglican Church is a shared community experience.

When death is announced, church leaders as well as members, neighbours and the Rek Apuk community at large flock to the family where fatal tragedy has struck to verify the news and assure the bereaved of their support. Involvement of various stakeholders ensures holistic comfort and support. Apuk community members provide labour such as pitching of the water, skin, tent, local shelter, cooking and baking, assisting with buying groceries and other errands while the church leaders or priests provide psycho-spiritual support. This period where the Apuk community members gather at the house of the deceased is a period of comfort and support with varying forms of tradition, culture, social and religious practices including the group's interpretation of its supportive function.

Similar practice of community involvement has also been recorded in other parts of South Sudan. From the time when death strikes, close relatives are usually the first ones to arrive and the whole community would begin to show up few days after at the deceased's home. Madhel Agei also highlighted the practice of community mourning among the southwestern Apuk, northeastern Apuk and northern Apuk Lith. Various investigations also recorded the performance of community rituals in the face of a death of a loved one in South Sudan. Agei also highlighted process of community comfort and support among the different cultures in the country at a time of death of a community member. He compared the burial and mourning practices of the Jieng and Apuk Lith communities in the northern, southwestern, and northeastern parts of South Sudan, which has been recorded by researchers and the Nilotic ethnic groups in Africa, which are reported to be more elaborate and lavish in their approach to death. Burial rites are among the most important and visible observances in cultural life.

Cultural Burial Method System

Mourning rituals have been a constant phenomenon throughout Jieng or Muonyjang history. Burial, also known as funeral or interment or committal, is a method system of final disposition anytime a person dies, lifeless body is placed under the ground, occasionally with objects, such as cows, sheep, pots, and calabashes, which is still on frequent practice in current rural settings.

This is usually accomplished by excavating a pit or trench grave shape, placing the deceased body and objects in grave. The knees of lifeless body are flexed, the hand is positioned under the head, in the position of sleep inside excavated pit hole shape grave in underground burial method system. The exposed ears are covered with skins so that dirt will not enter in them the body is covered over. A cultural funeral method is a ceremonial celebration party that accompanies the final disposition. The vultural burial method system is often seen as indicative of respect for the dead. It has been used to prevent the odor of decay from spreading, to give family members closure, prevent them from witnessing the decomposition of their loved ones, and in many cultures, it has been seen as a necessary step for the deceased body to enter the afterlife or to give back to the cycle of life. Soon after putting the dead body on the excavated pit grave, placing the deceased body and objects in grave, and covering it over.

Apuk Lith method systems of burial are heavily ritualized and include natural or spiritual burial, and the use of containers for the dead, such as shrouds, hides, grave liners, and burial vaults, especially for divine masters or master of the fishing spear. All can retard decomposition of the body. Sometimes objects or grave goods like cows, sheep, pots, gourds, and calabashes are buried with the lifeless body, which may be dressed in ornamental or ceremonial attire. Depending on the culture, family status and clan, the way the body is positioned may have connotation and importance.

Apuk Lith Community Making Change Adaptable

Bereavement rituals and burial ceremonies address the adjustments in role and status, community tensions, reliving previous losses and relocation of the deceased into a new role and task in Apuk Lith community. This means that the bereavement rituals facilitate an adjustment to the change in role and in status of the deceased. According to Apuk Lith culture, when the person that has died is a husband, his wife becomes a widow and there is a specific dress code that she must wear. This is also accompanied by certain behaviours and actions, and the first-born son becomes head of the family. Death upsets the social equilibrium of the society, therefore certain stipulated rites, animal sacrifices and ceremonial celebration parties are used to restore the disturbed balance. Bereavement rituals including animal sacrifices and offering prayers are most often used to facilitate relinquishing of relationships and transition to a new role.

Apuk Lith Community Displaying the Bereaved

In Apuk Lith and other Rek communities, rituals such as burials, prayers, ceremonial celebration parties and memorial services serve as a community acknowledgement that a death has occurred and they provided opportunity for the community display of bereaved. This means that in playing the bereavement rituals, the bereaved families show the people and the community that they are bereaved. The dress code becomes a symbol of accepting new social status and they carry a message that the person is now in mourning. The importance of ritual dress codes and prescriptions is that if there should be no social prescription, the bereaved people may behave in a way that does not position them as in need of support from others.

The Apuk Lith Community Branches and Symbol of Identity

Rituals are also vehicles through which Apuk Lith communities are delineated and distinguished from others. They symbolize how people identify with their culture, religion and also with the deceased[204]. In Apuk Lith, Rek and other Jieng communities where cultural and religious identities are emphasized, they serve to strengthen and reaffirm people or group identities. State, culture, and nationality are three factors embodying identity. The state or nation is the largest community.

Identity is anchored in a particular social context or in a specific set of social relations[205]. The Apuk Lith goal of identity is social and political security. The logic being that people that have something in common are more likely to grow other interests together. They are connected by nativity rights, nationality identity and the issues of sovereignty. People must evolve enough to where they are no longer threatened by their differences of community identity, cultural identity, religious symbol identity, food, social traditions, clan divinities and divinity symbols. The dilemma of our culture lies in the non-existence of social justice services and the lack of social equalities. Therefore, the identity formation process involves a dialectical relationship between the individual and the society. This implies that we become who we are as a result of a particular form of socialization.

The Apuk Lith Community Identity

The Apuk Lith purpose of identity is security in common. Identity may exist along religious lines, ideological, geographical, ethnic, or national. In every case the bond between people sharing identity has in a security

---

204   Radzilani, M. S. (2010). *Discourse analysis on performance of bereavement rituals in a Tshivenda-Speaking community: An African Christian and traditional African perspectives,* Unpublished Doctoral Thesis, University of Pretoria. Pretoria: South Africa.

205   Dlukulu, P. M. (2010). *Black Urban Widows: Their experiences of and coping with bereavement in a transitional society.* Unpublished Doctoral Thesis, University of Pretoria, Pretoria: South Africa.

factor. "I know you because we have this common thing. I can trust you more because of these shared features."

The Apuk Lith communities have their symbol of identity within the Rek nationalities. They are Rek branches of the river, wetland, and lake Nilotic people. They were the original sources from which the Apuk branched out.

The *word Apuk* originated from a punishment blood fine according to Jang Rek or Muonyjang Rek ethnic language communities. Although just one word, it conveys an entire concept. Loosely, it is the method whereby homicides or serious breaches committed by clans' peoples, with or without implied consent from clan members, are resolved and ultimately forgiven.

The Apuk Lith communities are branches of the clannish Jieng, Muonyjang or Jang Rek of nationalities, falsely called "Dinka" in foreign language. They are the original root where the three Apuk Lith -Eagle were separated during migration periods.

The Northern Apuk Lith separated and settled on Sudd wetland in Western Nile River Valley of northwestern Jang Rek in Bahr Al-Ghazal in South Sudan.

The three branches of Rek Apuk Lith family speaking languages are inhabiting the Savannah Valley[206] in Bahr Al-Ghazal areas in the following locations:

There is Southern Apuk Lith, meaning *Apuk cieen in thong muonyjang, or thuongjang,* generally known as Apuk Juwiir or Apuk Agei Malek or Apuk Malek Agei, or puk Mathok Malek inhabiting savannah valley zone between eastern Sue River Basins, to Wanhalel River Basins, to the extreme eastern Bahr Al-Ghazal River Basin to Tonj South;

There is Northeastern Apuk Lith, meaning *Apuk tweng cueec in thong muonyjang or thuongjang,* commonly call Apuk Padoch or Apuk Bol Ayai,

---

206   Department of Arts of Africa, Oceania, and the Americas. *Trade and the Spread of Islam in Africa.* In Heilbrunn Timeline of Art History. New York: The Metropolitan Museum of Art, 2000- (October 2001)

inhabiting swampy land on western Machar Rek River or western Machar Achol River basins to Tonj North; and

There is Northern Apuk Lith, meaning *Apuk tweng in thong muonyjang or thuongjang,* commonly call Apuk Giir Thiik, inhabiting wider savannah valley land zone, Sudd swamp land zone (Toch wetland zones) and dryland zones on eastern loops of River Bahr Al-Ghazal (River Wau) on the western Nile River Valley of north-western Rek Dinka speaking peoples.

The findings of Madhel Agei study highlighted that Apuk Lith share a historical identity, cultural identity and have identical name. They are "Apuk Eagle", commonly known as *"Apuk Lith"* according to the classification of family speaking languages of Rek ethnic clans of nationalities[207]. The Eagle bird is symbolized in scores of ways in their lives and cultural practices and values of identity among spoken Jaang/Jieng languages of Rek as seen in annex table. The first function of defining Jieng ethnic identity is an exercise that must identify all the indigenous ethnicities where there is a branch of the Apuk Lith community.

South Sudan Identity
South Sudan identity and pride debates rage on unabated. Its identity is made up of a diverse society with multiple cultures, norms, rules, and values. Insights generated from the definitions and findings of the current exploratory study highlighted the significant perceptions, meanings, and feelings about the 'unique identities' or 'identities uniqueness'. While identity uniqueness is perceived as a celebration, the important functions of this identity were indicated as uniting, comforting, and supporting the bereaved and helping them to cope with the impact of loss of a loved one. On the other hand, others condemned the practice as totally disintegrative, disrespectful and that unique identity is insensitive of the people to hold a community. The most common feature of South Sudan

---

207   Agei, Madhel Malek (2020). *Apuk a State in Waiting,* Africa World Book, Australia. Page

identity, beyond comparative cultural similarities, is its history, without exception. Thus, South Sudan identity is found in its diverse cultures and nationalities. The findings of Madhel Malek Agei study highlighted those who are South Sudanese by blood and those who are South Sudanese by soil. Because they do not meet the narrow definition of a 'true' type, or selectively defining certain traits, such as Nilo-Hamitic speaking, Nilotic speaking, Afro Asiatic speaking or Sudanic to Kordofanian speaking simply ignores the complexity of genetics.

Madhel Agei emphasised that the people of South Sudan must accept that identities and terminologies change as circumstances change. If there's not any such thing as a 'historical South Sudan identity'[208], then the groundwork must be laid for the people to grow into a mutual identity. Within that framework, there can also be an Apuk identity, a Jieng identity, a Balanda identity, an Azande identity, a Rek identity a Nuer identity or a Kuku identity, a Moro identity or a Jie identity.

This is then melded to the unique identity South Sudan. Madhel Malek Agei highlighted that the most important facet of identity is "security". He emphasised that the identity does not have to equal the politics of hate. Being proud and defining the identity of the Apuk Lith or Rek or Jieng does not impose upon, threaten, or obscure the identity of the Bari, Kuku, Azande, Balanda, Nuer, Anyuak, Moro, Makaraka, Awan, Atuot, Agar, Lotuko, Luanyjang, Aguok nationalities and cultures. People must evolve enough to where they are no longer threatened by their differences of nationality identity, cultural identity, religious symbol identity, food, social traditions, clan divinities and divinity symbols. They do not have to be rejected using rivalry, hateful speech and subjugation.

---

208   The goal of identity is clan security, political security and social security. Something in common is people and clan interest to look for each other and shared association identity may exist along religious lines, ideology, inter-marriage, personal interest, political interest.

CHAPTER EIGHT

LAWS AND HISTORY OF CUSTOMARY AND COLONIAL LAWS IN SOUTH SUDAN

Introduction

This chapter aims to understand much of what is considered most central to and characteristic of the nature and behaviour of law. The concerned three principles for an understanding in this chapter are: First, an understanding of the traditionality found in almost all sixty-four laws of customary legal systems in South Sudan, not as a peripheral, but a central feature or characteristic of them. Second, a questioning of the post-enlightenment antinomy between tradition and change. Third, aims at understanding the undeniable senses of tradition, the traditionality of law.

The thesis about to be defended here is not merely that law includes traditions along with rules, principles, maxims, and so on, but rather that legal systems have to be understood as traditions, notwithstanding complex ones. As an example, the Jieng Dinka ancient legal systems are not only held to be traditional; modern legal positive orders are perceived or regarded as being traditional too. Conclusively, the origin of "communities of interpretation" is applied to the contemporary hypothesized statute laws, which are believed by many to be a distinguishing feature of modern legal systems.

Customary laws are central to the very identity of indigenous peoples and local communities, defining rights, obligations and responsibilities of members relating to important aspects of their lives, cultures and world views. Customary law can relate to use of and access to natural resources, rights and obligations relating to land, inheritance and property, conduct of spiritual life, maintenance of cultural heritage and knowledge systems, and many other matters.

Maintaining customary laws can be crucial for the continuing vitality of the cultural and spiritual life and heritage of indigenous peoples and local communities, who have also called for various forms of respect for and recognition of customary laws beyond the scope of their own communities. For example, in claims over land and natural resources. This can raise complex issues in fatal accident loss of loved one in road accident collision crash law.

This brief will explore the issues concerning customary law, traditional knowledge and property. "Traditional knowledge" is used in a general sense in this brief, embracing the content of knowledge itself as well as traditional cultural expressions[209].

Backgrounds of Customary Legal Systems
Introduction

Law is a profoundly traditional social practice, and it must be. I am not merely saying that a particular law embodies traditions, which of course no one would deny. Much of traditionality of law and life is unwritten history passed along by word of mouth. This and future generations should be aware of the inexorable customary law blood compensation, collectively defined as *apuk in Thuongjang*, unless otherwise, indicated. Specific laws and awards of blood life compensation *apuk* exist in most customary law systems.

The earliest historical records come from Anglo-Egyptian Condominium

---

209   *Customary Law, Traditional Knowledge and Intellectual Property: An Outline of the Issues,* WIPO Secretariat, 2013. www.wipo.int/export/sites/www/tk/en/resources/pdf/overview_customary_law.pdf.

sources, which describe the land upstream towards the south as "wretched."[210] South Sudan is part of the territories of the Ancient Kush King, Meroe and the Jieng nation- states of Nilotic descendants which is older than Ancient Egypt or Sudan. It had a dominating political structure and a significant influence over its neighbours for centuries and their traditional belief practices remain important ancient studies.

It is important to understand law of customary legal systems or Islamic legal systems or customs in the context of South Sudanese people by discussing the following issues.

- Sources of Custom and Purposes of customary legal systems
- Classifications of Laws of Customary Legal Systems.
- Historical Development of Traditional Customary Law Legal Systems.
- Blood wealth compensation, Divine wealth, its origins and purposes.

Origin Sources of Custom

The four origins of custom recognized to exist are[211]:

1. 'Practice', defined as a custom or tradition that has been repeated over many generations or passed through the word of mouths from generations to generations at the community rather than individual level.
2. Binding or persuasive decisions from Courts. This source is particularly broad in that 'Courts' include not just customary courts, but statutory courts which are empowered to preside over customary law cases in accordance to laws of customary legal systems
3. 'Religious beliefs' or 'spiritual beliefs' have particular significance in the treatment of matters such as incest and adultery.
4. 'Morality' and moral principles.

It did not take long for the colonizers to realize that colonial **law** was

---

210   S. O. Y. Keita (1993). *"Studies and Comments on Ancient Egyptian Biological Relationships"*. History in Africa (JSTOR) 20: 129- 154. Retrieved 2015-04-11.

211   Wuol Makec, John., *The Customary Law of the Dinka People of Sudan*. Afroworld Publishing Co. 1988. At 31.

not always appropriate or convenient for the colonized in dealing with instances of everyday life.

There are two fundamental legal sources that have shaped law of customary legal systems as it exists in South Sudan.

The first law of Colonial regime introduced by the Anglo-Egyptian Sudan administration, that had an enduring and deep impact upon all forms of social practice, statutory law and customary law systems.

The second law was what they called "Living Law", refers to the current lived customs of South Sudanese peoples and Sudanese peoples. The customs of the time will usually be clearly reflected in contemporary law of customary legal systems and it is from this that provides the dynamism and flexibility inherent in law of customary legal systems.

Classifications Law of Customary Legal Systems

A clansman or clanswoman commits criminal homicide if he or she intentionally, knowingly, recklessly, or with criminal negligence causes injury, severe injury, personality damage, integrity damage, death of a clansman or clanswoman.

Criminal homicide is murder, revenge killing, killing attack on a clansman or clanswoman, capital murder, manslaughter, or criminally negligent homicide, organized murder on behalf of other or collective community.

Criminal offenses in greatest contemporary African countries are defined in criminal or penal codes, a sweeping exodus from the uncodified English criminal law where a lot of these codes are based. Because of their origins, these codes rarely reflect the penal assumptions of the original colonial power. The major franchises to South Sudan traditional values or problems are the inclusion of statute law against various law of customary legal practices, notably Azande witchcraft practice; the extension of the criminal law in South Sudan customary clans and subclans with planned economies to cover economic crimes against the society or clan; and as a consequence of the soaring rate of some kinds or crime, special provision for certain offenses, for example, armed robbery prevalent in South

Sudan. Different court of law or courts, committees, hearings or panels not subject to the ordinary rules of procedure, have been established in South Sudan laws of customary legal systems to deal with such offenses.

The word "Adequate cause", which can be translated as *long, longcok or wetcielic* in *Thongmuonyjang or Thuongjang* explains cause which a clansman or clanswoman would commonly argue as a degree of anger, rage, resentment, or terror in a clansman or clanswoman of ordinary temper, sufficient to render the mind incapable of cool reflection.

Separate Law of Clannish Legal Systems

A separate clannish ethnic group in South Sudan has its own distinct body of cultural traditional customary law legal system. In effect there are approximately sixty-four (64) separate laws of clannish ethnic bodies of traditional customary legal systems.

It is justifiable to continue classifying multifarious sixty laws of traditional customary legal systems into custom courts that reflect the customs of the victim's family and customs of the guilty family. These allow for a reflection of a mixture of common interests, customs, ethnicities, and practices as well as culture, traditional regulations, family language and proximity in South Sudan. In fact, customary and specified strict sacrificial rituals exist in every clan and subclan determining for everyone the appropriate traditional behavior in the face of death in South Sudan.

These traditional customary legal systems classically comprise clans and or sub clannish units where local individual chiefs and subchiefs or committees, normally of kinship networks, exercise core social and legal powers. Wherever an individual has killed or severely injured or crashed and killed another whilst involved in a domestic or internal or civil dispute, the courts and the community recognize that the clan family member was acting as a member of a clan family or society or community in carrying out the crime act and that the clan family or society or community bear collective responsibility.

Nilotic ethnic classes of peoples with different clans and subclans[212], and in particular ethnic Jieng, have established specific traditional customary rules and regulations whereas Azande of Bantu ethnic language speakers, have fewer regulations for blood compensation claims. Criminal charges are less likely to result from a fatal accident caused by a factor out of a driver's control, such as poor road conditions, unpredictable mechanical failure, or an "Act of God." These practices come out of cultural priorities and the meaning of the compensation benefitting survival. When **someone dies at the scene due to a car accident** fatality, incurs severe injuries that leads him or her to suffer, or survives long enough to receive medical treatment but later succumb to their injuries, the person driving may face criminal charges, such as vehicular manslaughter.

This does not happen for every accidental fatality that results in death at the scene, or when the victim suffers from long-term severe injuries. However, it will still leave the "at-fault" driver with criminal liability, particularly in rural environments. The decision whether or not to charge a driver with a crime in a fatal car accident rest with the local district legal representatives. This may be a local traditional judge or justice chief and/or king, who will assess a variety of factors to determine whether a driver was "criminally culpable" in causing the death at rural highway roads or feeder roads.

In my exploration I have chosen the Jieng and Azande law as a case for investigation, as they are distinct ethnic groups whose customary law systems are similar. Balanda Bviri and Nuer customary legal systems are covered for the purpose of comparison.

A court case was launched against an Azande clan person who, by his wrongful act or neglect, may have caused the death of a boychild in Apuk Rek family. In these situations, it is often-times right and expedient that the Azande wrong doer be answerable in blood compensations for the fatality death so caused by him. As a result, I have attempted to compare

---

212   Encyclopedia Britannica, Inc.

and contrast Azande of Central Sudanic Bantu ethnic peoples and Apuk Rek of Jieng Nilotic ethnic peoples to demonstrate major differences in customs, laws and process.

See also section 6 and other annexes for references. Punishment of Common Offences Under Domestic Statutory law and Sharia Law is included in these annexes.

Historical Development of Customary Law
Introduction
Primarily, the law of customary legal systems is derived from home-grown customs and usages of traditional Africa. In the anglophonic areas of Africa, including South Sudan, customary law now includes Islamic law. Changes in traditional customary law took place primarily after colonial governments arrived in South Sudan. It did not take long for the colonizer to realize that colonial law was not always appropriate or convenient for the colonized in dealing with requests of everyday life, like family marriage and divorce law.

Universal law now applies to the entire country, but customary law still varies by area, region and constituency. Customary law is enforced in separate courts in which the judges are politically appointed clan chiefs, clan kings, or clan judges or clan justice.

In greatest English-speaking countries, the customary legal systems are based upon English common law. Common law functions on standards and practices, established by judges that date from early in English history.

Modern Customary Legal Systems
Customary law is an accepted source of law within jurisdictions of the civil law tradition. According to the Common Law of England, "Long usage" must be established for customs to become common law. It is a broad principle of property law that, if something has gone on for a long time without objection, whether it be using a right of way or occupying land to which one has no title, the law will eventually recognize the fact

and give the person doing it the legal right to continue. The legal criteria defining a custom are precise[213].

Law of customary legal systems of the Jieng Nilotic peoples feature all over the exploration because their laws have been examined and recorded much greater detail compared to other clans in South Sudan. The exploration identified marriage, adultery, divorce, child custody, property, social obligation, and procedural law under the domain of traditional customary law legal system in South Sudan. Interaction between statutory law and customary law in various bodies in society is crucial in the change towards a stable and secure society in South Sudan.

Customary law systems exist in an unaltered form in the rural mono-ethnic regions of the south. Questions of harmful cultural practices, draconian martial law, lack of professionalism and jurisdictional uncertainty plague the administration of justice. Customary law in South Sudan largely embraces reconciliation and community harmony. However, the traditional values and community structure that reinforce them are under siege in post-conflict South Sudan.

Wanhalel Jieng Traditional Customary Law

Before the Jieng Apuk homeland was invaded by the Anglo-Egyptian-Sudan forces, the customary and traditional trial skills of the clannish ethnic groups were the primary source of law to the peoples of South Sudan214. The invasion was the first in a chain of events, which brought colonial influence to bear over the traditional customary practices and law systems.

The Wanhalel Dinka Customary Law adopted in 1927, was a traditional and basic law, whose stated purpose was "to entrench within basic law the values of the clan customs in South Sudan as a traditional society".

---

213   *"Customary Mooring Rights"*. Associated Yacht Brokers. Archived from the original on 13 April 2015. Retrieved 19 April 2015.

214   Lufti, G. A., *The Future of English Law in the Sudan. The Sudanese Judgment and Precedents Encyclopedia*. Sudan Judiciary, Khartoum. At 2.

When the British colonial administration established the Tonj District in 1903, The Commissioner appointed Traditional High Court of Appeal members and chiefs believed to be priests, divine masters, or masters of the fishing spear to determine the *apuk* price for a killing offence. The Commissioner adjudicated several clan offences regarding judicial disputes resolution and compensation in cattle.

The heads of institutions of the government of Anglo-Egyptian Sudan Condominium gave approval after Wanhalel conference. There were several important recommendations made in that conference were215 regarding the acknowledgment of customary laws in the judicial system. The customary "judicial system" is as much a social convention as it is a judicial trial procedure. Efforts were carried out to define customs together with customary law.

Colonial Law

Countries with majority Muslim populations have adopted diverse legal systems. Those that were once English colonies such as Sudan, South Sudan, Pakistan, Bangladesh, Jordan, and Egypt adopted English criminal law and civil law systems and procedure. The group retained or later adopted Islamic law called Shari'ah law; with few or no reforms. It was almost totally an Islamic revolution in Sudan from 1820 to 1899. As an example, Deim Zubeir city is also the first location Islam, Qur'anic or Koranic teaching and Shariah laws "took root and floured"[216] in South Sudan. Deim Zubeir king of slave-traders of Bahr Al-Ghazal critically shaped the Arabic, Islamic, Quranic and Shariah laws as institutions and systems between 18th to mid-19th centuries in the South Sudan. Living conditions were particularly hard in Deim Zubeir city since the area

---

215   Agei, Madhel Malek (2020). *Apuk a State in Waiting,* Africa World Book Company Lt. Australia. Pages

216   Klein, Martin A. (1998). *Slavery and Colonial Rule in French West Africa.* Cambridge University Press.

was heavily infested with tsetse flies, which transmit sleeping sickness[217]. Zubeir claimed that his rule as king of slavery was a civilizing mission in the name of "Islam" and "life" service. President Nimeiri imposed Sharia Law on September 26, 1983, which he called the "Islamic revolution". He also stated that "With the proclamation of the Islam laws, the rule has become God's or Allah's rule and disobedience to the ruler, disobedience to God or Allah."[218]

Prior to the 1820 invasion of the Sudan by Egyptian forces led by Mohamed Ali of the Turkish regime, the custom and traditions of clannish ethnicities were the primary source of law to those peoples of South Sudan.[219] That invasion was the first in a chain of events, which would bring their own unique influence to bear over traditional customary practices and laws. Successive colonial regimes under the Anglo-Egyptian Sudan condominium rules resulted in the enactment of a series of statutory instruments designed to codify, formalize and ultimately to control application, effect and scope of customary laws throughout the country.

Following restoring order and the government's authority, the colonial government devoted themselves to creating a modern government in the condominium. Judges or Jurists adopted penal and criminal procedural codes similar to those in force in British India. Administrations established land tenure rules and adjusted claims in dispute because of grants made by successive governments. Taxes on land continued the basic form of taxation, the sum assessed depending on the nature of irrigation, the quantity and variety of agriculture crops and the size of herds. In spite of this, the rate of taxation was fixed for the first time in history.

---

217   Lewis, D.J. (1949). *"The Tsetse Fly Problem in the Anglo-Egyptian Sudan"*. Sudan Notes and Records. 30: 189 – via Sudan Open Archive.

218   Le Moy, Pa Scale Villiers, *"Nimeiri plays the Islamic Cord"* Middle East (The), No. 112 (February 1984), pages 22-23.

219   Lufti, G. A., *The Future of English Law in the Sudan. The Sudanese Judgment and Precedents Encyclopedia*. Sudan Judiciary, Khartoum. At 2.

Quranic Sharia: An Islamic Law

The word 'Sharia', 'Shari'a' or 'Shariah' means Islamic law which is a theocratic legal system believed to be derived from God, which can be translated as "Allah" in the Arabic language. It is based on the teachings of "Mohammad" or "Mohammedan" as in the 'Qur'an', 'Quran' or 'Koran'. In fundamentalist Islam, law is also derived from the teachings of Mohammad that are not explicitly in the 'Quran'. Laws do not originate from secular sources, like kings or legislatures or 'Long usage'. The Shariah serves as a criminal code that lists several *had or huddud* crimes, or *Alms* and *Zakat* based on Sharia; a lot of Islamic economic principles, or offenses for which punishments are fixed and unalterable. Thus, ***Tariqa or Turuq* for** a Sufis Islamic Sharia order, demands teaching of discipline, the communal life, and all share ritual as the only way to Allah. It is the path of Islam according to Muslim followers.

During the 16th and 17th centuries, slave raiders began to raid the region downwards to the south as part of the Islamic and Qur'anic Shariah expansion. There were a number of Nile River slave routes[220]. Their captives were enslaved, Islamized, converted into Islamic traditions, and shipped to the Mediterranean. They went to Europe along Atlantic coast, Arabia along the Mediterranean coast, slave ports and factories, along the Congo Rivers[221], western South Sudan, northern Sudan, Egypt, or to the coastal Red Sea and Mediterranean.

The southwards slave raid and Islamic expansion pressure increased domination by Dar Fur Sultanate (18th to mid Turkiya 1821-1885), who established the first Koranic teaching school. Islamic Law courts were established for the crimes of slaves and captive trials as well as to serve as a hanging place for slaves who attempted to escape from their captors

---

220   *International Business Publications, USA (7 February 2007). Central African Republic Foreign Policy and Government Guide (World Strategic and Business Information Library). Int'l Business Publications. page 47. ISBN978-1433006210.Retrieved 25 May 2015.*

221   Alistair Boddy-Evans. Central Africa Republic Timeline- Part 1:

in Deim Zubeir town. Zubeir coined the word "Dar Fertit"[222] for Fertit Communities in the Greater Deim Zubeir areas locally called "Juku"[223] or "Uyujuku"[224] location in Western Bahr Al-Ghazal in South Sudan. "Zubeir Rahma constructed a trench camp and a fortification where slaves were kept awaiting to be transported to various destinations along the Nile northwards"[225]. The trench was built underground almost four meters deep and three kilometers long; wood and mud were used in the construction in Deim Zubeir town, where the slaves were held during their grueling journey into Northern Sudan and on to Egypt along Mediterranean coast, to Arabia, but it also reflects the memories linked to this challenging time in human history. Deim Zuber town gives an opportunity to remember this historic moment in South Sudan. The tree that was notorious as the site of slave hangings remains next to the trench[226].

.The word 'Dar' means "home of", and "Fertit" does not define or portray any ethnic group, but was at the time a downgrading or harsh "word for non-Fur, non-Arab, non-Dinka or non-Jieng or Jaang and non-Luo groups in Deim Zubeir-Uyujuku areas in Western Bahr Al-Ghazal".[227] Fertit is false word coined by slave owners as a name for their slaves and "Dar" as a name for 'the home of captured slaves' at

---

222   Sikainga, Ahmed Alawad (1989). *"The Legacy Of Slavery And Slave Trade In The Western Bahr Al-Ghazal, 1850-1939".* Northeast African Studies. Pages 75–95.

223   Sharpe, R. Bowdler. *"Note on a Collection of Birds made by Herr F. Bohndorff in the Bahr Al-Ghazal Provice and the Nyam-Nyam Country in Equatorial Africa"* (PDF). Zoological Journal of the Linnean Society. Pages 17- 103 -421.

224   *"Deim Zubeir, Sudan- Geographical Names, map, geographic coordinates".* Geographic.org. 24 September 1993. Retrieved 31 July 2016.

225   UNESCO (4 October 2017). *"Deim Zubeir Slave route site".* UNESCO. Retrieved 5 October 2017.

226   UNESCO (4 October 2017). *"Deim Zubeir Slave route site".* UNESCO. Retrieved 5 October 2017.

227   Thomas, Edward (2010). *The Kafia Kingi Enclave. People politics and history in the north-South boundary zone of western Sudan.* London, Nairobi; -Rift Valley Institute. Pge 36, 103, 116.117. ISBN 9781907431043.

the time. The dwellers of Deim Zubeir-Uyujuku township included a substantial number of ex-soldiers and former slaves, who had lost their ethnic ties and converted to Islam with Arabic as lingua franca.[228] Deim Zubeir city is also the first location Islam, Qur'anic or Koranic teaching and Shariah laws" took root and floured"[229] in South Sudan. This gives way further east to the Sudd wetland, raiding captured slaves and many captives in Jieng population and driven to Deim Zubeir slave camp, an area of tropical wetland fed by the water of the White Nile.

As a result, slavery critically shaped the Arabic, Islamic, Quranic and Shariah laws as institutions and systems in the Sudans. When foreigners first arrived at the region and found that slavery was "well established" in the region, used to "feed the courts of Azande kings as it was used in the medieval empires of the interior". Between the process of capture, enslavement, and "incorporation into a new community, the slave had neither rights nor any social identity." As a result, the identity of people who were enslaved "came from membership in a corporate group, usually based on kinship."[230]

The 1902 code of civil procedure continued the Ottoman separation of civil law and Sharia law, but it also created guidelines for the operation of sharia law courts as an autonomous judicial division under a chief translated as *qadi, gadi* or *kadi* in Arabic language, appointed by the governor general. Religious judges and other sharia law court officials were invariably foreigners in the Sudan colony. For example, apostasy requires a death sentence, extramarital sexual relations require death by stoning, and consuming alcoholic beverages requires eighty lashes. Other lesser crimes like *ta'zir* allow judges discretion in sentencing offenders.

---

228   Sikainga, Ahmad (1996). *Slaves into Workers: Emancipation and Labor in Colonial Sudan.* Austin. Pages 53–54.

229   Klein, Martin A. (1998). *Slavery and Colonial Rule in French West Africa.* Cambridge University Press.

230   Klein, Martin A. (1998). *Slavery and Colonial Rule in French West Africa.* Cambridge University Press. Page 1.

The earliest of such instruments[231] in the Sudan colony was the Sharia law court referred to as "Mohammedan Law Courts Ordinance 1902" which sought to empower Sharia Courts to entertain the following matters:

- Any question regarding marriage, divorce, guardianships of minors or family relationship, provided that the marriage to which the question related was concluded in accordance with Mohammedan law or the parties are Mohammedans.

- Any question regarding gift, succession, wills, interdiction or guardianship of an interdicted or lost person, provided that the endower donor or the deceased or the interdicted or lost person is a Mohammedan, or Muslim.

- Any question other than those mentioned in the last two successions provided that all the parties, whether being Muslims or Mohammedans or not, make a formal demand signed by them asking the Court to entertain the question and stating that they agree to be bound by the ruling of Mohammedan law or Islamic Shariah law.

Relative autonomy was also provided to formal Islamic lawmakers in that the same ordinance authorized the Grand Judge or Jurist translated as Grand *Kadi or Gadi in Arabic language*, pending the approval of the colonial Governor-General, to make regulations governing the decisions, procedure, constitution and jurisdiction of the Mohammedan Law Courts.[232]

In practice, being a Muslim means attending Koran schools, going to Friday prayers, keeping fast on Ramadan, claiming for "Dia" in Mohammedan Law Courts under Muslim jurists, judges, or justices or *kadi, qadi or kadi* in Arabic language, participating in public festivals and observing some of the rules governing naming and funeral ceremonies, marriage, inheritance and the conduct of women. Islam is commonly

---

231   Ibid. At 6.

232   Ibid.

found in towns only in the country because its practices are unpopular and are strongly opposed in the rural areas of South Sudan.

Fatal Accidents Blood Compensation Claims

The Fatal Accidents Act of 1855 stipulates that on the death of a person caused by the "wrongful act, neglect or default" of another person, the personal representative of the deceased can maintain an action for blood wealth compensations or bloodwealth payable on behalf of the wife, husband, parent or child of the Deceased[233].

Traditional customary law has one potential concern of a universal move toward those who should embrace customary and indigenous laws and protocols as part of a wider set of tools to trace that traditionality of law.

These tools may encompass existing law as tradition, native law and customs, traditional customary legal systems, Quranic Sharia Law Court Ordinance 1902[234], adapted Civil Justice Ordinance 1929, the Chiefs' Courts Ordinance 1931, colonial statutory law and customary law systems, civil law, and criminal law systems[235]. With new standalone blood wealth and divine wealth legal systems, such practices are an act that requires the perpetrator to pay the injured parties blood wealth compensation as well as are an issue of collective responsibility, and blasphemy.

Amongst the principal attributes of traditional customary law may, depending on context, be its legitimacy, flexibility and adaptability. In some countries it is recognized as a source of law, in others its role is limited to the exercise of internal autonomy or self-government by indigenous peoples and local communities. Suggestions made after investigations conducted by researchers include the following factors:

- The custom must be of immemorial antiquity. The responsibility,

---

233   Act No. 13 of 1851 (27th March, 1855). The Fatal Accidents Act, 1855.

234   Ibid. At 6.

235   Ibid.

obligation and duty of its antiquity should be on that individual who asserts the application of the custom. The proof is easier in this way, if its origin cannot be remembered. The responsibility of refuting it lies upon the party against whom the custom is being applied.

- The custom must be certain, precise, reasonable and have been enjoyed as of the fundamental legal basis or source of law for a community's legal rights and knowledge traditions;
- a factual element in establishing a community's collective rights;
- one element of the definition of knowledge traditional, or can otherwise establish the relationship between the knowledge and a community that is central to the concept of 'law as traditions and pass knowledge';
- a means of determining or guiding the procedures to be followed in securing a community's "free prior informed consent" for access to and/or use of laws as traditions and pass knowledge;
- the basis of specific user rights or exceptions, exempting a community's continuing customary law uses and practices from legal restrictions;
- a guide for the assessment of cultural or spiritual offence or damage caused by wrongful act, negligent or inappropriate actions use;
- a determinant of or guide to how benefits from the blood wealth payable as compensation claims and should be shared equitably within a victim family;
- a means of determining appropriate remedies, sanctions or restitution;
- an avenue for resolving disputes over ownership or other forms of custodianship for reconciliation and harmony amongst communities or societies;
- a guide for the transmission of rights through knowledge of 'tradition' from generation to generation.

Whatever makes knowledge "traditional" can be the same occurrence or truth that it is fostered, maintained and disseminated in a customary, generation to generation perspective or distinction, and often that distinction will be defined and shaped by customary law. Thus, at the same time the basic question in discussing knowledge of tradition to be protected can involve an understanding of customary law. This is one reason why indigenous peoples and local communities have consistently argued that measures for the knowledge of tradition should be protected against misuse and misappropriation should be based upon and support enforcement of their customary laws. Customary norms grew out of developing practices which became binding as result of general use. Local judges, justice or chiefs or kings did not feel that community practices could by themselves generate binding norms.

The purpose for a particular custom to acquire the binding force of law is by passing a test of reasonableness.[236] For years the courts defined the "reasonableness' of a custom as its conformity with 'justice, equity and good conscience". The objection was based on its weakness that it allows only the judges or lawyers to decide whether a custom is 'reasonable'. They in turn must make judgments about the concepts or values of a society in the light of their own values of that society.

Fatal Accident Laws and Customary Law

Over eighty percent of the population of South Sudan is living in rural areas. They have no idea about cars, or car accident fatalities. Some have never heard of any car accidents. Many traditional chiefs' courts have not seen or settled any injury or crime related to fatal road accidents at the rural level. No action or suit is maintainable in some of the rural traditional chief occurs against a person who, by his wrongful act, neglect, or default, may have caused the death of another person, because vehicles do not travel to these places. When new cities emerged at rural villages, road accident occurrences became common without arrest or court hearings. It is often-times expedient that the wrong-doer in such case should be

---

236   Wuol Makec, John., *The Customary Law of the Dinka People of Sudan.* Afroworld Publishing Co. 1988. At 31. At 26.

answerable in blood compensation claims for the injury so caused by him on rural highway roads or rural feeder roads.

Representatives of Indigenous people and local communities have been actively participating in committee, traditional court hearings and folklore meetings on the fatal accident regimes and access to blood compensation claims in customary law courts.

South Sudanese customary law systems have traditionally dealt with homicide as an offence that is both a tort issue, an act that requires the perpetrators to pay the injured party reparations or blood life compensations, and also an issue of collective responsibility. Indigenous people and local communities have frequently made the case that their customary laws and practices are in essence fatal accident regimes specifically crafted for protection of their families.

This book suggests a new fatal accident regime establish to protect the families of persons for loss occasioned to them and to grant a "right to the restitution of families, persons, cultural, religious and spiritual property" "in violation of fatal accident laws, traditions, and customs". Access to indigenous collective responsibility or law of obligation is subject to prior informed consent obtained in accordance with customary laws. When roadway accident occurrences arise, "customary laws and practices shall be used to resolve the fatal accident dispute.

One objective of the fatal accident regime would be to introduce a protection regime derived from the collective responsibility and law of obligations of Indigenous communities with intend "to promote the fair and equitable distribution of the payable blood wealth, divine wealth by the guilty party and blood wealth benefits to the victim party. The law shall provide that the traditional exchange between communities or indigenous peoples of the collective fatal accident responsibility shall not be affected.

CHAPTER NINE

LAWS AND HISTORY OF BLOOD COMPENSATION CLAIM AND ORIGIN OF CUSTOMARY LAWS IN SOUTH SUDAN

Blood Life Compensation for Fatality Death Occasioned to Family
When someone dies due to a car accident on a rural highway road the "at-fault" driver may face homicide criminal charges, but not always in rural environments in South Sudan.

Survivors of a car accident often face overwhelming emotional strain, and struggle to know where to turn for help. The legalities surrounding a blood life compensation claim can be complex and challenging in the urban fatal accident homicide crime court hearing sentences. Filing such a blood life compensation claim while you are still grieving can make it that much more difficult. Not only will you have to navigate your way through complicated urban legal systems but you will also have to deal with answering numerous personal questions pertaining to death occasioned to loved one, which can be emotionally draining.

Every bloodwealth compensation claim or court case shall be for the benefit of the wife, husband, parent, and child, if any, of the person whose death shall have been caused and shall be brought by guilty party. In every such action the court judges may give such blood compensations as it may think proportioned to the wealth blood life loss resulting from such death to the victim. The blood recovered, after deducting all costs and expenses, shall be divided amongst the before mentioned parties, or any of them, in such shares as the Court by its judgment or decree shall direct.

The current urban homicide crime courts provide a statute of limitations for filing fatal accident case law. There is a limited period given for filing bloodwealth compensation claim. This limitation period commences from the date of death or from the date the death was linked to the accident or exposure. If the deceased was in the process of dealing with their personal injury blood compensation claim when they passed, the period, could be a 1 year, 2 year or 3-year deadline. This is to allow the family to continue with their claim. Statutes are deeply embedded, along with customary and judge-made law, in the highly traditional practices of law.

Road accident fatalities shall be brought to urban legal judiciaries for hearing one at a time, and in respect of the same subject-matter of complaint. The representative of the deceased may insert a claim for damages caused by road collision crash accident fatalities and recover any financial or monetary loss to the property of the deceased occasioned by such wrongful road collision crash act, neglect or default, which sum, when recovered, shall be deemed part of the properties or possessions of the wealth of the deceased.

Chiefs Courts as the Second Ordinance 1931

Criminal offenses are defined in criminal or penal codes, a radical deviation after the uncodified English criminal law based on these codes. These codes reflect the penal assumptions of the original colonial power. The primary concessions to local tradition values are the inclusion of legislation against various customary practices, notably witchcraft practice in Azande culture. There is an extension of the criminal law to cover economic crimes against the community; and, as a consequence of the soaring crime rate, such as special provision for certain offenses like armed robbery. Special tribunals, not subject to the ordinary rules of procedure, have been established in many regions to deal with such offenses.

The Wanhalel Traditional Jieng Customary legal systems retained a greater role for traditional, or customary law, than most other communities in South Sudan. After the former Anglo-Egyptian Condominium ruled territory obtained independence in 1956, Sudan adopted a "general law" based on colonial common law and on the statutes of the national legislature. Most of the population lived in rural areas and largely were governed by what become known as "customary law".

Sudan and South Sudan established a tripartite system of criminal law and criminal justice as well as Sharia Islamic law system. Its criminal code is based on colonial common law, but there is also a penal code based on the Shari'ah or Quranic Sharia Islamic law and a customary law based on custom of local communities. Customary law is enforced in separate courts in which the judges are politically appointed clannish elders in the communities.

According to Attorney General Umar Abd al 'Ati, it has been decided that urgent amendments were made to some provisions of the current penal code, to prevent the duplication of penalties, and nullify many violations caused by the penal code introduced in 1983. He stated that the amendments do not mean a direct return to the 1974 codes as some may think but are intended to remove the violations which occurred as part of the country's supreme policy which still adheres to the Islamic Sharia Law as a source of codes. He added that it has been decided to retain the Islamic law penalties for manslaughter, theft, adultery, prostitution, fornication, corruption and war against Muslim citizens[237]. It has been decided that correcting the application of these penalties will be thoroughly discussed during a conference of Muslim Ulema from inside and outside the country.

President Nimeiri imposed the Holy Sharia Law on September 26, 1983, which he called the "Islamic revolution". He said that "With the

---

237   Attorney General Announces Islamic Law Amendments GF301935 Text Khartoum (SUNA) in Arabic 1730 GMT 30 December 1985

proclamation of the Islam laws, the rule has become God's rule and disobedience to the ruler, disobedience to Allah or God[238]". By October 1984, the number sentenced into limb amputations in the Shariah law courts had reached 58 amputee persons who were amputated, including 12 cross amputee persons given "cross amputations", with their right-hands and left feet amputated and one public hanging.[239]

In some ethnic communities, local criminal courts handle the more-serious criminal cases. While customary courts handle most civil cases and less-serious criminal cases. Customary courts differ widely throughout South Sudan. There are no lawyers and few formal rules of procedure, and the courts' decisions often conflict with the colonial law. In other parts of the South Sudan, in addition to colonial criminal courts, customary courts are authorized to hear civil cases and criminal cases involving children. In rural areas they often hear the entire range of criminal cases, including murder or homicide. The Customary Law and Custom Courts ordinances created a Wanhalel Traditional Jieng Customary law court system that hears both civil law and customary law cases at all levels of the judiciary, including that of the Appeal High Court.

As an example, the Anglo-Egyptian colonization came with statutory law and, in particular, criminal laws dealing with issues that had hitherto been the remit of customary law. Although the judiciary allowed the laws of customary legal systems great leeway in dealing with day to day legal matters under *Chief's Courts Ordinance 1931* allowed:

The Chief's Court shall administer the Native Law and Custom prevailing in the area over which Court exercises its jurisdiction provided that such Native Law and Custom is not contrary to justice, morality or order.

In these ways, the first non-colonial laws were formally recognized by colonial powers. Laws of customary legal systems were also addressed with

---

238   Le Moy, Pa Scale Villiers, *"Nimeiri plays the Islamic Cord"* Middle East (The), No. 112 (February 1984), pages 22-23.

239   *"Is this Islamic Justice?"* Middle East (The), No. 120 (October 1984), pages 20-21.

the passage of the Civil Justice Ordinance 1929 and the Chiefs' Courts Ordinance 1931, such as Wanhalel Traditional Jieng Laws conferences 1927. The first of these Ordinances is the original predecessor to the current section 5 of the New Sudan's Civil Procedure Act 2003. The ordinance was a novel change and improvement in that it formally recognized customary Chief's legal system of authority to exercise customary jurisdiction in their traditional clannish ethnic group areas. According to Ordinance Section seven: "The Chiefs' or Kings' Court shall administer the Native law and Customs prevailing in the area over which Court exercises its jurisdiction provided that such Native law and Custom is not contrary to justice, morality or order".

Consolidate the Traditional Chiefs or Kings Power

The Court Ordinance 1931 under the Traditional Chiefs or Kings turned out to be of enormous political and legal significance to that period, with equal importance in modern South Sudan. Pragmatic colonial recognition was the foundation of a society at that period, with classes of clans and subclans of nationalities. The main focus on leadership and social order was the clannish ethnicity chief or king. An ordinance that gave formal recognition to and empowered the traditional chief or traditional king was a 'capacity building' measure of the day. In bald colonial terms it was an act aimed at ensuring the allegiance of traditional chiefs or kings to the colonial government. It also recognized the realities of traditional clannish ethnicity life. In the opinion of a number of modern judges, the overall effect was to consolidate the chief or king power of customary law within the nation-state.

The Court Ordinance fantasies of Chiefs or Kings and the recognition of the status laws of customary legal systems in South Sudan were also reaffirmed by central government legislators of the post-colonization period.[240] The Local Courts Act 1977 repealed the original but replaced

---

240   Wuol Makec, John., *The Essentials for the Role of Customary Law in the Southern Sudan*. The Sudanese Judgment and Precedents Encyclopedia. Sudan Judiciary, Khartoum. At 3.

it with an almost identical mandate. It is fascinating to note that the Criminal Act 1991 of Sudan actually exempted South Sudanese people from the application of Sharia penalties, replaced with criminal penalties conforming to the concepts of localized customary laws.

Origin of Laws of Customary Legal Systems

Customary law can be traced back to the time of memorial antiquity. It continued throughout Middle Ages in the kingdom to chiefdom or chieftaincy. A single Indigenous customary legal system court was set up for most of the clans and subclans. Like many other early customary legal systems, it did not originally consist of substantive rights but rather of procedural remedies. The working out of these remedies has, over time immemorial, produced the new legal system in which rights, truths or faiths are seen as primary over procedure.

The Jieng Rek, especially after the earlier accession of divine clan divinities and their emblems, connected to spirituality of all the cultures, had developed a body of rules the customary law or the Law of Obligation resembling those being traced to collective divine punishment of *apuk* as compensation claims after homicide, injury, or fatal accident. The fear of divine intervention and divinity punishment influence even those who had raided herds or had committed kinds of crimes to return them to their rightful owners before *yath, jak,* or *jok* would strike back at them for divine punishment, for crime clans, and for stealing the cows of *yath* from different clans and sub-clans. The clan divinity is the very nature of an ancestor. The symbols or emblems are the very nature of the clansman and clanswoman. Local customs governed most matters, while the clan divinity with spiritual powers and diviners or divine masters played a large part in government with dual roles and duties. Crimes were treated as wrongs, for which apuk as compensation was made to the victim, or else you will face a divinity punishment severely.

Diass describes how traditional customary law systems originate. He says: "When a large section of the populace is in the habit of doing a thing over a very long period, it may become necessary for the courts to take notice of it. The reaction of the people themselves may manifest itself in mere unthinking adherence to a practice which they follow simply because it is done; or again it may show itself in a conviction that a practice should continue to be observed, because they approve of it as a model of behaviour. The more people follow a practice the greater pressure against non-conformity. But it is not the development of a practice as such, but the growth of a conviction that it ought to be followed that makes it a model for behaviour."[241] Diass suggests that certain conditions have to be fulfilled for a custom, usage or practice to be recognized by a court of law as having the force of law.

Linkages Between Customary Legal Systems in South Sudan

Linkages between customary legal systems of the approximately sixty tribes or clans and the six groups are given as example, as have much more in common than they have differences. Differences tend to be ones of style rather than substance; mainly connected to differing values systems and in particular the basis of community wealth. Where communities are cattle herders the currency of the courts is cattle. In agriculturalist communities it can vary from tools, weapons and beads to contemporary money. A comparison of some criminal offences and civil cases under six customary law codes, together with a comparison of some criminal offences under statutory and Sharia law, are shown at Annex._

The single main important linkage is the basis of all customary law, the need to achieve reconciliation and to ensure inter-community harmony rather than to punish. Other common ground can be investigated under the few principle subject areas of customary law:

Family Marriage Law: In South Sudan customary legal systems have a common recognition of the scope and tenacity or drive to marriage. Marriage is recognized as a union between a man and a woman for life,

---

241   RWM Dias, *Jurisprudence*, 2nd edition., Butterworths, London 1964, p.142

with the driver or desire to producing children and in doing so both boosting, guaranteeing and safeguarding the continuity of the family. Polygamy is accepted as a legal practice. In this respect marriage is considered to be between two family groups rather than two individuals. Marriage laws of customary legal codes involves a 'bride wealth' payable by the man and his family. The payable 'bride wealth' complexity in its distribution is designed in part to make both divorce and adultery socially unacceptable actions. The latter is considered to be so serious an offence that it is both civil misdemeanors incurring a fine in compensation to the husband and also a crime punishable by a jail sentence.

Laws of customary legal systems have their contingencies for dealing with mixed marriages across clannish ethnic groups in the country.

Divorce: The divorce issue is accomplished in very similar fashion in all customary legal systems. Grounds for divorce are common: repeated infidelity; neglect of family duties by either party; gross misconduct by the wife; impotence of the husband; physical cruelty; and overall breakdown of the marriage. The key action in divorce is to return "bride wealth". Given the complexity of providing "bride wealth", particularly cattle, the logistics of returning the wealth often causes severe friction within families and is a strong force militating against divorce.

Custody of Children: Customary legal systems dealing with the custody of children are almost the same to each other. They also reflect the ethos of a patrilineal society. Children remain with their mother until they are seven years of age. Thereafter they will go to their father if he has paid dowry and to the maternal uncle if the father of that child has paid nothing.

Property legal Systems: Customary legal systems reflect the importance each clannish ethnic group place upon movable and immovable property. The Nilotes who are pastoralists place great value on land for grazing and on cattle as a symbol of wealth, power and pride. Pastoralists have more complex property laws than sedentary agriculturalists. All of them have common customary legal systems regarding ownership and inheritance of property. The aim of customary law is to ensure that all property stays within the family.

Law of Obligations: Customary legal systems have dealt with homicide as an offence traditionally. Law of obligations combines a tort law issue, like an act that requires the perpetrator to pay the injured parties blood life compensations and also an issue of collective responsibility.

Procedures: Although individual customary legal system courts may conduct their proceedings according to clannish custom, variations are more superficial. The motives for the shared aims of procedures lie in colonial history. The Constitution of the Chiefs' Courts governs the customary laws of the people of South Sudan.

Customary law assumes that all legal disputes should be settled outside of the court in South Sudan; a judicial proceeding is a last resort, signifying a deadlock that the council of elders cannot resolve. Even when the dispute comes before the judge the doors are not shut to settling the case outside of court. The elders who first heard the case will continue in court to try and find a compromise acceptable to both parties. Litigation, in the Western sense, is a contest where the court aims to find for one party over another, is concept foreign to South Sudan society.

The jurisdiction of each clannish customary legal system courts determined by the Chief Justice and defined in a warrant issued by his office authorizing their establishment. Their restrictions are often placed upon the jurisdiction of each clan court, which determine such issues as the value of fines or verdicts, the types of cases that can be heard and the territory within which the clan court may exercise its powers.

Written Customary Legal System Practices in South Sudan

The contemporary or modern codification of civil law came from the tradition of medieval customs, collections of local customary law that came or arisen in a specific constituency, district or township jurisdiction, and which were gradually pieced together predominantly from case law and later written down by local judges or jurists or justices.[242] The word "judge" or "jurist" or "justice" or "legal expert" means a clansman with expert knowledge of law as traditions used in customary law by clannish ethnic community; somebody who analyses and comments on law traditions. This clansman is often a specialist traditional legal scholar, not necessarily with a formal qualification in law or a legal practitioner, although in western world the word "jurist" or "justice" may be applied to a judge[243].

Customs acquired the force of law when they became the undisputed rule by which some rights, entitlements, and obligations were regulated between members of a community[244].

Customary law is not widely found in written form, taking into account its origins and its practice in South Sudan. Still with the beginning of literacy amongst the South Sudan people, attempts to reduce customary laws into writing were widely resisted. The primary motive assumed for this resistance to written law was a belief that customary law reflects the contemporary customs, practices and beliefs of a society or community. These customs and practices are assumed to change and laws of customary legal systems must be flexible as much as necessary to reflect this enthusiasm and zeal. Opponents of recoding laws had argued that an attempt to codify, document or reduce these laws of customary legal systems to writing would severely limit their flexibility and rigidity.

---

242   Vieto Piergiovanni (2000). *Comparative Studies in Continental and Anglo-American Legal History.* Germany: Duncker and Humblot. Page 236. ISBN 978-3428097562.

243   Gamer, Bryan A., ed. (2019). *"Jrist".* Black's Law Dictionary (11 ed.). St. Paul, Minn: West.

244   In R. v Secretary of State For Foreign and Commonwealth Affairs, (1982). All E.R. 118, Lord Denning said "These Customary laws are not written down. They are handed down by tradition from one generation to another. Yet beyond doubt they are well established and have the force of law within the community.".

Advocates of written laws argued with strong and growing belief that laws of customary legal systems should be written down. This came as a result of varied surveys conducted by researchers. The need to write down the few customary laws was based on the fact that all law is prone to interpretation, unwritten law is more susceptible to misinterpretation and bias. Some researchers have described a number of other equally compelling arguments for the writing down of customary law as follows:

1. The enormous change in population of South Sudan has brought people of different customs and practices in close contact with each other, including refugees returning from the Diaspora. The consequence has been a marked increase in conflict between differing customary law systems. Lack of a written code of law has increased the complexity of the tasks of courts. It made the process of reconciliation very difficult between parties who may be ignorant of their laws of customary legal systems.

2. Wherever customary law is to continue to thrive, it must be incorporated within the domain of the judiciary. Judges at every level must have at least equal access to and knowledge of the body of a particular customary law code as they do to domestic statutory law or any other body of law. It is tricky to imagine how this can be accomplished unless it is in easily accessible, written form.

3. It is obvious that the law of customary legal systems will, in the future, have to be reconciled, on a frequent basis, with other bodies of law, particularly: domestic statutory law, Sharia law, international humanitarian law and, at least in the short term, military law in the country. These bodies of law are to be found in written form all. A written form of customary law would be better understood by external organizations and enable a closer harmony between the various bodies of law.

4. The appeals court process already has the effect of causing individual customary laws to be reduced to writing when higher court judges make decisions. Rationalizing precedent law with customary law would be much more effective where bodies of law are already written.

These key issues considered by the researchers, are the main issues of customary law. They deal with very nature of law of customary legal systems in South Sudan.

The investigation team concluded with few external observations that customary law differs deeply from colonial law, as well as from statutory law (which is based on colonial law) in South Sudan. This confusion is the foundation of considerable contemporary criticism demonstrated in the blood life compensation claims, human rights and other activist groups of international laws. The law of colonial legal systems approaches the issues of civil law and criminal law using two separate and distinct procedures. In customary law, both issues of civil law and criminal law are dealt with under the same body of law using the same procedures.

This is believable and successful because the ethical basis, aims and objectives of customary law differ essentially from colonial law known as Western law, predominantly in respect to criminal issues. In law of colonial legal system, the hypothetical or academic underpinning is that crimes against individuals or the society or community should be dealt through punishment of the offending party. This in turn should provide satisfaction for the aggrieved party and deter potential offenders.

This does require an elaborate and expensive penal system to deal with the incarcerated and removes individuals, often valuable breadwinners, from the society. This is not affordable either, according to the situation of South Sudan.

Reconciliation Culture

The important culture of African and exclusively law of customary legal systems in South Sudan is to achieve conciliation in civil law and reconciliation between the wronged and wrongdoer in criminal law. This requires an ethical outlook, rules and procedures manifestly different to law of colonial legal systems or even that of south Sudanese statutory law. The primary aim is to accomplish a sense of justice and resolution amongst the disputing parties especially disputing clans and subclans or disputing communities or societies and in turn to restore or maintain social stability.

The laws of a legal system that has, as its central aim the maintenance of social order and cohesion, must act in a manner that places the good of society above the rights of the individual. It is this basic ethical cultural difference that puts African and particularly customary law of South Sudan at odds with elements of the international community. Particularly those individuals and organizations whose central culture or cultural value is based upon the rights of the individual. There is no doubt that some aspects of law of customary legal systems, as they narrate to the rights of the individual and in particular women, must and will change. Thus, if the argument that law of customary legal systems is designed first and foremost to protect and strengthen social cohesion holds true, change can only safely come from within.

Rural Traditional Law of Obligations

One of the most unique customary law systems is the traditional law of obligations which is still functioning. It covers both social duty and liability within South Sudanese societies at the rural levels. A useful dictionary definition of **obligation** is: *"Subjection to a legal obligation or the obligation itself. He who commits a wrong or breaks a contract or trust is said to be liable or responsible for it."*

The Customary Law of Obligations is unique because it combines two aspects of law functioning at rural environments that in statutory law are considered separate branches of law: contract law and tort law. The distinction between contract law and tort law has been that duties in contract law are fixed by the parties themselves and are owed to a particular person or persons. In tort law, the duties are imposed by law and are owed to the public at large.

An example is within the Jieng law of obligations, where some applications of both contract law and tort law are peculiar to the custom and practice of different clannish ethnic groups in rural South Sudan. They are worthy of examination for they exemplify the social values of the society. According to some researchers, the *Jieng* (Dinka) customary law is the standard of the customary laws of obligation all the way through South Sudan society and hence a very useful example. The most common form of contract law within *Jaang* or *Jieng* society is known as *Amuk in Thuongjang*, which can be translated as 'owe" or 'have a loan from' which can be translated as '*hen ala kany kek yeen*', '*a ran kany*', '*a ran muk kany-die*' or *amuk kanydie* (singular) in *Thongmuonyjang (singular)*, which is translated as a creditor or *a kaany also* translated as creditors (plural*).* It is defined as[245]:

"Amuk is any property delivered by a debtor (raankoony) to a creditor (ran kony or amekony) as a form of security or guarantee for the repayment of a debt (keny) or discharge (cuot) of existing obligation."

"If the debtor fails completely to repay the debt at the fixed time, the secured creditor is entitled to own the property he possesses as *amuk* or *kaany* at a reasonable period, after the expiry of the said period, or at the period, which the court may consider to be reasonably long in the circumstances, if no fixed period for discharge of the debt was agreed upon at the time of the contract."

Limits for Filing A Fatal Accident Claim.

The main objectives of the book in this section is to understand the role of different customs in township environments, how urban communities approach road accidents, how they happen and meaning attached to blood wealth compensation payable in cattle equivalent prices in monetary finance, and to investigate the feelings of people about cultural effects of the road accident deaths on the mourners and how to prevent road accidents as a case in writing both at rural level and urban environment level in South Sudan.

According to Jieng ethnic groups and various Nilotic ethnic peoples, the time limitations for filing a claim, translated as '*amuk*', '*amukkany*',

---

245   The Re-statement of the Bahr Al-Ghazal Customary Law Act [Dinka Customary Law] 1984, Section 64(a)

'*kany*' or '*konykany*' in *Thongmuonyjang* or *Thuongjang* for blood compensation of the death occasioned, to a love one by fatal accidents usually encompasses injuries compensation claims caused because of negligent act by wrongdoers and cattle loan. The law requires that creditor exercise reasonable care for the safety of *amuk or kany or kany or konykany*, it is as a result the subject of much litigation in their courts.

The practice of the 'blood life wealth' penalty, payable in monetary or money equivalent after death of victim in fatal accident is a new phenomenon in the Jieng culture. Jieng people who are currently living in the urban environments are faced with immense challenges after family members are involved in fatal road accidents in the cities. They still resort to cattle equivalent currencies for payment for crimes or for their victim who can receive *apuk riem* in blood compensation payable in monetary money according to the urban court hearing sentences.

In the townships, dependents of the deceased are entitled to file a claim in any Court against a person who, by his wrongful act, neglect or default, may have caused the death of a loved one. This is often-times right and expedient that the wrong-doer in such case should be answerable in damages for the injury or other fatal accident so caused by him in cities. It has been suggested that a dependent or representative who may be:

- A spouse (wife or husband).
- A person who had been in partnership with deceased as husband or wife or as a civil partner for days, weeks, months, one year or more prior to the death.
- Blood children and other descendants including adopted children and children through marriage or civil partnership.
- Parents or ascendants including grandparents, great grandparents and those treated by the deceased as a parent.
- Brothers, sisters, cousins, uncles, aunts, nieces and nephews

What a dependent or representative can claim for in a roadway fatality case is different in every township or city. For example, Juba city court,

Wau city court, Malakal city Court or Kuajok city court may conduct different court hearing for fatal accident crimes among Rek Jaang or Jieng ethnic clans and subclans of nationalities. The exact compensation penalty in urban townships which victim can claim for will depend on the circumstances surrounding the accident and the other factors. In case of a fatal accident in road collision crashes, a victim or victim family would be able to claim for blood compensation for the following:

1. **Pain, suffering and loss of facility or property of the deceased:** If death was preceded by a disease, for example an asbestos-related diseases or if the deceased was bed-ridden because of medical negligence, or was caused by wrongful act or negligent, this claim will be blood compensation for the pain and suffering of the deceased during their lifetime as a result of the disease.

2. **Real or Physical body life losses:** This blood life compensation component provides for real or Physical body life expenditures incurred in caring for the injured person as well as any administrative expenses involved in dealing with their demise or their property. This covers physical body costs incurred such as hospital expenses, ongoing nursing care, medicines and medical aids, housing adaptations and the cost of travelling for medical treatment. Funeral expenses are also included.

3. **Loss of earnings:** In case the death was not immediate, loss of earnings during the time the deceased was alive but unable to work are also taken into consideration.

4. **Loss of services:** The victim or victim's family can also claim payable blood compensation for the loss of services that the deceased provided such as childcare, housework, gardening, and others. If the deceased was caring for another sick person in the family, the cost of hiring a replacement care may also be considered.

5. **Losses for dependency:** This is often the largest component of most fatal accident compensation claims. It is applicable if the deceased is survived by dependents who depended on his or her income, for

example a spouse, minor children or aged parents. The amount will vary depending on the deceased's income. The calculation may also take into account loss of pension as well as other bonuses and allowances such as healthcare benefits, use of company car and mobile phone usage.

People of South Sudan who are predominantly pastoralists have comprehensive customary legal systems dealing with tort law issues and liability for their animals.

These laws deal with damage done by one animal to another, damage done by an animal to a human and damage done by an animal to property other than animals. The basis for liability for the acts of animals are deemed under the laws which are threefold as follows:

- To put the plaintiff or applicant or petitioner in the economic position he or she was before the act was committed.
- The keeper of an animal has a duty of care to members of the public and their property.
- The keeper of the animals enjoys economic and social benefits from them and must therefore expect to be liable for their actions.

The Jieng people believe in a universal single God, whom they call *Nhialic* in *Thongmuonyjang*, 'Creator', 'Life King' or 'King of Life' and of the 'living' in "Heaven" and on "Earth" in the world spirit. They believe that the spirits of the departed become part of the spiritual sphere of this life. According to Oborii, "African religions tend not to be concerned with personal salvation or dogmas about God. They are instead religions of structure, in which self-realization arises through participation in the socio-cosmic web of relationships first laid down by God and the primal beings. God and the spirits are primarily worshiped because they, together with man, maintain the divinely established order"[246]. It must be clear that

---

246   Crim, Keith, Gen. Ed. *The Perennial Dictionary of World Religions.* San

man responds to a good and faithful God who initiates relationship and has extended grace to humans through the sacrifice of His Son.

Anderson also sees an opportunity to bridge the gap between Jieng traditional religious belief and Christianity by capitalizing on the Jieng understanding of God's sovereignty. According to Anderson, "The idea of God's sovereignty is seen clearly in the Jieng faith. They see lightning and other natural phenomena as coming from God. Deng observes that the Jieng peoples consider God to be whimsical. Sometimes He appears to be harsh. He may appear not to answer them, or to judge them. When problems continue, they may feel that He has refused their sacrifices. But they do feel that somehow good will come for it. The evil and good aspects of experience are merged into a positive image"[247].

Cattle have a religious significance and fundamental measure of wealth of Jieng (Dinka) society. Cattle are the first choice as an animal of sacrifice, but sheep may be sacrificed as a substitute on occasion. The family and broad social relations are primary values in the Jieng religious belief. Naturally, much of Jieng customary law is inextricably linked to both cattle and the family.

Customary Legal Systems Concerning Fatal Accidents Act

1. What systems of relationship between customary law and fatal accident act have been encountered in practice? What models could be explored?

2. What lessons can be drawn from recognition of customary legal systems in relation to other, or potential areas of laws and customs, and what do they have in common?

3. What experiences have been reported concerning the role of custom and customary law in relation to law of obligations concerning fatal accident act, providing a persuasive resolution for reconciliation,

Francisco: Harper and Row Publishers, 1989. Page 6.

247   Anderson, Joy. *"Behold! The Ox of God?" Evangelical Missions Quarterly; 1998,* Vol. 34, no. 3. Page 2.

forgiveness and healing?

4. What role for customary law has been recognised in existing and blood wealth and spiritual wealth laws for the wife, husband, parent, or child of the deceased killed in fatal accidents.

5. For the holders of blood wealth and divine wealth origin in culture, what is the preferred role or roles of laws of customary legal systems and protocols:

   a. As a basis for sustainable community practice-based development, law as custom, strengthening community identity, and promoting cultural diversity?

   b. As a distinct origin of law as traditions, legally binding in itself on members of the original community practice, and on individuals outside the community circle, including in foreign jurisdictions?

   c. As a means of truthfully guiding the interpretation of laws as custom, customary legal systems and principles that apply beyond the origin of traditionality of law to enter customary law and protocols?

   d. As a component of culturally appropriate forms of alternative concerning fatal accident act that provides dispute resolution for reconciliation and divinity healing?

   e. As a condition of access to traditionality of law for compensation claims?

   f. As the basis for continuing use obligations and rights, recognized as exceptions or limitations to any other collective responsibilities, obligations and rights granted over blood life wealth payable to protect and to strengthen social cohesion, reconciliation, spirit for forgiveness or related subject matter regarding historical identification and managing clan security and control?

   g. As the basis for maintaining action to provide blood compensation claims for the wife, husband, parent or child of the deceased occasioned by wrongful act, negligence act, fatal accidents?

A custom must be consistent with the general principles of 'law' which form the basis of every 'law' or statue which exists. These principles form the basis of ideas like Justice, fairness and liberty, and every custom must be in consonance with these.

'Customary law' does not split criminal cases and civil cases. A single 'customary law' proceeding will often result in a payable punishment for wrongdoing and or payable blood life wealth for compensation claims for the homicide, injury, hurt, price, cost or spoil done to the person who was wronged and victimized.

By the 17th century, statutes enacted by colonial government took precedent over common law. By the earliest 18th century, the word "Customary law" enacted by colonizing condominium arisen as self-governance rule together with indirect rule and dispute resolution mechanism adopted for South Sudan. It became a better way for communities to control their own lives. According to Professor Erica Irene-Daes, self-governance rule is "the freedom to live well". Customary law exists where a certain legal practice is observed and the relevant actors, players, performers or artistes consider such legal practice to be law.

A good number of customary laws deal with standards of community or society that have been long-established in a given environment. On the other hand, the word can also apply to areas of 'international law' where some standards have been practically 'universal' in their acceptance as correct bases of action. In a good number, yet not all occurrences, customary laws will have supportive court rulings and case law that has evolved over time to give extra heaviness to their rule as law and also to demonstrate the trajectory of evolution (if any) in the interpretation of such law by relevant courts.

A Strategy for Fatal Accident Occasions

If the basic premise of this investigation that 'change must come from within' is an acceptable hypothesis before any future strategy should be aimed at facilitating that change rather than attempting to impose it from the outside. A workable strategy might include a combination of three tactical approaches to fatal accident actions:

1. A social marketing initiative utilizing the standard tools for achieving public and community awareness of the fatality occasions in contemporary South Sudan.
2. A focused campaign on the occasions aimed at particular stakeholders; chiefs, lawyers, police, local government officials, community leaders and community activists.
3. An initiative by the judiciary to bring pressure for change through court decisions on case laws which in turn become precedent.

To achieve a synchronized strategy, it would be necessary to involve an array of experts from both within and without southern Sudan. A workable approach might be to use the medium of developing and propagating written customary law systems as a tool to focus upon the key stakeholders and to enlist the judiciary in the development of such a program.

Obligation, Reconciliation, Curse and Fatality Homicides

A fatality, a homicide, an injury, a misfortunate, or an event can never just happen in Apuk culture. Even if a fatality or homicide happens, it is a punishment originating from a divinity spirit, a divinity law, a curse, an evil eye, a curse made by devil spirit or a curse made by master of the fishing spear. There must be someone who cause d the fatality, accident or misfortunate to happen, whether it be a car collision that crashes a pedestrian dead, a snake that bites a person dead, a falling object that kills a loved one, a gunshot that shoots a victim dead, fatal and nonfatal motorist accidents, a roadway accident injury that causes death in a family, a mosquito bite that kills a child and so on.

The Apuk clan describes god spirits, divinity spirits, divinity law, ancestral spirits, bad devils, evil eyes, bewitching, clan sinning conditions and other spiritual punishments as the most common causes of fatalities or motorist accidents involving family members. When supernatural spirits and spiritual ancestors are offended, they can cause water drown, disasters, axe injuries, animal killings, spear injuries, and can cause firewood or poles to fall down on your shoulders to your feet and cut your feet severely for punishment. They also cause war death, disabilities, mental trauma or mental retardation, injuries, and even cause defeat at war any time anywhere. Death, injuries and fire disasters caused by thunder during raining seasons are all punishment from 'god' translated as *Nhialic* of 'ancestors' in *thuongjang*, the 'Creator' of all things. Curse, priest chief usage, pouring libation prayer by the spiritual masters, ritual sacrifice on life blood lost, sacrificing for evil suffering, talking with ancestors by use of spear masters, prayers and cleansing away wrongdoing and sinners from the clan members are ways of frequent causes of accidents or road car accident fatalities. The bereaved individuals and families could have failed to offer their ritual sacrificial animals, and libation by the use of fishing spear master or priest chief to lead in clan prayer for good health, to prayer for protection from evil spirit, evil eyes, bewitching and all forms of curses. It is a penalty causes by curse that results in harm, mental obstruction or mental impedance, severe injury damage or life loss.

When the Azande driver accidentally hit the pedestrian Mangong Akol Akot Anei, members of his family shared the same belief in the power of death which came through ill-wishing, evil eyes, and cursing. There were cases of car accident deaths believe they were under curse. They seemingly thought death might have been brought about to both Mangong of Apuk clan families and Jackson of Azande clan families by the curses of angry ancestral spirits, wrongdoings, disobedience to divine laws, or ancestors that had turned up in the homestead. Driver Jackson Gelua Anthony died few days later at his Zande homeland located in Tambura of Azande clan home village after he took leave to visit his parents. There are questions to be asked regarding his short time death because relatives of the child Mangong, pedestrian, was killed in Landcruiser collision crash on rural roadway on July 15, 2019, but driver Jackson Gelua Anthony also died on August 12, 2019, less than a month, at his Zande family homeland located in Tambura village.

With differences between customary law and statutory law, particularly colonial statutory law, perhaps the most contentious is the issue of fatal accident homicide. customary law considers some acts to be both a crime and a tort in South Sudan. Fatal road crash homicide falls into this category, in that the law considers there to be both criminal and civil aspects to murder. The law traditionally has allowed the relatives of the victim to decide whether they wish to seek justice through criminal proceedings or to seek blood life compensations through tort law action.

The basis for this argument lies in the religious belief of South Sudan peoples that the purpose of any legal action in regard to crime is to restore the social equilibrium rather than to punish the Azande wrongdoer. "The principle of a life for a life rarely leads to a permanent peace"[248]. Folk religion deals with meaning in this life and the problem of death, wellbeing in this life and the problem of misfortunes, knowledge to decide and the problem of the unknown, and righteousness and justice and the problem of evil and injustice[249].

The moment you have a religion you have organization. Two inseparable concepts, as one creates the other. Organized rituals make culture. Organized spirituality makes a religion. It is believed it was ancient native religion, and not agriculture, that gave rise to 'Apuk' as a "law", an "identity", a "spirit forgiveness, a "divine healing", a "peace-making", or a ""name" for Apuk Juwiir in the southwest of western Nile Valley of Rek, Apuk Padoch in the northeast of western Nile Valley of Rek and Apuk Giir or Apuk *Toch* in the north of western Nile Valley of Rek Jaang respectively.

This was followed by centralized political and military organizations, economies, and identities. Created thusly were centralized values, customs, laws as traditions and divine laws for what would have been otherwise disparate peoples. The commonalities allow for greater cooperation and collective objectives.

---

248   P.P.Howell, *A Manual of Nuer Law*, Oxford University Press, 1954, p41

249   Hiebert, Paul G., Shaw, Daniel and Tienou, Tite, *Understanding Folk Religion, A Christian Response to Popular Beliefs and Practices.* Grand Rapids, MI: Baker Books, 1999. Page 74

CHAPTER TEN

EXPLORATION OF ROADWAY ACCIDENT TRAFFIC INJURIES

Introduction

The aim of this chapter is to investigate the blood life wealth payable to families for loss occasioned by the death of a person, pedestrian after accident fatality occurrences, to understand the connections between blood compensation, fatal road accidents and what causes roadway accident fatalities, and how roadway accident fatalities happen.

In South Sudan in particular, road traffic injuries are one of the top two causes of death from unintentional injury, with the highest rates among aged 15–19-year-olds, who are at greatest risk of roadway accident traffic injuries, with the roadway traffic fatality rates increasing with age[250]. This reflects both increased exposure and differences in the way children of different ages use the roadway. South Sudan bears a large share of the burden, accounting for one of the highest percent of annual deaths and the disability-adjusted life years (DALYs) lost because of road traffic injury[251]. As long as roadway traffic injuries affect large percentage of between zero

---

250   *World report on child injury prevention.* http://www.who.int/ violence_injury_prevention/child/en/

251   World Health Organization (WHO) and World Bank, *"World Report on Road Traffic Injury Prevention,"* accessed online at www.who.int, on Feb. 6, 2006.

and 45 years old, this burden is creating enormous economic hardship because of the loss of family breadwinners.

Road traffic fatality death rates have decreased since the July 2011 because of successful interventions such as seat belt, safety laws, enforcement of speed limits, warnings about the dangers of mixing alcohol consumption with driving, and safer use of roads and vehicles. But rural highway road traffic fatalities increased during the same period by approximately 20 percent in rural roadway traffic fatalities in Bahr Al-Ghazal and Equatoria regions, for instance.

Besides, the disability burden for this age group accounts for 60 percent of all the disability-adjusted life years (DALYs) are lost because of road accident traffic injuries[252]. The costs and consequences of these losses are significant. Several poor families who have lost a member to road traffic fatalities, narrated a decrease in their standard of living, and more than fifty percent narrated they had to borrow money to cover expenses following their loss of family breadwinners[253]. The World Bank estimates that road traffic injuries cost 1 percent to 2 percent of the gross national product (GNP) of developing countries, or twice the total amount of development aid received worldwide by developing countries including South Sudan[254]. Motorist impairment is an important component of road traffic accident fatalities. Motorist at excess speeds, while under the influence of alcohol or drugs, while sleepy or tired, when visibility is compromised, or without protective gear for every single one vehicle occupants are major factors in crashes, deaths, and serious roadway injuries.

In general, pedestrians, cyclists, automobiles, motorists and motorcycle riders are the most vulnerable road users as well as the heaviest users of

---

252   Margie Peden, Kara McGee, and G. Sharma, *The Injury Chartbook: A Graphical Overview of the Global Burden of Injuries* (Geneva: WHO, 2002).

253   Babtie Ross Silcok, *Guidelines for Estimating the Costs of Road Crashes in Developing Countries.* (London: U.K. Department for International Development, 2003).

254   Margie Peden and Adnan A. Hyder, *"Road Traffic Injuries are a Global Public Health Problem,"* British Medical Journal 324, no. 7346 (2002): 1153.

roads in poor countries. On the whole people who use public transportation, bicycles, and *boda boda* riders or motorcycles or who habitually walk are poor, illuminating the higher risk borne by those from less privilege. In Bahr Al-Ghazal and Equatoria regions, for instance, motorized automobiles and *boda boda* riders will make up the anticipated growth in numbers of motor vehicles.

On Monday July 15th, 2019, a car accident death of a boychild resulted from the careless or reckless actions of a driver in Rural highway road traffic in Apuk community in Warrap State. It demonstrates the higher proportion of deaths among these groups in South Sudan.

Under South Sudan customary law including domestic Islamic Shariah law, it is illegal for local brewers, local bars and restaurants to serve alcohol to a patron or driver who is visibly intoxicated. Violating those laws and legal systems can saddle those customary legal systems with legal liability for wrongful death if a patron causes a roadway drunk driving accident fatality.

The justification for using this exploration is to determine the nature of the phenomena that is under investigation which is the people's experiences and descriptions of the blood life compensation claim payable after fatal accident death, burial, mourning, and grieved. The scope of this book covers the Azande of Bantu language speaking community in Equatoria and Apuk of Jeng Rek language speaking community in Bahr Al-Ghazal together with diverse customs, culture, and practices. The Azande driver of the fatal roadway traffic accident acted carelessly or recklessly on Gogrial rural highway road in Warrap State. The decision whether to charge the Azande driver with a crime for the fatal car accident rests with the local Apuk court law attorney or judge. It is his job to determine whether a driver was "criminally culpable" in causing the death, under Wanhalel Jieng customary law and judicial procedures.

The judges of Wanhalel Customary law in the Apuk court will use cultural experts to make cultural arguments about blood life compensation price practices, burial rituals, mourning together. The Legalities surrounding filing a fatal accident claim for blood wealth is complex and challenging.

The chapter tries to examine how the existing compensation law between the two diverse ethnic communities came into being in the early 19ᵗʰ -20ᵗʰ centuries or in the Turkiya regime and Anglo-Egyptian colonial periods.

The present-day customary law between Azande and Jieng ethnic communities is principally the result of the customary trial skills that replace the Mohammedan Law court Ordinance 1902 functioning in Shariah Courts in South Sudan. Wanhalel Jieng (Dinka) Traditional Customary Laws were adopted in 1927, Civil Justice Ordinance in 1929, The customary trial skills of the traditional courts of the Chiefs Ordinance in 1931 and the Anglo-Egyptian Sudan condominium enactment. The latter is a series of statutory instruments designed to codify, formalize and ultimately to control application, effect and scope of customary laws throughout the two countries or "the Sudans".

At present, there is confusion and controversy in South Sudan, particularly, after the independence in July 2011 between the current sixty -four (64) ethnic clans and subclans of nationalities that resulted in South Sudan. According to various media reports, in the ceding of complex sixty-four ethnic laws as traditions of their customary legal systems and customs created issues as the boarders between the diverse identities and communities is unclear.

This chapter explores the conflict of historical background of blood life compensation between Jieng of Warrap State and Azande of Western Equatoria State in South Sudan. In the case of the guilty driver of Azande, payable blood life wealth to the victim family of the boychild Mangong Akol, cattle numbering thirty-one cows.

Investigation of Roadway Accident Traffic Injuries Approach

This section presents the investigation approach used in the current fatal road accident occurrences investigate in this chapter. The explored hypothesis pursued in this investigation is qualitative. Hypotheses or themes are all encompassing customs and legal systems of consistent practice and thinking that define for judicial judges the nature of their legal inquiry.

This can be carried out along three dimensions: (1) Fatal road accident occurrences, how fatal road accident occurred or happened; (2) Connection between fatal road accident, processes of legal claims for blood life compensation prices payable in cattle or monetary equivalent for surviving families; and (3) Phenomenological approach describing the practice of what is to be investigated, how the judges intend to practically go about occurrences to be investigated.

A phenomenological approach was selected to explore the experiences and the meaning that the respondents attach to particular social phenomena. In this investigation case, the experiences in *apuk riem, apuk weng, apuk wong riem* or blood life compensation after road accident fatality, what causes road accident fatalities to happen, processes of customary law court penalty and the meaning attached to blood life compensation prices payable in cattle or monetary money equivalent after fatal accident death, burial, mourning and rituals. These could serve as guidelines to explore the spiritual needs of the bereaved in rural home communities and urban township dwellers.

Investigative approaches are what makes social science scientific[255]. The approach used in this investigation which includes the community, Committee chiefs, how the control committee, and legal advice committee were organized and operated, methods of data collection, organize collection payable *apuk* riem or blood life compensation in cattle numbering thirty-one cows (31 cows) according to customs of deceased child Mangong in Padok clan of Apuk community and data analysis will also be outlined in detail.

---

255   Neuman, W.L. (1997). *Social science methods: qualitative and quantitative approaches.* Boston: Allyn & Bacon.

I will also discuss ethical issues considered when the investigation was conducted.

Investigation Target

An investigation target is a strategy or a blue print that guides and informs how the exploration will be conducted. This refers to the procedures by which we approach problems and arrive at answers. It also provides control over those factors that could influence the outcome of the exploration or investigation.

In this investigation, I will use information qualities or qualitative, descriptive, explorative, and contextual strategies to explore and describe the experiences of the people who have experienced the fatal accident claims for blood life compensation. The person whose death shall have been caused and shall be brought by and in the name of the survival or surviving family or executor, administrator or representative of the person deceased in the rural villages and in the townships in South Sudan.

A universal format of a phenomenological investigation of cognizance follows the fundamental procedure classified into three ways. The first procedure is the process of gathering descriptions from people who are having or have had experience under investigation. The second procedure is engaging in a process of analyzing these descriptions so the writer comes to a grasp of the constituents or common elements of what makes the experience what it is. The last third procedure is producing an explore narrative that provides an accurate, clear and articulate description of an experience[256].

Investigation Information Based on Quality

Academia defines qualitative investigation as a multi-method that involves an interpretive, naturalistic approach to its subject matter. This implies

---

256   Polkinghorne, D (1989). Phenomenological research Methods. In R. Valle & S. Halling (Eds.). *Existential Phenomenological Perspectives in Psychology (14-60)*. New York: Plenum Press

that qualitative scholars revise phenomena in their natural settings, attempting to interpret them in terms of the meaning people take from them. Qualitative investigation involves the use of a variety of information based on qualities, case investigations, personal experience, introspective, life story interviews, observational, historical, interactional and visual texts that describe experiences and meaning in individuals' lives[257]. It is an inquiry process of understanding based on distinct methodological traditions of inquiry that explore a social human problem. The scholar analyses words, narratives detailed views of informants and conducts the investigation in a natural setting[258]. The theses or themes are naturalistic, holistic and inductive, which means immersion in the details and specifics of the data to discover important categories, dimensions and inter-relationships[259]. It is also an exploration, elaboration and systematization of the significance of an identified phenomenon. Finally, it is an illuminative representation of the meaning of a delimited issue or problem.

The justification for using a qualitative approach in this investigation is the nature of the phenomena that is under investigation which is the people's experiences and descriptions of the blood life wealth compensation. The intention of this investigation is to gain a rich and complex understanding of specific social phenomena. I have used the phenomenological approach to qualitative descriptions of the people about the blood life wealth payable after fatal accident death, burial, mourning, rituals, ceremony, bereavement for death of loved and the meaning they make out of them. This was done by allowing them to 'tell their stories'.

---

257   Denzin, N. K., & Lincoln, Y. S. (Eds.). (1994). *Handbook of qualitative research.* Thousand Oaks: Sage Publications.

258   Cresswell, J. (1994). *Research design: qualitative and quantitative approaches.* London: Sage.

259   Kelly, K. (2007). *From encounter to text: collecting data in qualitative research.* In M. Terre Blanche, K. Durrheim, & D. Painter (Eds.). *Research in practice: Applied methods for the social sciences* (2nd edn.) (285-319). Cape Town: UCT Press.

Justification for Using Phenomenology

The aim of using the phenomenological approach is to determine the meanings of experiences of the people who have acquired the experience and are able to provide their descriptions. In this case, the people who have the experience of fatal accident claims for blood life compensation. Human beings attempt to make sense of all their experiences. Through the approach I have striven to understand the meaning upon the phenomenon as understood by the community and victim families.

Phenomenology investigations require community respondents to express what they experienced regarding the fatal accident phenomena. Hence, no objective reality is assumed. The operative word in the phenomenological method is 'describe' rather than explain. This approach seeks to describe subjective meanings instead of just behaviours.

Validity of Roadway Accident Injuries Investigation

Some confusion exists in the literature about how to apply the notion of validity to phenomenological exploration. Phenomenological exploration approaches validity from a more general perspective as a conclusion that instigates confidence because the argument that supports it is credible[260]. Credible investigation produces findings that are convincing and believable. The credibility of qualitative investigation is ascertained while the investigation is being undertaken because the scholar looks for discrepant evidence to the hypothesis, she or he is developing[261].

In this exploratory investigation, I have conducted interviews with the people who have had an experience of the road accident injuries, blood life compensation, mourning and bereavement. These individuals either were part of the party or watched what happened in such a fatal accident

260   Polkinghorne, D (1989). *Phenomenological research Methods. In R. Valle & S. Halling* (Eds.). Existential Phenomenological Perspectives in Psychology (14-60). New York: Plenum Press.

261   Creswell, J. W. (1998). *Qualitative inquiry and research design: choosing among five traditions.* Thousand Oaks, California: Sage.

act to provide blood compensation claims to families for loss occasioned by the death of a person caused by actionable wrong. The respondents' personal individual interviews and focus groups were conducted.

I have attempted to conduct focus groups or committee members on the same fatal accident injury phenomenon to gather the experiences of people and by recording first-hand information gathered from the experiences of community members participating and relating them with the findings from the literature. I have also used a theory to interpret the investigation results.

Selecting Committee for Claim Road Traffic Injuries and Lifeblood Wealth

An investigation population is too big to be investigated in its entirety, or this can be too costly or impossible because of many reasons. In this case, a smaller subset of the entire investigation population was selected to be investigated in the place of the exploration population in Equatoria and Bahr Al-Ghazal areas, South Sudan. The selected subset of the investigation population is called a control committee claim. This selection of a subset committee needed for the investigation question is known as Chiefs, Judges, and survivors Committee for claims for blood life wealth payable to the family of a loved person for loss occasioned to the victim parties by his or her death or injuries by actionable wrong.

In this investigation the chiefs, parents, and judges committee for claims are the selection of the executor, administrator, or representative respondents to investigation from an entire population. It involves decisions about which people, settings, behaviours, customs, civil laws, homicide criminal laws, statutory laws, domestic Islamic law, and customary law court processes to observe. Another group of evaluation were the traditional court chiefs, spiritual wealth, divine master oath process, as well as the experiences of those people about car accident injury claims and personal injury compensation claims after fatality death, burial, rite, bereavement ritual ceremonies.

The roadway accident crash, that killed the boychild on July 15, 2019, in rural highway road traffic collision crash in Bahr Al-Ghazal, is the subject matter of this investigation. It provides that in the event of the death of a person caused by the "wrongful act, neglect or default" of another person, the personal representative of the deceased can maintain an action for blood compensation or blood reparation on behalf of the wife, husband, parent or child of the deceased person.

In gathering the data, I used information-rich cases, which in this case are the people who had been to a single court system based on Wanhalel Traditional Jieng Customary law system.

These people were chiefs, survivors, elders, local authorities, judges and court clerks selected among Apuk, Balanda and Azande. They are people who are able to function as informants by providing rich descriptions of the experience being investigated. Chiefs, court clerks, administration officers and judges of South Sudan criminal law courts including Wanhalel Customary law court systems also have to have the experience of the topic of the investigation, have the capacity to provide a full and sensitive descriptions of the experience under examination. Some scholars specify six important competency skills that the investigation respondents must possesses, which are: the ability to express themselves linguistically with ease, to sense and express inner feelings and emotions without shame and inhibition, to be able to sense and express organic experiences that accompany these feelings, the experience of the situation under investigation at a relatively recent date, have spontaneous interest in their experience and lastly, the ability to report what was going on with themselves[262].

Traditional court chiefs and court Judges for bloodwealth claims were selected from Warrap State capital cities and northern Apuk community

---

262   Mndende, N. (2009, 19 January). Principal turns a beady eye on boy's tradition. In K. van Rooyen, Culture Shock. The Times. Retrieved, May, 19, 2009 from http://www. thetimes.co.za. Polkinghorne, D (1989). Phenomenological research Methods. In R. Valle & S. Halling (Eds.). Existential Phenomenological Perspectives in Psychology (14-60). New York: Plenum Press.

townships at rural a community level. Representatives were employed from the deceased boychild family, guilty Azande driver family and Insurance Company Administration. The insurance administration for road accident homicide crime acts was to provide blood life compensation to families for loss occasioned by the death of a child, pedestrian caused by action-able wrong. A person commits criminal homicide crime act if he or she intentionally, knowingly, recklessly, or with criminal negligence causes the death of an individual, a child, or pedestrian.

The respondents were approached, and the investigation aims were explained and they were requested to participate. Those who agreed to participate also referred others whom they knew.

The number of respondents selected for phenomenologically based investigations varied considerably. The first stage of data gathering consisted of individual interviews that were conducted with eight (8) people from different courts, clans, customs, cultures and townships. Since the investigation is explorative, I aimed at obtaining rich experiences from a variety of members of the diverse communities. The 'lifeblood wealth' claim after the death of boychild Mangong is considered an act of social homicide within the Apuk community in Luonyaker village. The second stage of data collection consisted of the involvement of five (5) focus groups that were conducted with mixed and heterogeneous groups from different road traffic fatalities and urban environments across Bahr Al-Ghazal and Equatoria areas in South Sudan.

Focus Groups of Committees

According to some academia, focus groups or focus committees are a qual-itative investigate method, and a way of listening to people and learning from them[263]. They are guided committee discussions to generate a rich understanding of experiences and beliefs of investigation respondents in

---

263   Kelly, K. (2007). *From encounter to text: collecting data in qualitative research.* In M. Terre Blanche, K. Durrheim, & D. Painter (Eds.). *Research in practice: Applied methods for the social sciences* (2nd edn.) (285-319). Cape Town: UCT Press.

the fields. They also create a line of communication. Focus committees work best when what interests the investigation team is equally interesting to the respondents in the committees. When the committee discussions are right on target there are even more benefits. Some of its strengths are that: (1) The focus committees imply forms of explore where one can learn a great deal without truly knowing what questions one wants to ask; (2) The settings, contexts and depths help me understand the background behind concepts and feelings of people; (3) An understanding of why things are the way they are and how they become that way; and (4) Focus committees initiate a process of sharing and comparing between the respondents.

I must prepare to offset limitations in the explore plan of the focus committees. Such limitations are that focus committees tend to require a competently skilled mediator in a roadway accident traffic fatality, which are often difficult to assemble, and the individual responses may not be independent on one another.

Claim for Blood Life Wealth Exploration Procedure
Claim for Lifeblood Wealth Facts and or Evidence Collection

Many academics argue that interviewing is the most commonly used form of data gathering of a qualitative nature[264]. This exploration is used in mini groups, one-to-one, and face- to- face interviews for facts, evidence, and information collection. However, the interview questions used were oral, and open, random questions that lacked rigidity followed one another. Participants were asked if the accident was a result of somebody else's error, as well as the nature of the claim in respect of which lifeblood wealth prices or damages shall be sought to be recovered.

Their experiences were also needed to determine the risk factor of children aged 10-19 years. The information collected was used as guidance

---

264   Kelly, K. (2007). From encounter to text: collecting data in qualitative research. In M. Terre Blanche, K. Durrheim, & D. Painter (Eds.). *Research in practice: Applied methods for the social sciences* (2nd edn.) (285-319). Cape Town: UCT Press.

about road traffic injury connected with poverty, irrespective of income level, in children under 10 years old, and are less able to make safe decisions on the road in many low income and middle-income townships, and rural environments across the county.

Before the commencement of all the interviews, issues related to security, local administration, custom, family relationships, customary legal system requirements, insurance coverage, culturally different between the guilty party and victim party were clarified and completed. These included explanation of the purpose of the exploration, law case judge, to file in the brief fact-based and authentic data, and the road accident collision crash fatality claim for blood life compensation penalty prices payable in cattle equivalent or monetary money to collect for the benefits of the family, relatives and the typical payout for pain and suffering in most involve small injury claims.

At the beginning of the process, I introduced myself to the candidates or respondents and allowing sufficient time for rapport building. The group and committee respondents were informed about the aims of the investigation, the benefits of the investigation and how their participation could make a valuable contribution in the process of understanding how the blood life compensation payable in bloodwealth after fatal car accident phenomenon unfolds. They were also informed about their right not to participate in the investigation, and likewise that if they felt uncomfortable at any stage of the investigation, they had the right to withdraw their participation in contribution without feeling obliged to source motives.

The interviews took place at the times when each interviewee or candidate or applicant had indicated that they were comfortable. All respondents were committee for claims, group and community members who had volunteered their participation in the investigation. All the interviews were conducted in the languages that the candidates or respondents were comfortable with, which is *Thuongjang, Thongmuonyjang, or Thongjang, Thongjieeng* or *Thongjaang,* Arabic and English languages.

Every year, hundreds of people die in fatal roadway accidents around the country. Many of them die on the spot or scene, whereas many more survive long enough to receive medical treatment, but tragically succumb to their injuries. This country is full with survivors of a driver or passenger killed in a fatal car or motor cycle- *boda boda* accident. They always face devastating emotional strain and struggle to know where to go for support.

I had a set of brief guiding questions for this investigation. We seek to answer one of their most fundamental initial questions which is a general open-ended question:

Can you tell me about your experiences of the blood life compensation claims payable in 'bloodwealth' collection cattle numbering thirty-one cows (31 cows) after the death of a loved one in a fatal road accident?

The "at-fault" driver may confront criminal charges under common law, customary law, statutory law, criminal law, civil law or domestic Islamic Sharia law, but this is not always the case in rural environment in this country.

Many fatal road accidents happen because a driver of one of the vehicles or motor cycles involved acted carelessly or recklessly. If that roadway accident leads to the death of a pedestrian, the driver may face criminal charges, such as for vehicular manslaughter in common law, customary law or civil law, statutory law or domestic Islamic Shariah law.

If a loved one dies in a car or *boda boda* accident, the surviving family members have the right under civil law, customary law or statutory law, or common law or domestic Islamic law to file a "wrongful death" claim or grievance or charge or lawsuit. Thus, desire as the victim could have filed an individual injury claim or charge and grievance for the injuries caused by the accident had he or she lived.

Here are the following relevant questions for investigation issues:

1. Do you have any experiences to please share with me about the "Dias or apuk riem compensation" after fatal road accident traffic action?

2. What is your experience of the "blood life compensation" payable in "bloodwealth" cattle equivalent after fatal accident traffic action?

3. What does the "blood life wealth compensation" price after fatal acci-
    dent action mean to you individually?
4. What are your feelings towards the "blood life wealth compensation"
    price after fatal accident action?

The above questions were asked to all committee and group respondents. There were additional follow-up and clarification questions used
when a new idea came out from the applicant. Similar questions were
repeated to members of the focus groups, but individuals were not taken
into the formation of focus groups. One must bear in mind the size of
the groups one will interview if one chooses to use focus groups. Several
criteria apply, for instance, choosing enough respondents so that the focus
group does not fall flat if some members choose to remain silent, being
aware of group dynamics, clearing friendship pairs, 'experts' or uncoop-
erative respondents, breaking into smaller groups within a bigger group
that could interfere with the smooth running of the group meeting, the
mediator or facilitator needs to be highly skilled and highly involved,
increasing number respondents to compensate for members not showing
up and ensuring groups heterogeneous. I aligned myself with the above
criteria in conducting focus group interviews. I personally facilitated
the groups myself, and for every focus group interview conducted, I, in
consultation with the chiefs, local judges, customary court clerks, opinion leaders and various group members, set the context and the ground
rules for the group members. Group dynamics and group processes were
observed. I took notes during the interviews, which had also been agreed
with the respondents.

The interviews contained collected facts, evidence and information
which were described and translated from Jieng, Azande, Balanda, Jurchol-
Luo to English. I was cautious not to distort meanings in the process of
translating, thus, assistance with translations was obtained from a member
of the local authority and judicial court in Kuajok capital and Gogrial
townships where the personal representative of the deceased person who

died has the right to bring the action "only for the benefit of the spouse, children or parents of the deceased" person.

Compensation for those medical expenses in Luonyaker hospital is typically included as part of a wrongful death claim as a result of the fatal road accident collision crash that killed the child in Luonyaker town in Apuk community in Bahr Al-Ghazal.

Facts Analysis for Blood Life Compensation

The movement from a collection of protocols to an accurate, clear and informative structural description can be a complex and difficult process[265]. The collection of protocols was broken into manageable units for analytical traditions that come under the umbrella of explanatory analysis. The familiar ones in the human sciences are phenomenology, grounded theory and thematic content analysis. Some Scholars argue that explanatory analytical patterns or qualities vary along a continuum from smaller statistical qualities to immersion or crystallization qualities.

When collecting facts and evidence for exploratory analysis, one may experience events or the things people say in linear, chronological order, which is necessary to divide this sequence so that events or remarks that were far away from one another are brought close together.

The final step is when I put together the interpretations in a written account of the phenomenon investigated. At this stage, I fine tunes the findings from the interpretations and finds out if I may find examples that contradict various points or another in the interpretation. This final part was also an opportunity for me to make my reflections on my role in collecting facts or evidences and conducting the interpretation.

---

265   Polkinghorne, D (1989). Phenomenological research Methods. In R. Valle & S. Halling (Eds.). *Existential Phenomenological Perspectives in Psychology* (Pages 14-60). New York: Plenum Press

Ethical Issues

I deal mostly with the interaction between me and the people I am investigating. The essential purpose of my ethics is to protect the welfare of the respondents. Ethical review is increasingly becoming mandatory for social science investigations. Most leading universities require that all social science investigation involving human respondents be reviewed by independent investigation ethics committee. A list of ethical guidelines that this research adhered to is provided below:

1. I observed respect for the rights of participant.
2. I informed all the respondents about their right to participate in the investigation and to withdraw from the investigation at any time.
3. This investigation information was based on facts, evidence and quality response to fatal accident death caused because the Azande driver was careless and ignored traffic laws. I did not prepare a written informed consent outlining my name, the place where I am investigating and the purpose of the investigation, like a law regarding claim for blood wealth compensation for fatal accident traffic death, suffering, pain, loss of services, actual expenditures incurred in mortuary and Children Emergency Civil Hospital where the body was pronounced dead. I did not indicate Apuk Giir Thiik where it happened in Gogrial in Bahr Al-Ghazal. I also did not say the title of the investigation fatal accident claims, the aims and objectives and their right to participate which the respondents read and when they agreed to participate in the investigation, they signed it.
4. I requested the respondents to share their contacts to allow me to take notes during the discussions or interviews, and I described the purpose to them.
5. I informed the respondents that their names are not going to appear anywhere in the book if let me know before considering acknowledgement for your contributing to knowledge and to the success of the book.
6. I informed the respondents that they have the right to access the

exploration findings once it is integrated and readable on manuscript.

7. I clarified my role as a writer of this book and informed the respondents that should any issue arise as a result of the interview that impacted negatively on the respondents, they were free to contact me who would refer them for further assistance to the relevant service provider, such as a source center information gathered and written down on this book.

Conclusion

In this chapter the methodology that was followed in this exploration was outlined. The next logical step is to present the findings of the study from the narratives of the respondents. Reference is made for readers to check appendixes.

CHAPTER ELEVEN

FINDINGS AND RESPONSES

Introduction

This chapter clarifies the fatality ruling results of the collected data. This is presented in terms of the theses or themes that occurred from the individuals and reflection from focus group respondents about the importance and value they attach to the law 'lifeblood wealth' or 'dia' and 'Divine wealth' compensation claims after fatal road accident deaths, injuries, burial, sacrifices, rituals, mourning and ceremonies. This is in line with the phenomenological approach used in this investigation. The chapter will commence with a description of background of the committee of respondents.

Description of Focus Group Respondents

Individuals were interviewed in a committee of eight respondents for this exploratory investigation. The focus group respondents are described in terms of: Personal Representative of the Deceased Person, long-term experiences, home language, religion, customs, values, cultural practices, church, work affiliation, place of residence, legal expertise, witness, and surviving passengers of the roadway collision crashes. Of the eight respondents in the committee, the majority were males.

All of them reside in townships around Bahr Al-Ghazal and Equatoria, in the geographical locations of Tambura, Nimule, Juba, Wau, Kuajok, Pankot, Warrap, Tonj, Luonyaker and Lietnhom.

In terms of ethnicity and language, the majority were Apuk Lith branch of Jieng Rek family. They commonly spoke the language of Amuk Apuk, followed by Buoyar Apuk, (Buoi-yar Apuk), Adoor Apuk, Biong Apuk, Nyarmong Apuk, Abior Apuk, Apol Apuk, Abuok Apuk and Jurman Anger Apuk (Jur-Man-Anger Apuk) of Nilotic ethnic people found in Bahr Al-Ghazal to Gogrial location to the east in the Sudd wetland zones of the west Nile River of Bahr Al-Ghazal. The population of the northern Apuk Lith is approximately 103,283 people[266], inhabiting an area of 6,178 Square Miles (16,000 Square Kilometers) in the savannah zone, further divided into the zones of the Pathuon Apuk homeland. This is known as zones of dryland and zones of 'Toch' Apuk homeland, sometimes referred to as the Sudd wetland swamp of the Rek Apuk speaking language community in Gogrial to the east.

With regard to clannish, customary, residential, uptown and faithful affiliation, respondents belonged to the Roman Catholic Church, Afro-Asiatic Arab Islamic Traditional Religious beliefs, and African Traditional Religious beliefs, divinity spiritual beliefs, master of the fishing spear or high priest chiefs and deities practices, Jieng Rek culture, custom, domestic practices, Madi custom and culture, Balanda culture, Keresh culture, witch doctor, Azande witchcraft, mangu or witch clansmen, custom and cultural practices.

Focus group respondents were also conducted and a total of 28 respondents, who made the sizes of the groups ranging from 3 members to 6 members participated in the interviews. The ages of the members ranged from 14 to 65 with the majority falling within the ages of 20 to 40 members. The group members also affiliated to different custom, culture, symbol of divinity spiritualities, beliefs, religious denominations with the highest being the Rek Apuk divinity spiritualists, followed by the

---

266   Gogrial East Profile 2019. (Not published)

Roman Catholic Christians and the other members belonged to the Afro-Asiatic Arab Islamic Muslims. The focus group members resided in the townships of Nimule, Tombura, Uyujuku or Juku-Deim Zubeir around western Wau, Wau, Kuajok, Juba, Warrap, Lietnhom and Luonyaker across sections of South Sudan.

Fatal accident collision crashes triggered public anger, emotional outcry among the Apuk community and aggressive violent attitudes avenge the death of Mangong Akol. The road death instantly precipitated crises to investigate faster to calm down public anger and agitation, for the victim party and survivors of road accident collision crash fatality to drop revenge approach for the death of Mangong Akol and to seek legal justice in court to claim blood life wealth payable in cattle equivalent to comport and support the bereaved community.

The exploratory investigation was the result of road accident injuries and death on the scene, which raised public anger and huge crowds. I was invited to investigate road accident fatality death involving Apuk community child Mangong Akol Akot Anei (or Mangong Deng Kon) and Azande driver Jackson Gelua Anthony on July 15, 2019, to find out what causes road traffic accidents (RTAs) involving children, pedestrian roadway users, drivers, passengers, and traditional practices, bereavement, grief, mourning, current trends in burial rituals and mourning practices.

A note to the reader is that the words 'blood life wealth', 'apuk riem' or 'dia', *and* 'divine wealth' or 'spiritual wealth', and 'lifeblood' compensation' are used synonymously to refer to claim blood life wealth. The jargon used by respondents varies according to the location of the township, community, as well as location of customary spiritual law punishments. The Apuk customary spiritual law punishment is consequently a highly effective deterrent.

Individual and Focus Groups were Asked with Few Questions as Follows
1. Could you kindly share with me any experiences you encounter about the 'blood life wealth' compensation penalty price payable to the

family of a person loss after fatal road accident death, injury, pain and suffering of the Jieng Rek rural people?

2. What are the causes of road traffic accidents and what can be done to prevent or stop them from occurrence or minimize occurrences?

3. What does the 'bloodwealth', 'apuk' or 'apuk riem', or 'dia' compensation penalty to the survivors or grieving and to those guilty parties and those who offer support to the bereaved personally mean to you? What does the 'Divine wealth' or 'spiritual wealth' mean to you?

4. What is your understanding of the fatal road accident injuries, claim for 'blood life wealth', 'divine wealth' and how do you feel about them? How do the Azande and Apuk speaking peoples feel about the blood wealth and divine wealth in diverse cultures with different interpretations?

Understanding of the Lifeblood Wealth Themes
Respondents' Experiences of Claims for 'Lifeblood Wealth' after Road Fatality Injury or Death

After the burial of a deceased body or a loved one, mourning and ceremony, a group of mourners go together to sit under the tree, in the house or in the camp nearby. There is a 'claim' lifeblood wealth (or compensation claim) or declaration revenge as well as an allegation of wrongful action, accusation of causing the death intentionally. This is followed by a statement of 'apuk' or 'apuk riem' in cattle, or indefinite number of years or 'munayat'[267] translated as life imprisonment. The latter may also be ten to twenty years of imprisonment charges at the home of the deceased. The 'apuk' or 'apuk riem' individuals come prepared in advance to attend the 'apuk riem' such as payable cattle herds numbering one cow to thirty-one cows to collect, leading to the dropping of the revenge approach.

---

267   Jieng Rek language defines the word "munayat as life imprisonment. Sometimes imprisonment of 10 years to 30 years imprisonment as *ran mac munayat hot*, where *hot* refers to room or prison building for prisoners, ran mac refers to a person jailed for life in the prison.

A new thing recently adopted in the culture is the burial celebration. When a person passes away, or there is a road accident fatality, after the burial is completed, there is music and variety of drinks which served. There may be animal sacrifices in a celebration at the home of the deceased. The 'apuk' or 'apuk riem' individuals come prepared to attend the 'apuk' or 'puk riem', deciding on the number cattle to collect. These burial celebrations can also end up being chaotic and disorderly, especially during debates for number of cattle, provision of quality of cows to be collected by surviving family members.

In their first lifeblood wealth discussion, many respondents were shocked at what they saw happen after a funeral, which, according to them, was unexpected at and totally foreign in Apuk of Rek speaking people, or in entire Jieng society.

The Apuk Based Laws of Cultural Punishment exist in native laws of the *apuk* which express the cultures, beliefs and practices that reflect the identity of the people. The origin of *apuk* traces its origin to realistic peace, the use of deity and sacrifice, and persuasion by lifeblood wealth, known as 'apuk" or 'compensation', 'reparation' for reconciliation and forgiveness.

The Perceptions of 'Blood Wealth' and 'Spiritual Wealth' or 'Divine Wealth' claim for the perceptions of the 'after road fatality accident death tears' ceremony-parties'
The Perceptions of 'Lifeblood Wealth' Claim

Both the individual and group respondents attached similar perceptions on the 'lifeblood wealth', however, the vast number of respondents perceived it as an 'apuk' or 'apuk riem' payable in cattle, girls, and or money. The person who is injured or killed creates a blood price, and this price results in some form of lifeblood wealth compensation.

The *apuk* punishment in the court of law is taken to be a sentence of the guilty party to pay 'blood wealth' in form of cattle, sheep, goats, money, and girl. Contemporary urban people often take 'blood wealth' in the form of money. At this point in time, currency is increasingly used to pay for blood wealth. There is a strong likelihood that the practice will widely spread across to more of the population, with new values and needs. There are substantial perceptions given for the institution of *apuk punishment* in "lifeblood wealth". According to an investigation done by Madhel Malek Agei some of the most important purposes of 'apuk riem' are described below:

Apuk, known as compensation payable to the relatives of the victim clan, has been considered in some ways to be payment for sacred life and spirit body. The physical body is dead, but the life spirit, living spirit and body spirit are live on.

The Apuk believe that when a person is killed, defamed, or injured, an animal sacrifice is to be used by the spear master or priest to pray for the member of the wronged party. The spear master shall receive "spiritual wealth" for supplication in the form of animals as gifts or donations for the apuk of his spiritual and ancestry divinities. Those whose powers have been transmitted to him and because the spear master possesses their powers, must be compensated.

The payable apuk for clan homicide of thirty cows to the family of the clan victim is the reimbursement for blood loss which is life and sacred.

The thirty-one cows paid for apuk re the deceased person are called "thirty-one cows of blood" or "spirit body", I named them as blood wealth based on explanations I made earlier. Cow of blood is the singular address (Wong riem) and plural address as (hook riem), cows of blood.

Payable apuk to the aggrieved clan victim is measurable by the degree of loss. This is usually determined by the chiefs of the traditional courts.

Defamation is a crime in the clan and punishable in courts because defamatory remarks can lead to conflict and death. Blood wealth and spiritual wealth are payable in cattle for an apuk penalty as their spirits will be invited to be used by spear masters who are in possession of the deity spiritually.

The payable apuk penalty for severe cases can be five to fifteen cows following assessments made by chief's courts, where the aggrieved person may die, lose memory, or lose limbs in the near future due to the injuries afflicted in the past.

In the Dinka language, we say blood cows ('Wong riem' or 'hook riem') or blood goats ('thok riem' or 'thook riem').

If more than two cows are paid as the apuk penalty, they are called blood cows, hook riem for "lost blood", I have collectively named them as blood wealth as this is how clan members address the apuk penalty administered by the master of the fishing spear.

If the victim killed was by mistake (manslaughter) and was a member of a clan family, then the decision will lie upon victim's brothers, father, or maternal uncle, who shall receive sixteen cows, in blood wealth for facilitating peaceful reconciliation by the use of spear masters and deities for harmony. The spear master shall receive the traditional spiritual wealth payment.

Of the thirty-one cows for apuk there is a ritual sacrifice to cut one cow into two equal parts where the homicide causing clan family takes away the front or forelegs parts of the bull and the victimized clan family takes away the back or hind leg parts of the bull. This is a sign of acknowledgement that blood, life spirit, body spirit and the living spirit of the clan victim has been reimbursed and is reconciled with ancestry spirits. The other thirty cows blood wealth collected by the victimized clan family members are quickly distributed proportionally among said family members. Spouses of their sisters must take a share of one blood cow, *toong wong yuom or wong yuom*.

The institution of blood wealth involves an element of prestige for the children, family and relatives. It also may be a disgrace for a family in some instances. A deceased person will be seen as a hero if he or she died in defence of the family, clan, community or for the nation-state's dignity and integrity.

In the event of a failure of payable apuk, due to lack of resources or refusal, the clan chiefs will order forceful eviction to collect the cows for apuk from the clan members. Apuk as a clan payment reduces looming tension and prevents disruptive violence, which frequently leads to damaging disputes and conflict. The clan and the sub-clan of the victim always think of revenge if payment of is not quickly done.

Any action, which threatens family cohesion in the clan, is viewed with great disdain and is dealt with harshly under clan customary laws and through clan divinity penalties with severe curses for wrongdoers and sinners.

The Perceptions of 'Spiritual Wealth or Divine Wealth' Claim

Both the individual and group respondents attached similar perceptions on the 'spiritual wealth' or divine wealth', thus, the vast number of respondents perceived it as a claim compensation or apuk for the purposes of reconciliation, forgiveness, peace and harmony.

As an example, all respondents perceived the spiritual wealth as a cultural gift to a master of the fishing spear and as one paid in cattle, goats, sheep and/or money. The divine master invokes the spirits *jak*, *yath*, and *atiep* to offer beast sacrifices for rituals on their behalf. The divine master shall receive spiritual wealth (divine wealth) on behalf of the spiritual powers which have been offered gifts in compensation for the spirit and ancestry powers to guide the life of the people.

A priest receives the divine wealth payable to lead ritual prayers in traditional ceremonies organized by the guilty parties, or the victim parties, or by a surviving family. This is for sacrifice prayers to transfer to spirits and ancestors for cursed families or parties to restore their life in the society. The family uses other spear masters to reconcile clan spirits and the creator of ancestors who chooses to empower the spear master to possess supernatural spirits. This enables healing for spiritual crimes, divine disputes, devil offences, oaths, homicides, bewitching, wrongdoings, and evil eyes that people perceive to have come through the creator.

All respondents perceived that divine wealth is the *apuk* payable to the spiritual priest and ranges in accordance with the retaliatory punishment for the specific spiritual crime and the circumstances of the victim party or family. Compensation is well defined. The divine wealth to be received by the spear master varies.

Youngsters and Civil Servants Initiated the 'Blood Life Wealth' Claims

Nearly all the respondents were uncertain of how the blood life wealth and divine wealth claims evolved. The majority had a general perception that youngsters grow and see or observe their world extending far beyond the home, environment and out into local roads. The respondents perceived that youngsters or children are exposed to hazard and risks. Since children use roads as pedestrians, cyclists, motorcyclists, 'boda boda' riders and vehicle passengers, their roadway environment is rarely developed with consideration for their needs. Perceptions of the respondents were for the fact that many children work, play or live on the road, and this exposure, along with other risk factors inherent to childhood, make them particularly vulnerable in rural highway road, and in city roadway traffic. The consequences of this are thousands of deaths or disabling injuries every year across the country. In South Sudan, roadway traffic injuries are one of the top two causes of death from unintentional injury, with the highest increasing rates between 2 years old to 45 years old.

'Lifeblood wealth' claims (or divine wealth claim) evolved, thus, the majority had a general perception that young people were the first to be seen having 'apuk' or 'apuk riem' claims for the loss of services that the deceased provided and loss of life of the loved one, 'provided that if the nearest relatives or blood children, or blood parents of the deceased opt for customary law 'blood life wealth' compensation known as "Dia" the court may award it in lieu of death sentence'.

Road traffic crashes cause more than one thousand deaths in young people and children aged 0 to 19 years. Road traffic injuries are the leading cause of death in 9 year olds to 45 year olds, which is the highest increment in occurrence and the second leading cause of disability adjusted life years (DALY) lost in South Sudan. Children road users as pedestrians are the most likely to be injured or killed. Children aged 2 years old to 19 years old are most at risk[268]. Cyclists, motorcyclists and 'boda boda' riders

---

268   The World report on child injury prevention. (2004).

make up over 2 % to 13% of injured children as cyclists and motorcyclists and 'boda boda' riders and account for 2% to 5% of all child road traffic deaths. Children as vehicle passengers account for up to 20% of all child road traffic deaths.

The perception of respondent is that the person who is injured or killed in road fatality or in crime of homicide action brings the blood price, and this price connotes some form of 'life blood wealth' compensation payable in cattle equivalent. The payable 'apuk' for crime of homicide action of thirty-one cows to the family of the victim parties is the reimbursement for blood loss which is life and sacred.

Unrestrained children are more likely to be killed in collision crashes than those using appropriate child restraints in South Sudan. Teenage drivers and *boda boda* riders are a high-risk group in South Sudan. They are about 17 times to 35 times more likely to crash than older drivers.

Young people were seen organizing funerals after death for celebrations at the homes of their dead colleagues. Apparently, young people acted in a scary way, gathering immediately at the graveyards drinking beers and soft drinks, boozing, playing loud music and even shooting into the air at the burial sites over a coffin with a dead body inside. Then teenage 'boba boda' riders, and lorry drivers took over. Even through this lacked the intensity of violence previously seen, they encouraged it to a point where ordinary people copied some of these after burial celebration party behaviors.

'Blood Wealth' is a Blood Price of Someone's Dead or Injury

There is an overwhelming acceptance between respondents that 'apuk riem' or 'apuk' a wealth of life lost. That notion, however, is only that it is customarily determined and accepted by the blood related family or the deceased person's representative after a burial, sacrifice, ritual ceremony, and bereavement. It is more about the people remaining behind rather than for the deceased person. The payable 'apuk' for homicide action of thirty cows of equivalent currency to the family of the clan victim is the reimbursement for blood loss which is life and sacred. 'Lifeblood wealth' is 'apuk', the price paid to the living spirit of the victim, as well as to the family or party of the body spirit of the victim. Some of the respondents perceived burial, ritual sacrifice, mourning after road traffic fatality death as a party to celebrate. People go to enjoy and party.

Some of the respondents perceived the 'blood life compensation claim' as a case of two extremes that would never reconcile. Here the extremes are described as a 'blood wealth' for the death of loved one which is very painful for the bereaved and on that same day, a divine wealth immediately after the burial. A burial in urban city environment ends up becoming a celebration party. The controversy arises because it occurs after a road accident to bury a dead body, followed by people gathering at the home of the deceased person after burial in order to make ritual sacrifices and mourn. Having a party means that these sad events are associated with celebrating when there is a loss of human life. At one extreme the people mourned and immediately after adopted a celebratory mood. The general feeling between the respondents is that people who attend burials in the recent times do not mourn but they celebrate. However, some of the respondents felt differently, as they saw the celebration as a way of celebrating the life of the deceased individual.

Young People and the 'Blood Life Wealth' and 'Divine Wealth' Claims

Many respondents had the belief that 'apuk' was a tradition started by the youth, for instance, young people between the ages of 10 to 15, and in the 20s and below 40s age range felt this way. The younger generation seem to be the ones driving and using roads as pedestrians. As well as this they seem to be the main demographic who are mostly involved in 'apuk' after traffic crashes and tend to sustain multiple injuries and deaths. Road traffic injuries or deaths are a leading cause of disability for the young generation. Boys are almost twice as likely as girls to be involved in road traffic crashes. Children under 9 years are less able to make safe decisions on the road.

Even when elderly groups drive, passengers in vehicles are still eligible for a pedestrian injury, or a pedestrian death claim if they were injured, or killed after road collision crash. There are claims that the events taking place in burial, animal sacrificial rites and mourning celebration parties after fatal road accident deaths are immature, childish, childlike, or young in the young generation.

The Elderly and the 'Blood Life Compensation and 'Divine Wealth' Claims

Many old people feel that after burial celebration parties are a disgrace to ancestors, life spirit for the dead one, dead body, tradition and culture and they are hurt by what they see occurring at those celebration parties in townships. Elders do not believe that funeral rite or burial celebration parties are a proper way to support the families to cope. Elders totally disapprove of the funeral rite referred to as burial mourning celebration party practice completely.

The Increased Occurrence of Fatal Death in Urban City Areas

The increased occurrence of severe injury or death in the present days is reported as the main reason for the changing attitudes towards death and the burials. Few respondents believed that nowadays the increased risk factor of severe injury or death is endemic, rife and common. People die in large numbers compared to the past and as a result, death is no longer a scary thing. Burial rituals or memorials these days are a daily occurrence in the townships.

Past and Present Burial Rites Compared

The respondents compared the manner burial rites or burials were handled in the past with what is done in the present. They showed that they were aware that in the past, burials were handled with respect and there were also regulations and policies connecting to how people must behave at the burials, while the era of young generation does not show that. The respondents also confirmed that things have changed. According to the respondents, people are no longer afraid of burials and ritual mourning ceremonies. When there is one, people behave like it is a normal and they continue to do whatever they want. What was done in the past is not practiced anymore and, unlike in the past when people would go home after the burial of dead body or corpse, they stick around at the burial home, for alcoholic drinks.

Respondents feel that death changes with fashion if you compare it in the past and in the present.

Traditional Mortuary Rituals House

The traditional burial house for symbolic action that respondents describe is the morgue or mortuary or burial house for the Apuk Lith of Jieng Rek speaking people. Respondents described that the Apuk of Jieng Rek do not celebrate death after burial and do not rumor, or speculation, gossip, or chat much with reference to death. They are not likely to bring burial rituals or ceremonies to the attention of others. When a person dies his or her decorations and ornaments are removed. His or her head is shaved and his or her body is washed and then anointed with oil. A skin or hide shield is put on the floor of the grave, and he or she is placed upon it. He or she is laid on his or her side with his or her head facing to the west. His or her knees are flexed and his or her hand is positioned under his or her head, in the position of sleep. His or her exposed ear is covered with a skin so that dirt will not enter in it. The burial party crouches, facing away from the grave, and pushes dirt into it with their hands. They then wash off their knees over the grave, and a relative place a mat over the grave.

Considering three days for a deceased male person or four days for a deceased female person, the family of the deceased person bring a small kid that is a twin, to the grave. They take beard or stubble from the hut or shelter or house of dead person, throw it near the grave and set it on fire.

According to Michael Lambek, "the smoke blows over the people, and the people, and the senior member of the family, or master of the fishing spear if he has been called in, walks round the people beating the living kid on the ground. He finally holds the bleating kid over the fire a little, and then makes an incision in its belly and takes out the entrails. Their contents area sprinkled over the people, and the carcass is thrown away for the vultures"[269]. This "fire smoking" of the people is known as *tol nyoor guop koc or tol nyor koc ke gup, tol nyarguop, translated* as fire-smoke for cleansing body survivors of the deceased person, and the kid is the *nyong ee tol-nyoor koc gup.* The respondents say that Rek Apuk of Jieng people offer *nyong tol* to please the deceased person and a twin animal is chosen because twins have a special relationship to Divinity Spirit. After another day a sheep or goat is sacrificed. This is known as *alok ciin* (singular) or *lokcin,* "the wash hands" (plural) for digging graves for burial. This lifts the prohibition upon drinking milk from the family of dead person. Someday afterwards a whole bull is sacrificed, and prayers are offered, and invocations made by a divine master or a master of the fishing-spear. The ending ritual sacrifice, known as *apek or har akeeth or apek* between the dead and the living in *Thuongjang,* propitiates the living spirit, life spirit, body spirit of the deceased person, who without it would be likely to injure his people and kill their cattle.

To put burial mourning ceremonies of ritual sacrifice into context, "In victimizing a bull or an ox the Dinka are aware of using or manipulating something physically more powerful than themselves; and through the identification of the victim with the divinities they also control something spiritually more powerful."[270]

Rural and Urban Burial Rituals

The burial mourning ceremony parties referred to "fire smoking" people, translated as *tol nyoor guop koc or tol nyor koc ke gup, tol nyar guop* and 'washing hands' of people which is translated as *alok ciin* or *lokcin* in

---

269   Lambek, Michael Ed. *A Reader In the Anthropology of Religion.* Oxford, UK: Blackwell Publishing Ltd. 2002. Page 334

270   Lambek, Michael Ed. *A Reader In the Anthropology of Religion.* Oxford, UK: Blackwell Publishing Ltd. 2002. Pages 377

thuongjang language are very common in townships as compared to burial mourning ceremonies 'fire-smoking' people held in the rural burial ceremonies at the rural areas or the villages. This means that there is still a lot of respect for the dead and their bereaved in the rural environments and in the villages, respect for the culture of burial ceremony fire-smoking people or *tol nyor guop* and the burial ritual sacrifices. There are clear indications or respect for the dead, for the burial ceremonies of fire-smoking people and for the families involved. The burial ceremonies of 'fire-smoking' people are also characterized by order and strictness and as a result the 'fire-smoking' ceremonies are for blood relations and grave diggers alone. On the other hand, some of the respondents have highlighted that they have experienced the after-burial mourning celebration after fatal accident death at the rural villages however, they were conducted quietly and with respect unlike in the townships.

The 'Fire-Smoking' People after Burial Rituals as an Old Practice
Some respondents in the groups have highlighted that the practice of the 'fire-smoking' bereaved people after burial has been there but done differently in the past. Originally, they were conducted differently; but, as time went on when things changed, they evolved. The modern trends of 'tolnyorguop' are argued to have no basis from culture or history as 'tolnyorguop' is held in modern people's own ways, or as a burial ceremony, on the same day, which was not the case in the past. Furthermore, people dance and do all sorts of activities that do not relate to mourning when viewed in the context of old practices. Current trends are not the old after burial rites functions that were held a few days when the family of the deceased has settled. The current form, which is 'tolnyorguop', is held immediately and people have fun. The 'fire-smoking' bereaved people after burial ceremony sacrifices have existed for a long time with different names and different formats.

The Meaning Attached to the 'Fire-Smoking' Bereaved Family After Burial Rituals

Some respondents feel that people have different agendas for attending the '*tolnyorguop*' after burial rituals. Both the individual respondents and the focus groups highlighted various reasons why they think the 'fire-smoking' after burial rituals exist in the townships.

A Coping Strategy

The meaning attached to 'fire-smoking bereaved people after burial rituals are that they are a way of helping the bereaved families to cope with the loss of their loved ones. For the focus groups, it meant a way of helping the bereaved cope with the impact of loss, especially when it is done jointly between the family and the friends and colleagues.

Social Support and Comforting the Bereaved Families

The respondents indicated that '*tolnyorguop*' or 'tol-nyor-guop' was introduced with the reason of comforting the family that has lost a loved one through death. The '*tol nyor guop*' are also believed to be some kind of support to the families that were mourning their loved ones.

Social Support and Comforting the Bereaved Families

The respondents indicated that '*tolnyorguop*' was introduced with the reason of comforting the family that has lost a loved one through death. The '*tolnyorguop*' are also believed to be some kind of support to the bereaved families that were mourning their loved ones.

On the other hand, the focus group respondents feel that the party reduces emotional pain. This is especially effective when it is done immediately after the deceased has been laid to rest.

Perceived Offenses Against the Actionable Wrong or Person

Punishments for serious offenses include imprisonment and death penalty. Nearly sixty to seventy different criminal homicide offenses are punishable by death, though the vast majority of death sentences are imposed for common crimes including murder, rape, robbery, traffic accident, assault, theft among others. Since the 1990s there have been a surging number or frequency of death sentences for drug crimes. There also have been a relatively small number of high-publicity death sentences for white-collar crimes such as embezzlement or stealing, cheating, counterfeit or smoke and mirrors.

Actionable Criminal Homicide Offenses

The focus respondents indicated that offenses or crimes were treated as actionable offenses in colonial law for which blood wealth compensation was payable to the family of a person for loss occasioned to it by his or her death by actionable offenses.

The first experience is colonial law body, introduced by the Anglo-Egyptian colonists, did not bring an immediate end to Turko-Egyptian Mohamedan Law Courts, which has had an enduring and deep impact upon all forms of social practice, statutory and customary law. A period of colonial rules and colonial criminal law bodies originated in the early Middle Ages of conquerors or colonizers produced change. Serious wrongs were regarded mainly as public crimes rather than as personal matters, and the perpetrators were punished by death and penalty of property, possessions and or belongings such as cows. The requirement that, in cases of sudden death, the local community should identify the colonial law body or "presentment of conqueror", and, therefore, of little account, or face heavy fines reveals a condition of unrest between the conquerors and their natives or indigenous subjects. The second, experience is the 'Living Law' refers to the recent lived customs of South Sudanese peoples. The customs of the time will usually be clearly reflected in contemporary customary laws and it is from this that provides the dynamism and flexibility inherent in customary law.

Factors of the Anglo-Egyptian Condominium law system that survived were the panel of adjudicators or jury, or judges, hearings, trials by physical tests or combat, the practice of putting a person accused beyond the protection of the law, and orders requiring a person accused to appear before a court. The basic sources of many customary laws for other criminal-law systems, which remain uncodified are commonly recognized[271] as: 'Practice', defined as a custom or tradition repeated over many generations in the society. Binding or persuasive decisions from Courts. This source is broad in that 'Courts' include not just customary courts, but statutory courts which are empowered to preside over customary law cases. 'Religious beliefs' have particular import in the treatment of matters like incest and adultery. 'Morality' and moral principles.

271   Wuol Makec, John., *The Customary Law of the Dinka People of Sudan.* Afroworld Publishing Co. 1988. At 31.

CHAPTER TWELVE

LAW FOR "BLOOD LIFE WEALTH" CLAIM AFTER ROAD ACCIDENT INJURIES AND CASE STUDY

Origins of Laws of South Sudan

Recent exploratory investigations have cited two legal origins that have immensely contributed into original birthplaces of current customary law, as it is now functioning in South Sudan today.

1. First, **the foreign law**: This foreign law was brought into South Sudan during the Condominium rules. It has had an enduring and deep impact upon all forms of social practice, statutory law and customary law.

2. Second, **the 'Living law'**: This living law means the currently lived customs of South Sudanese peoples. The customs of the time will usually be clearly reflected in contemporary customary laws and it is from this that provides the drive, vitality liveliness, spirit and flexibility inherent in customary law.

Criminal Homicide Law and Civil Law in Customary Law

One of the supreme understandable characteristics of customary law is the absenteeism or nonexistence of distinction between criminal law and civil law. Foreign law systems have a tendency to view criminal law and civil law bodies as isolated and discrete; recommending entirely different bodies of procedural law to govern their lawsuit or suitcase running. Customary law systems have a tendency to pool or trust their action, cure, or healing of civil laws and criminal laws. This merger or fusion of civil procedure and criminal procedure does not veto a family or victim from exercising their right to pursue civil compensation or damages, or alternatively a full-scale prosecutorial action under statutory law.

The definitions of crimes contained in a code must be interpreted in the light of many principles, some of which may not actually be expressed in the code itself. The definitions of particular crimes contained in a code must be interpreted in the light of many principles, some of which may not actually be expressed in the code itself. For example, many legal systems take into account the mental state of the person accused at the time the alleged crime was committed. Most legal systems also classify crimes for the purpose of assigning cases to different types of court. Social changes often result in the adoption of new criminal laws and the outmodedness of older ones.

Reconciliation and Forgiveness

The amalgamation of civil law and criminal law under a single code is validation that customary law differs largely from Foreign Law in a very precise fashion in South Sudan. The core point towards customary law is conciliation, forgiveness and dispute settlement in civil law and in criminal law, reconciliation and forgiveness between the victimized individual clan person or victimized clan family group on one side and individual clan person killer or clan family group offender on another.

In divergence, foreign law bows towards attribution of blame or guilt and penalization, commonly aims at retribution and deterrence.

At the same time as, Foreign Courts aim to obtain a satisfactory description or version of the truth from first to last adversarial presentation of argument, the 'truth' under customary law could often be of lesser concern. In customary law courts the main objective will virtually continually be to achieve satisfaction for as many clan members as possible. The underlying objective, proved from first to last Medieval Ages of experience, is to ensure a sense of justice and settlement or agreement between the disputing clan families or clans and clan members or groups or parties and yet this means, to restore or maintain social stability through reconciliation and forgiveness.

John Wuol Makec had identified basic principles of reconciliation, aimed at peace through compromise and compensation for wrongdoings committed that fashioned customary law practice[272] in a more different functions from foreign jurisprudence as:

- Efforts are made to reconcile disputes outside of Criminal Judicial or Jurisdictional Court, except those most serious cases and heinous of criminal homicide crimes.

- Every part of procedures is simplified to minimize logistic problems, expenses and collateral losses of the parties and to ensure expeditious handling of cases.

- Customary law procedure keeps an eye on an inquisitorial system with Chiefs or Judges actively engaging the parties during the decision-making process. This differs radically from English-style adversarial systems, where the Judge acts in an observer role.

Contemporary researchers and students examining South Sudanese tradition customary law are arguing that the goals, principles and fundamental concepts of new foreign Alternative Dispute Resolution (ADR) (a relatively new phenomenon) are strikingly similar. In foreign countries, minimum commitment of ADR is usually linked to a common desire to lower legal costs and greater control over a more expeditious process with a better chance of gaining a commonly satisfactory outcome. Within traditional African societies however, the primary motivation for conciliatory

---

272   Wuol Makec, John., *The Customary Law of the Dinka People of Sudan*. Afroworld Publishing Co. 1988. At 198.

approaches to dispute resolution has been identified as ensuring sustainable cohesion of the group. African dispute resolution has been described as placing a premium on improving relations on the basis of equity, good conscience and fair play, rather than the strict legality often associated with Western justice.

Customary and Statutory Borderlines

Customary legal systems possess usually progressive Alternative Dispute Resolution (ADR) processes and mechanisms. The impacts of ADR for the inclusive legal and political systems in future in South Sudan could hypothetically be significant and prevalent. In spite of this, much will depend on the opinions and decisions of judges presiding over lawsuits at the customary law borderline and statutory law borderline or boundary at the Transcend and High Court level. How these individuals interpret and foster these parallel systems of laws will ultimately determine to what degree jurisprudence in South Sudan accepts elements inherent to customary laws and integrates customary law and statutory law into the overarching customary law legal system.

There is already evidence of a growing vibrant between statutory law and customary law, all the way through the appeals process. Where lawsuits of customary law are implied or insinuated upwards to the higher courts and those courts rule on the appeal, a decision of judge sets a precedent, which in effect makes law. This process affects customary law. For example: (1) it causes the lawsuit to be written down and (2) it challenges the precise or exact customary law to change.

Taking a Written Appeal Addressed to a Court

A family member may begin proceedings by means of an oral or written petition or written appeal addressed to the court, chief of the court or judge of the court or president or member of the court. There is no strict format but the petition must show a right of action, if not, it will be rejected. The petition may be presented:

1. Directly to the chief of court, the President or member of court at any time,

2. Through the clerk of the court to the Judge or Chief, by way of petition,

3. By attending and addressing the court from an area reserved for complainants.

Once the Judge, Chief, or President of the court has examined the complainant, petitioner, appellant, or accuser or plaintiff and determined there is a container or an instance or a situation to answer, the container is admitted and summonses issued to the suspect or accuser or defendant and witnesses or eyewitnesses. The court retainer, an individual authorized to carry out specific policing duties on behalf of the court, will present the summonses. Failure to attend court at the time specified may result in detention or arrest or apprehension and seizure of property.

Most customary law courts conduct formal proceedings in a similar fashion. An examination of the rules of procedure of the Apuk, Rek or Jaang court, described by John Wuol Makec, provides a good example of typical customary court proceedings. The hearing is simple. There are no pre-hearing proceedings, once a written appeal is admitted to the court and a date is fixed and, on the day, if all parties or groups or persons or people appear the hearing, prosecution or judgement takes place. Justice Makec describes in detail the makeup of the court and the roles of its members.

- 'The court Judge or President or Chief and members are seated in a semicircle at one side of the court.

- The Judge or Chief sits in the middle and members sit on either side according to seniority till the line ends on either side with the most junior member.

- Traditionally chief court membership was elastic, its size depending upon the numbers of chiefs' present in court.

- But contemporary practice is for the Chief Justice to fix the size in the warrant of establishment. However, Bahr Al-Ghazal Region State courts comprise five members including the President. Three members amongst whom is the President, constitute a quorum.'

- The court clerk and police are seated facing the court. They put on record the summary of proceedings or the evidence given during the hearing...
- Agam-long is seated in the middle between the court members and the clerk...No trial takes place unless he is present to play his traditional ceremonial role...
- Every person who speaks in court, including the President and court members, speaks though him. Agam-long repeats aloud the words of each speaker. He is an orator who has command of the language of the court...it is part of his duty to direct the parties and witnesses and the court as to what steps to take at each stage of the proceedings...
- The plaintiff and his witnesses sit in front of the court at one side of community translator called Agam-long in thuongjang or in original language of Rek Jieng speakers. The defendant and his witnesses at the other side.
- Retainers and court's agents who maintain order, stand around the court.
- At the outer ring... members of the of the public who are always attracted by court proceedings, sit or stand.'

Formal Procedure for Hearing Lawsuit in Court

The process of hearing a lawsuit follows a similar pattern to statutory law courts except that Agam-long is the master of formal procedures. The oath is taken using a spear facilitated by a spear master, and is accompanied by an elaborate formal procedure. There is little attempt to reduce the evidence given by plaintiff, eyewitness or witness or defendant, even if it appears unconnected or inappropriate or immaterial. This tends towards very long and tedious hearings or trials. Investigation and cross-examination are a continuous process, led by the court President or Chief. When the lawsuit or suitcase is complete, each member of the court, starting with the most junior member gives his judgment. Finally, the President or Chief addresses the court, scrutinizing the other members judgments and giving his own. The decision of the court is given as a consensus by a majority of the members. The clerk of the court reduces decisions to writing, the President or chief signs and the judgment is dated.

Law of Responsibilities

The jurisdiction of Rek Jieng, Apuk, Azande and other ethnic customary courts have been determined by the Chief Justice and defined in the authorization issued by the Chief Justice authorizing their establishment. Always, restrictions were placed upon the jurisdiction of each ethnic court, which determine such issues as the value of penalty, fine or awards, the types of lawsuits or suitcase which can be heard and the territory within which the court may exercise its powers.

When it comes to opinions of Judges, those members in the judiciary interrogated shall have their opinions considered. As the judiciary grows in size, and experience, the influence of statutory law upon community at every level has also increased. As anticipated, customary law systems and statutory law are growing slowing into regular conflict. Likewise, past antiquity, to a great extent in evidence in the works or the texts or the writings or the books, increases influence to the argument that customary law and statutory law are by their very nature bound to come into dangerous conflict. A system based upon reconciliation must characteristically or habitually clash with one based upon penalization and deterrence. This is even more prospective or liable if the judges who interpret statutory law have a manifestly different cultural viewpoint from those who interpret and execute customary law.

Types of Actionable Criminal Homicide Offenses

Legal procedural processes include criminal offense act, posted in after a fatal accident, legal advice and tagged accident scene, eyewitness, witness for injury lawsuit, and witness statement.

- A person commits criminal homicide offense if he or she intentionally, knowingly, recklessly, or with criminal negligence causes the death of a person.
- Criminal homicide is murder, capital murder, manslaughter, or criminally negligent homicide act.

Intentional Murder Act

The most important general assumptions of criminal law are that a person normally cannot be convicted of a crime without any intention to commit the act in question. As an example, the person in not required to know that the act to murder itself is a crime, as ignorance of the law is no excuse for criminal behaviour. Thus, if a person believes that an act to murder is perfectly legal and intentionally performs that act to murder, the legal requirement of criminal intention is played.

The focus group respondents experienced that the colonial legal codes recognize insanity to be a state in which a person lacks criminal intention. There are versions of the law of insanity, but in the common version insanity may be defined as a mental disease or defect that causes a person either not to know what he is doing or not to know that what he is doing is wrong or criminal offense. According to the respondents, a legal finding of insanity results in an acquittal of criminal charges expressed as "not guilty by reason of insanity", simply, because the person lacks the required intention, despite the fact that a verdict that recognizes this defense is very rare in the societies. Another very rare situation that solely exempts persons from criminal liability is a procedure of unintentional conduct in which the conscious mind does not control bodily movements, such as in sleepwalking, thus rendering a person unaccountable for even serious consequences.

A sentence of capital punishment for people with mental retardation was unconstitutional; however, such people can be sentenced to life in prison without parole. The practice of not acquitting those with mental impairments but mitigating their punishments is found in many common laws.

The assumption of criminal intention is subject to many other exceptions and qualifications. Few referred to as 'offenses of strict liability' are abandoned completely or are not allowed. Only a limited scope of those offenses. As an example, employers may be held liable if employees are injured on the job, or roadway accident, regardless of how carefully the employers followed safety precautions, and manufacturers may be held liable for injuries that result from product defectiveness, even if they exhibited no fault or negligence in the manufacturing process whatsoever. As an example of offenses, the person should have a "specific intent" either to commit a crime, for instance, common definition of burglary involves breaking and entering a dwelling "with intent to commit a felony therein" or to achieve the consequences of an act, for instance, first-degree murder usually requires the specific intent to achieve the death of the victim.

The focus group's experiences indicated that a person or driver had been drinking or using drugs before committing a crime or traffic accident fatality criminal homicide crime is not in itself a defense, except possibly for crimes that require such specific intent. Provocation is not generally a defense either, except in cases of act to murder, where evidence of a high degree of provocation, for example, in English criminal law on which many of these codes are based, sufficient to provoke a reasonable person into acting in the same way as the accused, could result in a verdict of manslaughter, even if the killing was intentional. Apart from that, some "felony murder" statutes attribute criminal homicide intention to any deaths that occur in the charge of certain "dangerous felonies". This is similar to strict liability.

For complete treatment of precise legal aspects of crime, are treated through criminal law, civil, common law, court, police, and procedural law. Particular legal systems are also handled in Shariah of Islamic law. Aspects connected to crime are then addressed in criminal justice, criminology, juvenile, justice, parole, prison, and punishment.

Below is a summary of the types of criminal homicide offenses against the actionable offense.

a. Sufficient actionable cause of offense: means an adequate cause that would normally produce a degree of anger, rage, resentment, or terror in a person of ordinary temper, sufficient to render the mind incapacitated or incompetent of cool reflection.

b. Abrupt actionable anger of offense: means sudden actionable anger directly caused by and arising out of provocation by the deceased person killed or another acting with the deceased person killed which passion or actionable anger arises at the time of the offense and is not solely the result of former provocation.

c. A person commits an offense if he or she:

1. intentionally or knowingly causes the death of a person;

2. intends to cause serious bodily injury and commits an act clearly dangerous to human life that causes the death of a person; or

3. commits or attempts to commit a felony, other than manslaughter, and in the course of and in furtherance of the charge or attempt, or in immediate flight from the commission or attempt, he commits or attempts to commit an act clearly dangerous to human life that causes the death of a person.

d. An offense committed with intention or knowingly causes death, serious bodily injury, dangerous to human life is a felony or crime of the first degree.

e. At the punishment stage of a trial, the defendant may raise the issue as to whether he or she caused the death under the immediate influence of sudden passion arising from an 'adequate cause'. If the defendant proves the issue in the affirmative by a preponderance of the evidence, the offense is a crime of the second degree.

Other factors include the amount of insurance coverage available and the type of case. That said, from my personal experience is from the blood life wealth price to the family of Mangong Akol Akot Anei killed on July 15, 2019. The surviving traffic accident victim, for pain and suffering, received bloodwealth prices in most claims payable in cattle numbering thirty-one cows (31 cows). This is equivalent in monetary money market rate of SSP 2,790,000 (two million, seven hundred and ninety thousand South Sudanese Pound (SSP)), under Article 47 and 50 Traffic Act 2003 and Civil Law Procedure Act of 2007 of the South Sudan. This is because most claims involve small traditions for injuries, pains, sufferings, deaths or long-term deaths.

Testimony Eyewitnesses to a Fatal Road Accident Scene

Eyewitnesses are those people who have a first-hand account of an accident so as to be able to testify to its having taken place at the scene. They may provide slightly different testimonies and details of a roadway accident than others in a cause or before a judicial tribunal. Observations between one testimony eyewitness and another can potentially be opposite. In a roadway traffic accident, for example, one eyewitness may approximate a car traveling at 20mph and other 65mph. Particularly, where the crossways of one motor or more motors are crashed. The speed at which a motor or car is traveling is an important piece of testimony-evidence specifically.

Other eyewitnesses at the scene may testify for a roadside departure crash, which happens when a driver leaves the lane they are in and collide with another vehicle or a roadside object, or pedestrians walking on roadside lane. For instance, this could be head-on collisions and run-off-road collisions on road transport. They may testify on collisions at junctions like rear-end collision and angle or side impacts collisions, about collisions with animals. This is common in rural road or rural highway road crash collisions. Collisions involving pedestrians, bicycle cyclists and motor cyclists known as *boda boda* riders.

An accident collision which may rollover automobile can happen and result in excessive rates of severe injury and or death. These come secondary and happen after a collision with a run-off-road crash or a collision with another object or pedestrian or automobile. The term 'serial crash' may be used at several motors are involved. If many motors or cars are involved, the term 'major incident' may be used rather than 'pile up', as a result of improper left turn or right turn, violations of road traffic basic rules, speeding, and distracted driving.

A fatal injury resulted in the death of the child Mangong. This happened by a side impact collision, when the driver, Jackson, left the middle road lane he was in and collided with the child July 15, 2019 in the Apuk community in Gogrial around Bahr Al-Ghazal areas.

A Lawsuit for a Child Loss or Death

A parent fighting for the rights of a loss or death of a loved minor child in a fatal car accident is important. However, there are many customary and cultural differences in the customary legal process. The legal guardian or parent of a lost minor child will be responsible for seeking out and choosing a trusted customary legal court or local law court. Once a court is chosen, the legal team will work closely with the minor child lost or deceased; and in every such action the Court may give such damages as it may think proportioned to the loss resulting from such death to the family members or parties, for whom and for whose benefit such action shall be brought. The prosecutor performing lawsuit case for loss of the loved minor child or deceased minor child may act as a "guardian appointed act in lawsuit' for the child during the court process. When customary court takes on an accident injury death case, rest assured that best interest of victim minor child parties will be top priority, including full blood life wealth compensation claim to parents for pain, suffering, injuries and life lost for wrongful act. The insurance company who is paying for the claim of minor child lost may want court approval so they can release themselves from further liability. In addition, courts in South Sudan like to ensure that the rights of the minor child are protected.

Where a criminal homicide crime has been committed against another party it is commonplace to charge the accused under the customary court in lawsuit and if found guilty, to award both punishment under the Code and blood life wealth compensation.

Testimony Eyewitnesses and Witnesses to Minor Child Crashed Dead
In one case, a driver identified as Jackson Gelua Anthony, aged 34 years old, drove a passenger identified as Taban Kaps Robert, 45 years old, and another passenger identified as Mabuoch Khalid Kur, 37 years old. They were travelling on July 15th, 2019, northwards to eastwards on interstate in Wau Town. They were passing through Kuajok Capital. After checking his mirrors, driver Jackson slowly reversed out of a parking spot at the Kuajok town shops.

As the vehicle approached the workplace, less than a mile on rural highway road traffic, the driver applied the brakes and steered left, crossing over the road center lane and into the westbound lane. From there the left front of the car hit a minor child identified as Mangong Akol Akot Anei, 3 years old, who was on the road lane on road traffic behind his mother Aluel Deng Kon. After impact, the child Mangong was pushed forward and rolled over three times as the body rotated clockwise up to where his face faced south before coming to rest at the scene. Due to the impact, minor child Mangong sustained fatal injuries and died upon arriving to hospital. The driver Jackson of Azande did not also stop at the scene to follow proper post-accident protocol.

However, he sped to the police station to inform the police about the car accident collision crash. The driver and two passengers were wearing lap and shoulder seat belts and were uninjured when the car accident happened. The posted speed limit is 40 mph in Warrap State around Bahr Al-Ghazal areas. The driver Jackson had comprehensive insurance. He held a valid commercial driver's license and his medical certificate was current. He was operating within the regulated hours of service. The car and driver were all insured by the South Sudan Insurance Company.

The driver Jackson from Azande of Bantu speaking people, tried to resolve the dispute with Apuk County Commissioner Joseph Kuot and sent the bereaved family of Apuk community a letter of demand to pay for the cost of 'apuk riem' claims for damages for hospital mortuary, nursing, medical postmortem, burial expenses, and expenses of administration necessitated by reason of injuries causing death. Those medical expenses are typically included as part of a wrongful death for road traffic tragedy occurring in urban townships. Jackson has asked his witness to write a witness statement.

This accidental crash triggered public anger, emotional outcry among Apuk Giir communities. The road fatality instantly precipitated crises to investigate faster to calm down public anger and agitation, for the victim party and survivors of road accident collision crash fatality to drop revenge approach and to seek legal justice in customary court to claim blood life wealth payable in cattle equivalent to the family to comport and support the bereaved Apuk Giir community. Jackson Gelua Anthony knew this situation when he was asked to write a witness statement.

Eyewitness Testimony Statement by Joseph Kuot, Commissioner
I, Joseph Kuot, Commissioner of Apuk South County in Gogrial of Warrap State, around Bahr Al-Ghazal areas:

1. On July 15, 2019 at about 4:30PM, I was about to get into my house next to the administration office building in Pathuon Apuk along the rural highway road, Apuk County.
2. I noticed that a white Landcruiser Toyota Jackson was driver down the highway road lane behind me.
3. I saw a woman walking with a minor child going to direction of a car and collide with the white Toyota Jackson Gelua Anthony. The white car was moving at the time of the serious fatalities front crash collisions injuries with speeds up to 80 km/h.
4. After collision impact, the boychild Mangong was pushed forward and rolled over three times as the body rotated clockwise up to where I saw his face faced south before coming to rest at the scene.
5. I was walking on foot to my house opposite where the accident happened.
6. The boychild Mangong was hit and died on impact in hit crash collision by an oncoming car on July 15, 2019, Monday afternoon around 4:30 pm.

7. The driver Jackson of the white Toyota car did not stop at the scene to follow proper post-accident. He did not seem to be hurt.

8. The driver and front seat passenger were restrained with lap and shoulder belts and were not ejected. I saw the three passengers on the car all were wearing their lap and shoulder belts and were uninjured at the time of the road traffic accident injury death. The driver Jackson and the white car involved on rural road traffic accident were detained in the road traffic police station.

9. The driver Jackson a passenger in the same car Mabuoch Kalid Kur, and another passenger in the same car Taban Kaps Robert, all survived in the road accident. He also said that the body of the child Mangong Deng Kon has been deposited at Luonyaker Hospital mortuary awaiting postmortem.

10. Mayuot Deng who was travelling behind the minor child Mangong had rushed to the accident spot and joined Joseph Kuot. They all shared their details they saw when accident happened at their present in the scene.

11. Mayuot Deng of the RRC said "Did you see the accident?". I (Joseph Kuot) said words to the effect "I saw it". Mayuot Deng then said "We can rush the child to hospital, just in case we need to save his life". I replied "Yes".

12. I called a few persons from the crowd to join Simon Akot Kuot. Mayuot Deng at the time lifeless body Mangong was rushed to Emergency Children Hospital. His dead body was then transferred to mortuary where I pronounced deceased on July 15, 2019 at around 7:00pm to the parents, relatives and crowds gathered around the Hospital.

13. Soon after the lifeless body was announced dead, I saw the crowd of people running to where they started abusing the arrested driver at the Traffic Patrol Police Station. I followed them immediately and tried to convince them that it was not his fault. It was just a traffic accident.

14. It was a sunny day on July 15, 2019.

15. The speed limit in the Landcruiser Toyota car parked at the Traffic Patrol Police Station was 80km per hour. The white Landcruiser Toyota car seemed to be travelling faster than that.

16. I noticed damage and severe injuries. But nurses and doctors had confirmed hit crashed impact compressions of the body, severe and catastrophic injuries, damaged spinal, spine, the disks in the lower body part of the spinal column, head and severe brain injuries.

17. I received doctors report of damage to the back-left side of the minor child, suffer from soft-tissue injuries.

18. I believe that the contents of this statement are true and correct.

Signed: Joseph Kuot, Commissioner of Apuk County, and Mayuot Deng, Coordinator of Relief and Rehabilitation Commission, Apuk County, Warrap State.

Dated: 17 July 2019.

Emergency Children Hospital in Luonyaker Township

Family members and neighboring communities all rushed to the road traffic accident spot. The crowd joined nurses, workers, traffic police, doctors and rushed to the Emergency Children Hospital where the injured child Mangong was transported. Doctors and nurses entered and took injured child to check, test severity of fatal injuries and damages caused to the body. Doctors and nurses shared specialties were bonesetters, whiplash, hearing damage, broken shoulders, brain damage and head trauma and fracture specialists who appear to make the arrangements after death of the loved one.

They transferred the lifeless body of Mangong to mortuary for post-mortem test, where he was pronounced deceased. There were people who blanket or wrap, pray, craft or construct the coffin. Their help was evidence not only of solidarity but also of necessity, for there were no commercial changes in the burial procedure. In addition to these nurses, workers, Akol of Palakyow sub-clan, Padok sub-clan family, there were other, less visible helpers.

Lifeless Body Grave

There were those who dug the lifeless body of Mangong Akol a grave. There were those who carried his lifeless body down to the world spirit side or world ancestor side. In addition to the traffic police, doctors, local authorities, and specialists who appear at death came to the scene. There were those who came before, such as healers and prayer persons and divinity spiritual high priest chiefs and those who come after, like invisible spirits and again spiritual masters and deities. All comprise a generous response to precise ecological conditions, but they are much more: links between nature and the life spirits of physical body, the sick and the healthy, the living and the dead, and the deities, prophets, saints and the high priest and the witchdoctors.

Family House After Burial of the Child Mangong Akol

The family house continued to have fundamental value after burying the lifeless body Mangong. According to the culture of Apuk Rek, the dead belong to the clan family house as do the physical body spirit, life spirit, body spirit, flesh spirit, blood spirit or lifeless body spirits. When a clan family house is inherited, all of its dead body spirits or lifeless body spirits come along with it. Everlasting rest, the payment of pending responsibilities, and the motionlessness or rigidity of the dead are transacted by means of the clan family house.

The continuity of the cooperation between the living and the dead is a result of their mutual dependence as well as their mutual identity. For instance, what remains of the dead in surviving clan family house and what the dead have taken away in surviving clan family house that is theirs as members of that surviving clan family houses.

Sgt. Adolmuot Tong Wol Inquiry of Rural Highway Traffic Fatality

Sergeant Major Adolmuot Tong Wol, Highway Road Traffic Patrol Police Officer soon arrived to the fatality scene and got busy with the usual road traffic accident procedures and injury site formalities.

1. The statement from the Traffic Police Sgt Major Adolmout Tong Wol was that "minor child Mangong was caused by the carelessness, speeding and recklessness of the driver and his ignorance and negligence of the road traffic rules".

2. I asked the name of the victim child to record correct name in investigation and I was informed that the deceased child was immediately registered as "Mangong Deng Kon" when the lifeless body reached the hospital. His maternal grandfather is identified as "Deng Kon". This is reported and recorded in the death certificate as 'Mangong Deng Kon'.

3. Relative emerged in the crowd at the scene to tell me that the biological father of victim child is called 'Akol Akot Anei' from Padok clan and he lives in Pinydit village in Apuk.

4. He again side to me that the child 'Mangong Akol Akot Anei' is living with the mother Aluel Deng Kon and grandfather Deng Kon.

5. When this minor child was involved in car collision crash on rural roadway traffic in Pathuon Apuk, it was my responsibility to investigate what causes fatal roadway accident to record true story by starting to ask for exact names of passengers and victim hit in road collision.

6. I was called on the phone by Joseph Kuot, Commissioner of Apuk County who present at the scene.

7. I arrived to fatal road accident side and began with the investigation about what cause the tragic road injury. The crowd arrived to the scene and some people started abusing the car driver.

8. I met Joseph Kuot, Simon Akot Kuot, Mayuot Deng before they performed life saving measures on victim child Mangong and transported him to Emergency Children Hospital.

9. I requested them to intervene to calm down angry crowd gathered on the scene on rural highway roadside, where I am investigating traffic accident fatality occurrence. They accepted my appeal and convinced angry crowd that it was not the fault of driver. It was just an accident.

10. The driver and other two passengers were taken to the police station

and their statements were recorded. Passengers Taban Kaps Robert and Mabuoch Khalid were let off.

11. I kept the driver Jackson Gelua Anthony in custody causing a horrific road accident. I detained the white Toyota Land Cruiser at the Rural Highway Road Traffic Patrol Police Station.

12. Driver Jackson Gelua Anthony lost control of white Toyota Landcruiser vehicle and veered off roadway and hit the child Mangong Akol (or Mangong Deng Kon) when such fatal road accident injury death tragedy occurred.

13. I confirmed through many reports the vehicle was speeding while I have been continuously urging motorists to follow speed limits of 20mph, especially at all curves.

14. I found out in my investigation that the child death was caused by the carelessness of the driver and his ignorance and negligence of the traffic rules. Investigation confirmed the driver Jackson Gelua Anthony may have been under the influence at the time of the vehicle collision crash.

15. I called the father Akol Akot Anei to my office on July 16, 2019 when he arrived together with maternal uncle Gabriel Arol Deng Kon Kon, and nephew Aru Madau Aru and took statement. I informed them to follow up the Customary Court hearing sentences penalty regarding apuk riem' compensation claim payable in cattle equivalent by guilty driver Jackson Gelua Anthony of Azande to comfort and support parents of Mangong Akol Akot Anei

The first witnesses and passengers have written down everything they saw and heard with the road traffic police. Others provided testimony of the driver negligence and proof of the child killed in fatal roadway accident at the judicial hearing and trials before the judiciary judge of Apuk Law Court in Bahr Al-Ghazal in South Sudan.

One of the first witnesses, Simon Akot Kuot was delegated to facilitate the court hearing so that eyewitness testimony and witness statements provided for fatal road accident collision crash are finalized and quickly brought for court hearing in the Apuk Law Court. Gogrial Highway Road Traffic Patrol Police reported to the Judge Heaven Key Lino those eyewitness testimonies and witness statements emphasizing carelessness of the Azande clan driver Jackson Gelua Anthony and his ignorance and negligence of the road traffic rules as the main cause of sad killing of the child Mangong in rural roadway traffic accident fault.

The road traffic patrol police reports, witness statements provided by the parties involved in the roadway collision crash said that the death of the child Mangong was caused by the recklessness of the driver Jackson Gelua Anthony who is an Azande or a Zande. The deceased boychild Mangong came from Apuk Rek customs of belief systems and practices. The child had died in fatal road traffic collision because he was too small to judge the oncoming sound of a car. Meanwhile the driver Jackson was ignorant and negligent, as he did not observe the basic rules of the road traffic accidents. The driver Jackson therein, violated vehicle code contravention section 44 and 50 of Traffic Act 2003 of South Sudan Laws.

Judge Heaven Key Lino collected evidence and statements witnesses to prove that the driver was negligent for the car accident death. He also collected evidence provided by the parties involved in the car accident, examined traffic police report prepared after the car accident and evidence of the police officer's findings on traffic violation committed by the driver.

Statements emphasized carelessness of the driver and his ignorance and negligence of the traffic rules as the main cause of death in road traffic accident.

The driver may have made statements such as "my brakes were not working," or "I was on cell phone," or "I was checking my seatbelt," are counted admissions against interest and are strong evidence of negligence.

The Apuk Law Court in Apuk Lith clan is a custom law legal system, which allows a victim surviving family member to decide to seek justice and blood wealth. The Apuk court settles disputes between citizens and different nationalities so that they repent they cannot resolve on their own. For example, in common law systems, same as custom law systems, most criminal suspects are allowed to a hearing convened before a panel of traditional chiefs and designated prominent noble groups or councils. This emerged when the foreign government attempted to use their power to deprive the accused clan member of life spirit. Customary rules of criminal procedure provide rules for lawbreaker suspect hearings or trials.

In these Apuk custom law legal systems, the responsibility for supervising the investigation in the police into whether a clan crime has been committed falls on an examining chief, judge or magistrate who then conducts the trial. The idea is that the truth is more likely to emerge from an impartial and exhaustive investigation both before and during the trial itself. The examining chief acts as a crossexaminer who directs the facts-gathering process by questioning witness, interrogating the suspect, and collecting other evidence.

Those observations from Judge Heaven Key Lino carried the great deal of weight when the time came to sort out who was at fault for the killing in car accident fatality in Apuk Customary Court hearing.

The examining chief acts as a crossexaminer who directs the facts-gathering process by questioning witness, interrogating the suspect, and collecting other evidence.

The *apuk* of killing in criminal judicial system requires the perpetrator to pay blood compensation of collective responsibility for victim party member and that this blood compensation must have traditional recognition.

The house of the bereaved family members is not lonely in its sorrow but is supported by the general Apuk Lith Communities. At a certain point, death becomes a collective event, both in requiring a house to live up to its obligations and in supplying it with its due. First the sick clan person, then the dead clan person, becomes the center of the community. Notably, the cares are similar: a visit and offerings, for those who are born and those who are dying within clan family houses. Complex transactions are organized between those of the family house, those from the nutritional character, and those from the outside. The doors of the

254 MADHEL MALEK AGEI

family house are open, and so its store, more or less according to the different intensities and levels of social collaboration or teamwork and topographical vicinity. In the burial procedure all levels of social relation or cooperation are present, openly distinguished and clearly differentiated.

Driver Jackson paid out all blood wealth compensation and other claims to family members of Mangong Akol. When the same guilty driver Jackson Gelua Anthony was released in jail. He died slowly peacefully on natural death on 12th August 2019 in Tombura area, in the Azande family house.

I Want to Ask a Few Questions
"What makes a person to die on violent or slow and peaceful death?" "What makes a clan child to die on violent death or painful death in a car collision?" "What makes a car driver in Azande clan to die on peaceful death? Or slow death?

CHAPTER THIRTEEN

'APUK RIEM' WEALTH IN CATTLE EQUIVALENT

How Public Customary Justice Principle of Criminal Sentencing Works
The principle of public customary justice is that justice is executed, accepted, and witnessed. Customary law court must process, administer, or direct justice in public: under trees or open spaces. Public customary justice is a legitimate principle that is a foundation of that shared common and civil laws as noted by the Wanhalel Dinka Customary Law adopted in 1927. Peace and harmony are achieved through a process of compromise and payment of blood life compensation for wrongdoing. A number of the key benefits of public justice include ensuring public confidence, acceptance and respect in democracy and the administration of justice, as well as deterring people from committing crimes.

A transparent criminal justice process allows the public to understand and accept what is ensuing in the courts. Under the criminal procedure rules the customary law court will release factual evidence or knowledge. It is said in the mouth in open court and then contained within a customary court document that is open to public inspection. The court can release all factual evidence notifying others of the decision of the court. The customary court must provide details including the results and date of any hearing in public, where the relevant evidence or report is available, and it is not prohibited by a reporting restriction.

Customary law, in common with other modern legal systems, recognizes where a person has a cause of action, that is where he can show a prima facie case against the defendant, he is legally entitled to raise a civil suit against that defendant. This is known as a right of action. In modern legal systems there is usually a statute of limitations governing every action, setting a strict timeframe within which action must be taken if at all. Customary law does not recognize such a period of limitation for action and with the exception of certain specific circumstances; right of action will prevail over the passage of time.

Jieng Customary Law Court

The Chiefs' Courts Constitution governs the customary laws of South Sudan. The Chiefdom of Rek Apuk hosted a Conference in Wanhalel and adopted the traditional laws, popularly addressed as "Wanhalel Dinka Customary Law". It became the first time the state had involved itself in the laws of traditional judicial system.[273] The "People's Local Courts Act 1983" repealed the original ordinance, but replaced it with an almost identical mandate, which remains in practice in most parts today, modified under the Laws of Procedure of the South Sudan. The Ordinance created the following courts: The Chief sitting alone, the Chief as president with sitting members, and Special Court. The first two Chief's courts listed are permanently established by means of warrants issued under the hand of the Chief Justice.

The most common type of customary law court is that with the Chief as president and with sitting members. There are two types of court established under this construction: a Chiefs' court, also known as an A-court, and a regional court, also known as a B-court. To some extent, this is

---

273   Wuol Makec, John., *The Essentials for the Re of Customary Law in the Southern Sudan.* The Sudanese Judgment and Precedents Encyclopedia. Sudan Judiciary, Khartoum. At 3.

confusing in a way that the Regional or B-court is higher than the Chiefs Court or A-court.

The Jurisdiction of Rek Apuk Customary Court

The jurisdiction of court is a key subject in any judicial system. When a case appears before a court the first step is to determine whether that court has the jurisdiction to hear it. Jurisdiction is described as[274] the power of the court or judge to entertain an action, petition, or other proceeding and as the county limit, such as Apuk County Court within which the judgements or orders of a court can be enforced or executed.

The jurisdiction of specific court is determined by the highest justice and defined in the warrant of their establishment. Occasionally, restrictions are placed upon the jurisdiction of each court, which determine such issues as the value of fines or awards, the types of cases that can be heard and the territory within which the specific court may exercise its powers. The original Chiefs' Court Ordinance provides detailed and complex guidelines, still in use today. Hence, original Chiefs' Court Ordinance is now modified under the traditionally Laws of Procedure for South Sudan, and for the highest justice concerning what subjects and over whom the separate or specific court has jurisdiction.

The Terms Used for Criminal Road Traffic Offense

The given term or name of the roadway traffic offense varies from jurisdiction to jurisdiction and from legitimate to everyday terminology. The specific road traffic criminal offense is exceptionally termed driving under the influence. Thus, the given name is "driving while intoxicated" (DWI), "operating while impaired" (OWI) or "operating while ability impaired", "operating a vehicle under the influence" (OVI) and so on[275]. The criminal homicide offense caused in roadway traffic is generally considered crime

---

274   Osborn's Concise Law Dictionary, John Burke.

275   http://www.courtinfo.ca.gov/forms/fillable/tr220.pdf

when it is punishable by imprisonment or even death. As an example, driving related offenses that are classified as crimes include: driving under the influence of alcohol ("DUI").

For out of country drivers in South Sudan, just the speeding and reckless driving charge can be devastating. South Sudan has several reckless driving speed traps. For example, fatal drunk or drugged driving accidents frequently lead to criminal traffic violation charges against the driver. Offenses in criminal traffic violation are classified as either misdemeanor or felony. Each community in South Sudan has its own classification system. In South Sudan, the criminal traffic offense court is common, and speeding can count as low as travelling 85 mph in a 60 miles zone. As with crime, the first step is an initial appearance or an arrangement before a judge of a lower court or magistrate, or chief court at rural village environment level.

For one thing, the process is vastly different depending on the severity of the crime. Generally, the more important the offense, the more elaborate the process. The most serious crimes are felonies, crimes such as robbery, assault with a deadly weapon, and sexual assault, for which the punishment on conviction is imprisonment at least a year. Misdemeanors are less serious crimes, such as simple assault, driving while intoxicated, and trespassing, for which punishment on conviction could be a term of incarceration of less than a year, usually in a local jail.

The customary court for an offense concerning criminal traffic violation case has at its core, the principle of conciliation. This is like the Wanhalel Dinka-Jieng Traditional Customary Law court justice practice Bahr Al-Ghazal areas by Rek ethnic groups as traditional societies.

The criminal traffic violation is when the person causes the offense in criminal traffic violation while operating the vehicle. Criminal traffic violations include reckless driving, driving while license is suspended, driving under the influence, refusal to submit to breath test, habitual traffic offender, leaving the scene of an accident, no valid driver's license, expired driver's license, racing on a highway, attaching tag not assigned, expired vehicle registration, no valid registration, unlawful use of an identification card, no motorcycle or *boda boda* rider endorsement, unlawful display of a license, and permitting an unauthorized person to drive.

The case will be heard in criminal court if the driver was accused of a more serious driving-related offense like driving under the influence (DUI), reckless driving, and vehicular homicide or manslaughter. Minor traffic offenses include running a stop sign, running a red light, texting while driving, and an unsafe lane change considered infractions or civil offenses, whereas the charges that end up in criminal offense court are usually misdemeanors or felonies.

Township Justice Court

More serious charges, such as a driving under the influence ("DUI") or instances where the person in question may be responsible for injuries to another, may require the person to appear in customary court regardless of their plea. Some cities, towns and rural village environments process guilty pleas of this nature without the presence of a real judge, whereas others may require one to appear in court. Often these charges are handled by the better criminal court. Each community handles criminal traffic matters in its own way. In most of South Sudan communities, for example, criminal traffic matters are heard in the court for the city, town, or rural village environment court where the alleged criminal traffic violation happened. The town and village courts are known as custom Justice Courts.

Bargaining Among Azande and Apuk families

Azande and Apuk speaking communities have different feelings about the blood wealth, divinewealth, customary law court system process. Many Judges presiding over criminal traffic violation court cases usually encourage parties to resolve cases out of court by having both sides come to an agreement. This process is known as negotiating a plea or plea bargaining. In most jurisdictions it resolves most of the criminal cases filed.

Plea Bargaining is Prevalent for Practical Reasons

1. The defendant can avoid the time and cost of defending his imprisonment term, bailing cost and court fines at customary court trial as well as the risk of harsher punishment blood wealth compensation claims, and the publicity a trial could involve around Rek Apuk community.

2. Respondents and defendants can agree in blood wealth compensation claims price payment, per one cow for the purchase of thirty-one cows (31) sentenced in the customary court trial of criminal traffic death after the Second negotiations and use plea bargaining to determine cattle numbers.

3. The prosecution can save the time and expense of a lengthy court trial in criminal traffic violation cases against the convicted such as in the case of Jackson, driving drunk at a speed of more than 85 mph on a crowded rural highway.

4. The Apuk Law Court prosecution can save time to announce the completed verdict and can decide by the end of justice court trial.

5. The defendant can enter a plea bargain in proportion blood life wealth compensation claims sentenced in court fines, and payment 'apuk riem' in cattle prices of thirty-one cows (31 cows) determined by the judiciary.

6. Representatives can plea bargain to negotiate with the Insurance South Sudan Company. For example the payment of reparation may have a monetary currency money equivalent of SSP 2,790,000 (Two million, seven hundred and ninety thousand South Sudanese Pounds).

7. The Plaintiff or respondent representatives can agree to negotiate lifeblood wealth compensation verdict payment in cattle, determine cattle market value cost, type of cows and cattle price per cow charge purchase in cattle marketplace value in Luonyaker town.

8. Azande and Rek Apuk communities can spare the uncertainty of going to court trial of criminal traffic violation.

9. The court system can save the burden of conducting the trial for every crime charged.

10. The Prosecutor can agree on an acknowledgement of the proposal's negotiation with representatives of the deceased, especially traditional chiefs of custom court. That can begin steps in the legal court direction that adopted the Wanhalel Dinka Traditional Customary Laws in 1927 to immediately and unconditionally implementation.

11. Joint ownership of all property, even in the largest families, provides security, a sense of ownership and responsibility for all, thus, the family members use their property in discharging major obligations.

Part of a dispute can be settled, with the remaining issues left to be resolved by the judge or jury or council of elders in the community. Criminal cases are not settled by the parties in quite the same way customary court cases are. The government may decide to dismiss a case, or be ordered to do so by a court. The defendant may decide to plead guilty, perhaps as a result of negotiations with the government that result in dismissing some of the charges or recommending leniency in sentencing. Plea bargains are a very important and efficient way to resolve criminal cases.

Settling Criminal Homicide Death by Negligence Accident in Customary Court

Relatively few lawsuits go through the full range of procedures and all the way to trial. Most customary justice cases are settled by mutual agreement between the parties. A dispute can be settled even before a lawsuit is filed in court. Once a lawsuit is filed in court, it can be settled before the trial begins, during the trial, while the jury or judge is deliberating, or even after a verdict is rendered. A custom settlement doesn't usually state that anyone was right or wrong in the case, nor does it have to settle the whole case.

The process of hearing the misdemeanor death case follows a similar pattern to statutory law courts except that *Agam-long* or court translator is the master of ceremonies in court. The oath is taken using a spear and is accompanied by an elaborate ceremony.

Not many attempts have been made to reduce the evidence given by plaintiff, witness or defendant, even if it appears irrelevant. This leads to tendency towards very long and tedious trials. Investigation and cross-examination are a continuous process. When the case is complete, each member of the court, starting with the most junior member gives his judgment. Finally, the President addresses the court, analyzing the other members judgments and giving his own. The decision of the court is given as a consensus by a majority of the members. The clerk of the court reduces decisions to writing, the President signs and the judgment is dated.

Fatal Road Injury Death of Mangong in Apuk Lith Community
The Child Traffic Criminal Death Case Charged Against Sentencing

I will now refer back to the case of Jackson Gelua Anthony who, as discussed in the previous chapter, was convicted in criminal traffic violation. His case was seen before the Customary Law court system, presided over by magistrate Heaven Key Lino on July 17th, 2019, in Luonyaker. The plaintiff, Deng Kon, who represented the deceased child, had filed the first complaint in the Rural Highway Road Traffic Patrol Police for the negligence leading to a traffic collision death, and to claim blood life wealth compensation.

The complaint stated the plaintiff's version of the facts, the legal theory under which the case was brought. It outlined that the driver Jackson Gelua Anthony was driving under the influence and exhibited negligence, careless, and ignorance of the road traffic rules. The complaint also asked for certain damages in the form of *apuk riem* compensation, this was cattle numbering thirty-one cows and other relief. The plaintiff filed with the Apuk Customary Law Court clerk.

The request was given that a notice was to be issued to the defendant driver Jackson, who was at this point in the custody of Traffic Patrol Police station in Luonyaker. The deputy sheriff served the summons. It notified the defendant, Jackson, that a lawsuit has been filed against him in Apuk Customary Court in Luonyaker in Apuk Giir community. After the Jackson was notified, he was given the period of seven days to file an answer admitting or denying the allegations made in the complaint petitioner Deng Kon on July 16, 2019.

The judge listened to the traffic patrol police officer and the plaintiffs representing the lost child Mangong as well as the respondents representing Jackson. The Judge considered what sentence was appropriate, the testimonial evidence and the customary law. As a result, a sentence lead to payment of blood life wealth compensation payable in cattle numbering 31 cows, court fines and other claims was imposed.

The Azande defendant pleaded guilty to the criminal traffic violation charges of reckless driving due to speed and was found guilty of child traffic fatality death on July 15, 2019, after the court trial. The court awarded seven days to the defendant to report back before the court for "sentencing hearing".

Defendant Jackson Arrested in the Traffic Police Custody in Luonyaker Town

The fatal road traffic criminal offense drunk driving charges against the driver Jackson has been classified as misdemeanor or felony homicide actions punishable by imprisonment or even death. His reckless disregard of the substantial risk resulted into the sad death of the road user Mangong. The arrested driver Jackson was brought before the judge for an initial appearance on July 17, 2019. He was kept in the Traffic Police custody for protection from surprise revenge attach by the surviving relatives because of negligence death of their son in Luonyaker town.

Initial Appearance in Customary Law Court

During the initial appearance, the Judge Heaven Key Lino determined the name driver Jackson Gelua Anthony and his address in Tambura in Equatoria area before the court in Luonyaker town in Apuk Giir community in Bahr Al-Ghazal area. The magistrate Heaven Key Lino informed the defendant Jackson of the fatal road traffic misdemeanor charges caused by recklessness with criminally negligent homicide.

The magistrate presided in the courtroom of Apuk Customary Court in Luonyaker small town. He allowed family members of the deceased child Mangong Akol of Apuk community and those family members of the guilty driver Jackson Anthony of Azande community to attend initial appearance in the courtroom of Apuk Customary Law Court in Luonyaker town.

Survivals of misdemeanor or felony traffic homicide actions are implicit in Jieng customary law because all members of families are also considered to be party to the injury, severe injury, damage, and death caused by negligence misdemeanor traffic fatalities. Legal scholars have highlighted practice that a criminal homicide offense case raised against a person is a case raised against the family or group of families. Every member of the family or families was invited to attend court hearing concerning the deceased child Mangong of Rek Apuk community by negligence.

The initial appearance action was in effect a representative action in court trial. Any member of the family was invited to attend court trial at any point in the hearing as he or she is party to the lawsuit by virtue of family membership. The principle of family unity also dictates that an individual may be subject to a court decree even if they have not been parties to the case.

Officers of the Apuk Law Court System

The magistrate Heaven Key Lino presided in the courtroom on July 18, 2019. He ruled on points of law and gave instructions to the council of eight respondents, informing them about the Wanhalel "Jieng-Dinka" Customary Law that governs the case.

The court clerk and bailiff administered the oath to Apuk Law Court magistrate Judge, traffic police officer, respondents representing Apuk community, surviving parents and the guilty family members of Azande community and witnesses. The clerk in charge of physical exhibit vehicle involved in fatality death of the deceased child Mangong was introduced into evidence and was responsible for other administrative aspects of the trial.

The bailiff kept order in the courtroom, called the witnesses and was in charge of the respondents in the council, as directed by the judge. It was the duty of translator and bailiff to be certain no one attempted to influence the respondents of council.

The court reporter recorded word for word everything that was said as part of the formal proceedings in the courtroom, including the testimony of the witnesses, and the ruling of judge on them.

The lawyers were trained for both sides and are also officers of the customary court. There is already evidence of a growing dynamic between statutory law and customary law, through the appeals process. Where cases of customary law are referred upwards to the higher courts and those courts rule on the appeal, a judge's decision sets a precedent, which in effect makes law. This process affects customary law in two ways: it causes the case law to be written down and it challenges the particular customary law to change.

Lawsuit Case Death by Negligence

The lawsuit case of, Mangong Akol Akot Anei against Jackson Gelua Anthony F/I/R/No:130/2019, occurred before the Customary Law Court of Apuk Couty settled date: 18/07/2019, in the Apuk County in Warrap State, Bahr Al-Ghazal area.

The accused defendant Jackson was charged against criminal homicide death because driver Jackson Gelua Anthony was recklessness, carelessness and ignorant of traffic rules. He was thought to have caused a fatal road traffic accident due to the use of a particular plant to act as a 'love charm' to 'an old man'. It was alleged that the initial result [of the administered plant] was the 'old man' lost his teeth. He was then alleged to have died 'two years later'.

Despite the dubious nature of the evidence, the length of time between the administration of the drug and death and the deceased being an 'old man', the lower court awarded *Dia* to the relatives of the deceased. The decision was upheld on appeal to Payam, County and High Courts. The appeal moved to the Court of Appeal, which overturned all previous findings and dismissed the case against the accused. *Dia* was returned. The precedent set enables all future awards of *Dia* from customary courts to be appealed to Court of Appeal for scrutiny.

The Magistrate-Judge Heaven Key Lino passed his sentence based on the Apuk customary law court system verdict. His sentencing reads: "Whereas this criminal case has been submitted before me, I, Heaven Key Lino, Second Grade Judge, F.I.R.NO:130/2019, under section 44 and 50 Traffic Act 2003, year 2019, for judgement, do hereby issue these orders":

1. The defendant convicted Jackson is sentenced to three months imprisonment with the effect on detention date 15/7/ 2019 for contravention sections 44 and 50 Traffic ACT 2003.

2. The defendant convicted driver Jackson Gelua Anthony of Azande community is sentenced to pay court fine SSP 50,000 in default of payment one-year imprisonment for contravention sections 47 and 50 Traffic Act 2003.

3. The defendant Jackson sentences shall run consecutively.

4. The defendant Azande Jackson Gelua Anthony driving speeding white Landcruiser vehicle caused collision with the child Mangong Akol killed in fatal roadway Luonyaker town shall pay the Complainant or Plaintiff *apuk riem* known as blood life wealth compensation payable in cattle numbering thirty-one cows (31 cows).

5. Defendant Jackson shall pay *apuk riem* blood wealth first class four (4) value cows in currency monetary market price in accordance to the Dinka-Jieng Customary Law. Blood life wealth compensation of the deceased child Mangong Deng, shall be paid and be obtained by way of civil procedure Act 2007. Issued under my signature and the seal of Court on this day: 18/07/2019.

Signed by Judge Heaven Key Lino, Second Grade Judge, Apuk South County Court. Luonyaker, Gogrial State, South Sudan.

Respondents, representatives, court clerk and chiefs pleaded to the Insurance Company to pay lifeblood compensation claims, and relevant representatives to organize collection *apuk riem* in cattle according to the Padok clan and subclan customs. Liability fell on: the clan family members guilty for the collision crash crime act that resulted to death of the child Mangong, Apuk Giir community; the kin clan family of the guilty defendant clan family members; and the guilty Zande of Bantu classification language speaking community.

Payment Blood Life Wealth Compensation in Cattle of Thirty-One Cows

The Blood life compensation claim payment was negotiated and a plea agreement was settled even before the lawsuit was filed on July 17, 2019. When the lawsuit was filed, the blood wealth compensation claims negotiated to be worth 31 cows. This could be done while the Magistrate-Jude Heaven Key Lino was deliberating, or even after the verdict was rendered.

Criminal cases in Azande customary law court system are not settled by the use of cattle in quite the same way Apuk customary court system cases are. However, not every criminal homicide case goes to a local court trial in Apuk Giir. The types of cows, value cost per cow price and total number of cows ordered by the court to be purchased in the marketplace values and price costs in Apuk community market have been outlined below for reference.

Table Showing Type of Cows and Market Value Price Cost

S/ No.	Type of Cow	Number of cows	Value cost per cow	Total SSP
01.	Third birth cow	4	60,000	240,000
02.	2nd birth cow	4	70,000	280,000
03.	1st birth cow	4	90,000	360,000
04.	Pregnant Heifer	4	150,000	600,000
05.	Heifer size two	5	120,000	600,000
06.	Heifer size one	5	80,000	400,000
07.	Bull size two	3	70,000	210,000
08.	Bull size one	2	50,000	100,000
	OVERALL TOTAL	**31**	**690,000**	**2,790,000**

This payment of *apuk* blood life prices of SSP 2,790,000 was made through from the Insurance Company amount of SSP 5,580,000 (five million, five hundred and eighty thousand South Sudanese Pound only). It was done in such a way to conform to clan customs they believe were laid down by the clan spirit, or other clan deity who governs according to principles of ancestral worship in ritual sacrifice, truth, and justice. Some family members of the victim child killed in road accident claimed for a pay of apuk blood life price known as *apuk riem wei akuen*, numbering fifty-one cows (51 cows). But the presiding court magistrate Judge Heaven Key Lino was quick to rule out any payment of *apuk* blood life wealth compensation prices 51 cows. He said he will not accept any payment of *apuk price* beyond Dinka Customary Law Court system which limits payment of fatality to *apuk price* 31 cows only. The family members each submitted a claim for their transport charges to the adjuster Committee Road Accident Negotiation which represents their expenditure bills multiplied by the number of family members plus them out of pocket expenses attributed to prescriptions. Accurate records of monetary amount spent were available with Committee Road Accident Negotiation.

Collection of Court Fines and Blood Life Wealth Compensation Claims

The Apuk Law Court collected court fee charges and penalty fines which were paid in cash by the guilty defendants on behalf of relatives and family members of Jackson Gelua Anthony. The payment covered all their collective responsibilities.

Judge Heaven Key Lino supervised the release sentence for the period of payment of three months. He ordered payments before the guilty driver imprisoned for three months could be released from prison as detailed below:

1. Court fee fines, guilty car fines, guilty driver fines and Road Traffic Charges totaling an amount of SSP 28,850 SSP (Twenty-eight thousand eight hundred and fifty South Sudanese Pounds only), must be duly or fully settled before the guilty driver in prison is released to his freedom according to the sentence verdict announcement.

2. The funeral expenses incurred by the family of the deceased child totaling an amount of SSP 50,000 SSP (Fifty thousand South Sudanese Pound only) must be refunded before court hearings clearance certificate is issued out by Apuk Law Court Clerk.

3. Expenditures of different charges spent on July 16, 2019, in the hospital examination, Road Traffic Patrol Police investigation, mortuary preparation and death certificate processes reached a total amount of SSP 50,000 (Fifty thousand South Sudanese Pound only), and should be refunded before the final court clearance certificate is issued by the court Clerk in Apuk Law Court.

4. Restitution or other refund of reclaims for relatives which amounted to a total of SSP 2,790,000 (two million, seven hundred and ninety thousand South Sudanese Pound only) must also be settled in monetary money cash. This is different from the blood life apuk price (blood

life compensation price) in cattle number thirty-one cows (31 cows). It has to be paid to relatives of the child Mangong killed in car crash on Pathuon Apuk road, Eastern Gogrial region.

Customary Court Case Apuk Riem Procedure

The party may begin proceedings by means of an oral or written petition addressed to the president of court, or member of the court. There is no strict format, but the petition must show a right of action otherwise it will be rejected. The petition may be presented over directly to the court president or member or magistrate at any time. Through the clerk of the court to the magistrate or judge or president by way of petition, by attending and addressing the court from an area reserved for complainants. When the judge or magistrate or president of the court has examined the litigant and determined there is a case to answer, the case is admitted, and summons are issued to the defendant and witnesses. The court retainer, an individual authorized to carry out specific policing duties on behalf of the court, will present the summonses. Failure to attend court at the time specified may result in arrest and seizure of property.

Term Blood Life Wealth

For the people of the Apuk clans, blood life compensation is often paid in cattle but sometimes can be paid in sheep and goats. Clans of Apuk people residing in towns and cities are changing the way blood life wealth can be paid or collected, which is taking the form of monetary currencies. Now, monetary currency is widely growing up even in rural villages.

Because the Zande clans are agriculturalists with a history of conflict with Jang Rek clans, particularly the Apuk Lith clans, and Malual Rek clans, they have abandoned cattle keeping and practice an agricultural farming system. Hunting is especially important, and both sexes take part in the agricultural work. They use monetary currency in customary law system actions.

Custody of Child in Marriage and Divorce Family

Custody of child is a contentious matter in marriage and divorce family in South Sudan communities. It is bound up together with 'bride wealth' marriage and payable cattle for divorce case. The child during divorce will determine payable cattle. In Apuk Lith and any other Rek family divorce case, 'bride wealth' paid during marriage cannot be return when there is a child in the marriage. Others may divide the 'bride wealth' with the maternal family to demand the return of some cows to the father of child.

The girl child may make matters more complicated, because she may attract a significant number of 'bride wealth' to a custodian family upon marriage. If a young woman becomes pregnant and the man refuses to marry her, that child shall remain under the custody of maternal uncle or father of the young woman. There are cases when the child will belong to the husband who married the mother to raise with other children born in a different marriage. It is not uncommon for a young woman to become pregnant and then have a man refuse to marry her. If a man refuses to marry a girl after she is pregnant, she and her child would remain with her parents.

Where the child is a girl and grows up attractive, marriageable, and valuable girl in that family, the biological father could think of claiming the girl as his daughter in customary law court. Such case has appeared in a number of customary law courts, where the biological father claimed custody before the court and was found in his favour.

As an example, several cases have appeared in a number of Jieng and other Rek Apuk custom law courts, where the biological father claimed custody before the court and was found in his favour. In turn these cases had appeared before the Court of Appeal, which found in favour of the defendant or plaintiff or respondent who was proven to be the legitimate guardian of the child.

The finding was a strong warning or caution that in future, a time limit of ten years should be placed upon all claims for paternity and redemption of child or children. This limitation would, the court believed discourage an unscrupulous, dishonest, corrupt, or deceitful man from neglecting his biological child until he was able to make financial gain from that child.

Mangong in the Custody of Maternal Family

Custody of Mangong was under his maternal grandfather, Deng Kon, in the Apuk Lith community. Aluel is the daughter of Deng Kon and mother of the child Mangong Akol. Aluel Deng Kon got married with more than 30 head of cattle paid to her parents as 'bride wealth' by Akol Akot Anei, father of her child Mangong.

Mother Aluel's Story

All her life, Aluel Deng Kon hated herself because of her mental sickness associated with the psychiatric and psychological problems she had. In psychological terms, the death of her child was immediately equated to mental health crisis because it was a stressor that forces an individual to respond and adapt in some way. Mental illness had caused Aluel such an embarrassment to family house.

The deceased child remained with Aluel's parents together with the rest of her children living in the house of her father Deng Kon Kon. Mother Aluel Deng Kon aided a small business at a flea Pathuon Apuk Market in Luonyaker township. She collected little firewood, green vegetables, foodstuff, and such to sell. Anything for the money they needed. She cooked for local brewery women and alcohol consumers to support the family. She was considered an embarrassment. Here are some quotes for the father and mother of the child Mangong.

There was one day, during cultivation season, when mother Aluel came to say hello to her son's father Akol Akot Anei in their clan family house at Pinydit Village in Apuk. Father Akol was so embarrassed. "How could she do this to me?!" He ignored her, threw her a hateful look, and ran away from her.

He confronted her that day and said, "If you are only going to make me a laughingstock, why don't you just leave me alone?"

Mother Aluel remained silent. Akol did not even stop to think for a second about what he had said, because he was so full of anger. He was oblivious to his wife, Aluel feelings. He wanted her out of his house.

Akol Akot Anei guessed he felt a little bad, but at the same time, it felt good to think that he had said what he had wanted to say all this time. Maybe because he had paid his dowry of 'bride wealth' to the parents. Akol did not think that he had hurt the feelings of Aluel very badly.

That morning, Akol woke up and went to the farmhouse to complete a tillage of groundnuts garden at Pinydit homestead. Aluel was sitting there under the trees at the farmhouse, and she was crying quietly, as if she was afraid that she might wake Akol Akot Anei up.

"How dare you come to my house and cry to curse me? You came to curse me to curse my garden?" Akol Akot screamed louder at her. "Get out of here now!".

Mother Aluel quietly answered, "Oh, I am so sorry. I must have the wrong house."

Mother Aluel got up, and walked away, holding hands of her son Mangong Akol Akot Anei. They slowly made their way down rural feeder road and disappeared around the corner until they reached the house of her father Deng Kon in Luonyaker township.

So, Akol Akot Anei told himself that he would work harder and become successful, because he hated embarrassment and poverty.

Akol really worked harder. He built a clan family house of his own. Now he is living happily as a successful man. He likes it here, because it is a house that does not remind him of Aluel Deng Kon with embarrassing illness.

Death of Mangong Reached his Father Akol Akot Anei

The grief reactions for the roadway accidental death of the child Mangong was accompanied by strong emotions and performance of a grief ritual. During mourning, groups of people joined father Akol Akot to express words and behaviours symbolic of support and comfort.

On Tuesday July 16th, 2019, in the evening hours, the deceased child father identified as Akol Akot Anei was informed about the death of his son Mangong in road traffic fatality injuries on rural roadway on Monday July 15, 2019 in the afternoon hours in Luonyaker township.

"What?" "Who killed my only son?" Akol said as he loudly cried out on air.

"It was caused by the reckless driver Azande called Jackson Gelua."

It felt as if the whole sky was falling down on Akol Akot Anei. Akol ran away crying like a crazy man. Akol said he wanted to see his son before burial, and he cried. When he got there, his son was buried at the house, where his grandfather Deng Kon Kon was resided. The mourning crowd which had already gathered around the burial site in the house told Father Akol Akot Anei that the Azande driver collided with the child on roadway in the afternoon hours.

"I always knew Aluel would let my son die! I really wish that was Aluel to die. Aluel is more than an embarrassment woman in this family. She has now crushed me and my family good" said Akol with a lot of emotions and tears dripping down in his eyes.

An insurance representative, Anjelo Kom Agoth, approached him and gave him the condolence letter sent to the bereaved family. The condolence letter was read to the father Akol Akot Anei. There was a lot in the condolence letter, but Father Akol Akot could not continue hearing messages. When the condolence letter was given back to Akol, the condolence letter felt from his shaking hands and he collapsed to his knees, sobbing like a little boy, and sat closer to his son's grave.

Father Akol Akot Anei sat on his son graveside and said: "My son, I think my life has been devastated enough now. I wanted to visit you few days ago, but it is now too much to miss you forever. I was glad to see your face once again. I miss you so much. You mean the world to me. I have always been so proud for you, my son. I am sorry that the increase in psychiatric and psychological problems are associated with mental health implications, and that Mother Aluel was such an embarrassment to family house life. Mother Aluel turned to suicide death because of your death.

God ancestor is watching to revenge you, your precious life."

Akol Akot Anei made that statement and collapsed on his son's grave. He was carried away on the grave. But he did not accept going away. He came back and said: "Your mother Aluel has worked against our own family, because Aluel had been diagnosed with post-traumatic stress disorder. Your death now is the psychological wound and pain of the bereaved family members and members of the community burdened by the painful loss of the loved son".

"Aluel returned you only to die! You are to be buried in maternal house, not mine".

"When you love someone, their happiness is far more important than your own."

Conclusion to Mangong's story

The investigation highlighted the Apuk cultural belief that every person has blood, flesh, life and life spirit which will curse the guilty driver who sadly killed Mangong, a member of the Padok clan of the Apuk community. Akol Akot Anei also believed that the clan divinity has created every living thing with physical body, blood body, lifeblood, and life spirit.

Akol said that life spirit and body spirits of the deceased son is still surviving and shall invisibly guide family for bad for worse. They are all preserved with great respect as they are understood to have a distinctive relationship with the living, raw life spirit, the body spirit, the dead spirit in ancestry world spirit and other world spirits.

This is fear and is the bottom line of the story of this sad fatality.

Respondents and representatives that negotiated and pleaded for the Apuk Law Court case verdict for payment of life blood wealth compensation claim with cattle numbering thirty-one cows (31 cows) collected by the family members are shown on the annex table.

The family members of the child Mangong Akol needed to participate in a ritually organized ceremony for oath in blood sacrifice. The victim family members of Apuk are required to take the back part of the bull used for blood sacrifice, while the guilty family members of Jackson of Azande should take the front part of blood bull. This is usually done before blood wealth is collected home to be distributed between the paternal clan members and maternal clan members having closer blood relations with the child Mangong killed in criminal traffic offense. It is reported to have been carried out when the process *apuk* price 31 cows were completed and fully paid.

Clan victim and clan homicide families bring revenge disputes and unhappiness. They will cause their own clansmen's desires to be exercised if the aspirations of the blood wealth spirits are not fulfilled. According to Madhel Malek Agei, they will cause the victim and homicide clans to be destroyed by body spirits, *jak*, *yath*, life spirits and divinity spirits[276].

CHAPTER FOURTEEN

DISCUSSION OF THE FINDINGS, CONCLUSION AND RECOMMENDATIONS

Introduction

This chapter presents the discussion of the main themes that emerged during data analysis. Insights were generated from in the experiences, perceptions, the meaning attached and the feelings about the blood life compensation promoted through a judicial process emerging in recent road accident occurrences in South Sudan

This included the factors that cause accident injuries to happen, malfunction or failure of instruments, claim for blood wealth compensation prices payable in cattle equipment, automobile collisions, deficient maintenance, hazardous environments, and weather as well as animal accidents. There is an emergence of the blood wealth compensation after a death and 'after tears' parties in South Sudan urban and rural environments.

The aims and objectives of the current study were to understand the perceptions of the people living in rural Apuk communities and to explore their psychological needs in connection to road accidents and how they happen, mourning the dead in the urban townships and modern rural environments as opposed to traditional Apuk setting during the process of mourning the fatality death of their loved ones by: -

Exploring their experiences of the 'blood life wealth' compensation penalty prices payable to the family of Mangong Akol lost after fatal road collision crash.

Understanding the perceived causes of Mangong death on July 15, 2019, after road crash and the meaning attached to the blood life wealth cattle herds payable to the family of deceased child Mangong Akol by the guilty driver Jackson Gelua Anthony and prevent road traffic accident occurrences.

Understanding the roadway traffic accident fatality and blood life wealth compensation effect it has on them and the diverse Apuk and Azande cultural practices.

If you have had an accident or been injured or assaulted, you may be entitled to petition compensation claim court judge or solicitors offer for a free. There is no obligation consultation on the legal entitlement to injury petition compensation. Personal injury cases are a customary law and statutory law specialty and there are confidently integrated customary law and statutory law judges who offer the absolute best possible service.

Discussion
Experiences of the Blood Life Wealth Compensation Penalty

One of the significant themes extracted was how the focus groups respondents described their experiences of the blood life wealth payable after fatal roadway accident deaths or injuries. They explained that immediately after the road collision crash, a boychild Mangong Akol collided with the car on rural highway road traffic accident where he died instantly within Apuk community.

A crowd of people gathered on spot. Some people started abusing the car driver. Commissioner Joseph Kuot tried to convince them that it was not his fault. It was just a traffic accident. The driver did not come to rest, but sped to the police station to inform the police about the accident. Soon the highway road traffic patrol police reached the accident spot. A few individuals, good-hearted volunteers, gathered at the crash scene.

From the crowd joined local government workers and rushed the child Mangong Akol, (also called Mangong Deng Kon) to the civil hospital mortuary or morgue in Pathuon Apuk, in Bahr Al-Ghazal area.

Soon the traffic police reached the road traffic accident spot with a team of doctors and authorities. The driver Jackson Gelua Anthony was detained in the police station. The car involved on Apuk rural highway road traffic accident was detained in the road traffic police station. Their statements were immediately recorded. The two passengers were let off. People in the crowd all started abusing the driver. The Apuk Commissioner Joseph Kuot and his extension worker Simon Akot Kuot intervened to convince them that it was not his fault. It was just a road accident. A few people from the crowd joined Apuk Commissioner Joseph Kuot and extension worker Simon Akot Kuot and rushed the body to Pathuon Apuk Civil Hospital.

The Apuk Commissioner explained to the crowd what had happened. The driver and front seat passenger were restrained with lap and shoulder belts and were not ejected. The three passengers were all wearing their lap and shoulder belts and were uninjured at the time of the Apuk rural highway road traffic accident death and injuries. The posted speed limit is 40 m.p.h. in Apuk County in Bahr al-Ghazaal. The driver held a valid commercial driver's license and his medical certificate was current. The driver was operating within the regulated hours of service.

Commissioner Joseph Kuot announced that the deceased body has been deposited at Luonyaker Hospital mortuary awaiting postmortem. The traffic police arrived and become busy with the usual procedures. The car, driver Jackson Gelua Anthony from Azande of Bantu classification language speaking community, and Taban Kaps Robert from Madi language speaking community were all detained together by the traffic patrol police in Rural Highway Traffic Patrol Police Headquarters in Apuk community, Bahr Al-Ghazal.

The people I interviewed explained that the dress code for the burial celebration had changed from dressing modestly, covering the head and shoulders, to dressing up with black clothes and the latest models for the

burial of late Mangong Akol. After the burial rituals and ceremony celebrations, some have an extra pair of clothes to change for the after-fatal
road accidents, burial rites, sacrifices, ceremonies, and blood life wealth
compensation. This confirms observations by Posel[277] and Maluleke[278].
Some focus group respondents used the expression of 'shock' and 'surprise'
when they attended the customary legal court hearing verdicts. Burying
rituals, sacrifices, mourning ceremony celebrations and grieving after
fatal roadway collision crash in homicide action crime law court verdict
sentences to blood wealth happened for the first time in the rural village
of Apuk community of Jieng Rek. It resonated with Mndende, in Van
Rooyen, that South Sudan is experiencing a 'culture shock'[279]. Social learning theory explains this phenomenon as socio-cultural diffusion, which
occurs when societies are continuously faced with pressures to change
some of their traditional practices in efforts to improve the quality of
life[280].

In line with the concept of modeling in social learning theory, the focus
groups described the behavior that they observed in urban townships
were modeled by certain subcultures such as Roman Catholic Christians,
Coptic Christians, Protestant Christians, Afro- Asiatic Sufis Muslims,
Sunni Muslims, and Buddhists. African Traditional religious believers, and
others, were later imitated by other people. Observing others' behaviors

---

277   Posel, D. (2002). *A matter of life and death: Revising "modernity" from the
vantage point of the "new" South Africa.* Draft Manuscript. Johannesburg. Wits Institute
for Social and Economic Research. Retrieved, August, 13, 2009 from http://www.wiser-
web.wits.ac.za.

278   Maluleke, T. S. (1995). *Urban Black Townships A Challenge to Christian Mission.*
Missionalia, 23(2), 162-183.

279   Mndende, N. (2009, 19 January). *Principal turns a beady eye on boy's tradition.*
In K. van Rooyen, Culture Shock. The Times. Retrieved, May, 19, 2009 from http://
www. thetimes.co.za.

280   Bandura, A. (1986). *Social Foundations of thought and action: A social Cognitive
Theory.* New Jersey: Prentice Hall.

and doing what they do or using another person's behavior is a stimulus for an imitative response[281]. Modeling has always been acknowledged as one of the most powerful means of transmitting values, attitudes and patterns of thought and behavior. Not all behaviors observed will be imitated. Observing the actual fulfillments of others also involves the consequences that those behaviors have for them, which could also involve judgmental standards.

Beyond the psychological understanding of the meaning of blood life wealth, is the strongly emerging culture which seems to be gradually wiping away and replacing the past Jieng lifeblood wealth payment practices that have existed for centuries. People appear to be quite dissatisfied about the bloodwealth compensation price after a fatal car accident death, caused by actionable wrong. There seems to be little done to prevent the law of bloodwealth compensation. Future research on the blood life wealth compensation, burial, sacrifice, and mourning rituals could focus on the factors motivating the careless drivers as well as how societies could preserve and sustain the values of traditional blood life compensation and mourning practices.

From the literature reviewed, the understanding of mourning in African culture as expressed by academia, is that mourning a dead person in the family does not end with the burial. There are traditional customs and rituals that need to be fulfilled even after the burial and there is a stipulated family mourning period[282]. When a death has occurred, everything must be done in moderation. Talking loudly and inviting visitors to pass near to a graveside is not allowed. Eating too much, laughing or even being angry are also not allowed.

Today, social, economic, and political changes have in turn changed the face of death rituals in modern and technologically advanced societies. As

---

281   Flett, G. L. (2007). *Personality Theory & Research*. Canada: John Wiley & Sons.

282   Mkhize, N. J. (2008). *Example of indigenous healing: African grief therapy*. Power Point Presentation. Retrieved, May 14, 2010 from www.psychology.unp.ac.za.96

a result, some rituals appear to have diminished in South Sudan contemporary townships. The results of various studies on the traditional African mourning practices completed in response to deaths show that an observed surge in psychiatric and psychological problems connected with incomplete mourning and unresolved grief. This could be connected with the psychosocial inadequacies of newer family mourning processes. The social learning theory and observation model describe these changes according to the social diffusion theory and innovation model.

Understanding the Perception of the Fatal Roadway Injuries and Deaths
Significant understandings were generated from the customary law courts blood wealth compensation interpretations. These understandings are based on the roadway accident and subsequent blood life compensation in the case Mangong Akol.

The findings appear to be consistent with some academic assertions about characteristics, types, and features of urban townships. They generated a variety of sub cultural forms which included youth subcultures, peer groups, gangsterism, truancy and crime. These aspects were later perceived as a threat to the social fabric of the town. Furthermore, there is concern that criminals who had committed homicide had become role models for the young groups.

Other significant perceptions highlighted that the life loss, burial rituals, mourning, and bereavement after a fatal roadway is in and of itself a blood life wealth price in cattle equivalent of previous life. This is consistent with customary law court which outlined the purpose of modern township traffic fatalities, burial, ritual sacrifice, and blood life wealth is about more than 'mourning the dead' and celebration. There is more talk now of 'moving on' and 'letting go' rather than remaining stuck in the sorrow of those who died such as in the past traditional era. This also appears to support academic assertion that due to the practicalities of transitional societies in the urban communities of South Sudanese cities, there is demand that bereavement should be brief and intense. Blood wealth compensation and mourning ceremonies should be resolved as quickly as possible so that the person should go back to normal life as soon as possible. This phenomenon is something that could be perceived as anti-cultural practice in South Sudan communities

Focus groups highlighted that urban township environments were not really 'home'. No one cared to respect the premises and they could not fulfill rituals, sacrifices, ritual *apek* prayers, and the mourning ceremony of fire-smoke. In support of academic assertions, focus groups in the Rek Apuk community confirmed that millions of people no longer live in their original rural homelands for a number of reasons. Many people live in multicultural urban cities in places such as Luonyaker, Juba, Wau, Kuajok, Rumbek, Lietnhom, Jonglei, Yambio, Tombura, Awiel, Tonj, Yei, Torit, Malakal, Bentu, Gogrial, Warrap among others.

In these places there are many economic forces, acts of government terrorism, and acts of colonial power. Survivors of a roadway traffic accident often face overwhelming emotional strain and struggle to know where to turn for help in most cities. The "Value" of a wrongful death depends, in part, on the financial resources of the party with liability and victimized parties' ability to pay for judge and court expenditures.

Bloodwealth compensation and proper grieving sometimes may not be possible because claiming 'apuk riem' compensation in lawcourts and grieving involve engaging in a lot of rituals and legal processes. If the social and the physical environment do not support those like *apuk riem*-compensation claim and grieving, they can be difficult for the bereaved.

Many scholars highlighted the contradiction of life and death in the new rituals of mourning and celebration which have recently been documented in some urbanized townships environment, particularly among the affluent societies. According to the Social Learning view, the environment shapes, maintains and constraint and maintain behaviors but people are not passive in the process; they can create and change their environments. This could describe the emergence of new practices in urban environments such as 'after fatality road accident-death tears' parties.

Such as in the case of Mangong Akol's death, it is not unusual for a person to attend several funerals or burial rites in a single day. The most common form of crime in the urban environments of South Sudan is loss of life caused by careless *boda boda* riders, medical negligence, drink driving and 'murder'. People die like flies, especially on the weekends. The exploratory investigations also seem to support focal groups and academia investigations of the child injury and mortality death rate among South Sudan communities. Child deaths occur as a result of injuries caused by car crash occurrences, inter-community violent conflicts, violent civil wars, armed crimes, Ebola, HIV/AIDS, and endemic malaria parasites.

In the rural areas people still have a lot of respect for blood life wealth, burials, ritual sacrifices, and mourning ceremonies as compared to urban areas. Their blood wealth payable cattle herders, burials and funeral rites are characterized by strictness and order and as a result there is celebration after a fatal road accident. Some focal group respondents mentioned that they had attended a burial celebration in rural areas, but they were conducted quietly and with respect unlike in the urban areas.

Understanding the Effect of Blood Life Wealth After a Death

The focus group respondents highlighted significant insights into what the understanding of blood life wealth 'after fatal road injury deaths' effect to them. African indigenous churches highlighted the supportive role of the community, in the event of death of a family member, from a religious perspective. Upon knowing that a member has died, community members flock to the family to offer different kinds of support. The Balanda and Azande use money as the currency of customary law action as in most claim sentences with a penalty of blood life wealth payment. Their traditional religions and beliefs do not permit a mourner to be alone in his or her sorrow after death by fatal injury.

There seems to be contrasting understanding regarding the social support provided by bloodwealth. Some people did not agree that burial rites and blood life wealth compensation are forms of social comfort and support to the bereaved families. The nature of burial gatherings and compensation rituals is that they are held far away from the home of the bereaved families. In several urban settlements in South Sudan, there are contradictions in the reported purpose of the after-death rituals and burial ceremony. This concurs with argument that social comfort and support from friends and family are important during bereavement. Thus, it is the **quality** of social comfort and support that is important, not just the presence of rituals and ceremonies.

The blood life wealth compensation, burial, sacrifice, mourning, and ceremony is as a coping strategy for the bereaved. It is a social gathering for relatives and friends who have lost contact with each other. It allows people to reconnect and can be a platform for people to 'show off' their social status and social identity. This confirms the opinion that township funerals have become cultural events where everyone attends a funeral. The size of the crowd seems to reflect the social status of the person organizing burial and the deceased. It may also reflect the lifestyle of the individual's friends in urban cities.

One of the focus group respondents remarked: "Burial ceremony celebrations go concurrent in amount to your status. If he or she was a person that used to attend the after-fatality injury death burial ceremonies, who used to dress up, then the burial ceremony would differ from ordinary burial ceremony celebrations. If the burial is for a person with certain identity, even celebrations will follow that identity to some degree."

The outcomes of the current investigation, regarding the perceived gatherings of the burial ritual of the after-child road crash death ceremony celebration, are comparable to other explorations into gatherings at some of the traditional mourning rituals.

The outcomes of the investigation conducted on the widow's experiences of performance of traditional rituals, highlighted that the mourning customs prescribed by the society were stressful for them and the mourning process as isolating and discriminating against women[283]. Similar results were recorded on the investigation conducted about violent victim widows and performance of death rituals in South Sudan. My previous investigation on Nilotic ethnic women's experiences of burial rituals highlighted that while tradition on its own is not bad, it can be a tool to oppress women. Scholars further recommended that there should be flexibility on how people would want to express their grief in order to allow for the discrepancy or assortment of individuals. Some academic findings about the Balada and Aande widows indicated that whereas some women found the fulfillment of the mourning rituals healing, curative and medicinal others fulfilled them because they feared that misfortune will befall them.

From the social learning perspective, fulfillment of certain behaviors can occur because these behaviors are imposed on them, and people want to avoid negative reinforcement. Behavior doesn't necessarily occur because people accept and understand the reasons for the fulfillment of those behaviors.

A Customary Religious Perspective

The social background is just one aspect to the procedure of death according to divinity spirit. The conceptual or religious aspect: - in what manner it is described, evaluated, and predicted; helps community understanding in different ways.

The old physical body dies naturally without illness. People die from old age, when their bloodlife, their vitality, healthiness, vigor, and stamina wear out. They disappear without causing trouble for the survivors and can even help with small tasks. The old physical body in clan divinity spirit sees death and calls for to be buried alive. This is to leave behind good health, prosperity, and life spirit to the community after the person joins the world of spirits and ancestor spirits.

---

283   Manyedi, M. E., Koen, M. P. & Greeff, M. (2003). *Experiences of widowhood and beliefs about the mourning process of the Batswana people.* Health SA Gesondheid, 8(4), 69-87.

A regrettable death is one in which the natural procedure is interrupted by human causes, external causes, or accidental causes. Death by suicide and accident are perhaps the least "natural" and most "cultural" way of death.

What it means to die differs between the clan definition, medical definition, and belief systems. Regarding the sad story of the three-year-old child, Mangong, who died in a car collision, the most interesting aspect of violent death lies in its clan definition. According to the clan definition, the spirits of the life of Mangong did not disappear when his physical body died. Instead, they continue on a long passage that began in life.

The factors that contribute to the maintenance of the physical body spirit or life spirit are feeding habits, good health, concern in activity and service, financial independence, the intensity of clan family house and friendship relations, customary and mental health, among others. Contrastingly, with tiredness, impotence and passivity, death is preferrable to life. Though belief system how to die and how to live is outlined, but the boundaries between the life and death are vague. There is no clansperson in the culture, who shall say where life is to end and to start. This is the work of Divinity Creator in the spirit world and the ancestor world.

Life is a gift from Clan Divinity Creator. Life is a gift, a pleasure in everything, a participation, and a struggle. According to customary belief, the child born in the family house stays in the clan family house at first, only slowly venturing out to get involved in clan obligations and gathering relationships beyond the clan family house and outside the clan family house. In the bounds of death of clan person, this process is turned around. There is a slow separation from public life, from celebrations and entertainment, from relationships with friends and neighbours, and from work and consumption, drinking, feeding, or bothering.

Many theologian writers mentioned that "LIFE" is a gift from the clan divinity gods, but so, too, is a lifeless body a "MISFORTUNE". From this point of view, violent accidents are not bizarre as is customarily believed in the clan norm to be.

Although it is believed the spirit lives beyond physical death, a person does not become publicly and mentally dead when they have lost their lives. A spirit is evidence of the existence of death in life. A Spirit is the extension, of life after death of physical body. The spirit of the living is the cultural self that has died, divorced from the physical body. It is the self that is still alive. This is exactly what the customary belief in the clan family house divinity spirits of the living means. Above all, clan communities can begin to belong to the world of spirits, of the dead and ancestor spirits before having a lifeless body death or medically proven death. It is possible that many of clanspersons whose deaths are increasing through motor driver carelessness, negligence, human causes and other common causes, joined this class of the living dead when they loss their grace in clan family house.

Testimony for the clan duality of spirits is visible at community level. Spirits do not come in one identical standard or representation. To a certain extent, spirits come in many types. These types range from animals and trees to divine clan people. Anthropological writings and sources may portray spirits as belligerent, antagonistic and uncompromising, but it is the spiritually powerful clansman or clan spear master who will desire to ask the question:

Are all these evil spirits?

Are bad Devils and witchdoctors invading our clan? Or is the Spearmaster undermining their nature as adjudicators and patrons.

These oversimplifications leave out the different kinds of spirits, for both living and dead, as well as the different ages of the spirits.

The symbol of the clan divine is selected based on gender and the process begins on birth night. If the child is a boy, clan family house members will put a spear as a symbol on the right-hand side of the door for six days. This is for the mother to use as a symbol for the spirit. The mother will then go for six days without taking the newly born baby outside the house. If the child is a girl, then a stick will be put as a symbol on the door, which will be a symbol for the spirit. Similarly, the mother will go for six days without taking the baby girl out of the house. When this long journey ends, the spirit becomes the life of physical body.

Spirits secure a cult, worship, or sect from the living. We find the same punctuations in the range or specialists who talk with the dead and deities, from spiritisms, healers, witchdoctors and prayer clansmen. These mediators try to maintain a difficult balance between the spirits and the outside, and between this living spirits world and other ancestor worlds.

Thus, the focal group respondents felt that from their personal experiences, the after-burial celebrations were very painful when the death had occurred in their own families. Thus, the death celebrations were experienced as hurting the bereaved families and were seen as hurtful and insulting towards the bereaved. The blood life wealth price and hurting the practice of apuk riem after fatal road traffic injury and death suggested lack of respect for the bereaved families. This is unlike in the past where burial rituals and blood wealth were conducted with respect. It should be noted That the 'after accident-death tears' party can be a source of valuable support when conducted properly, respecting the deceased and the bereaved and helping them to cope with the impact of death.

Conclusion

The investigation conducted was an attempt to explore the experiences of people who and interact with blood life wealth compensation claim convictions after road injury deaths, burial rites, and ceremony celebrations. Phenomenology was followed as a research method which its aim was to explore the blood life wealth understanding, meaning, perceptions and the feelings of the people regarding the practice of the blood life wealth.

The results indicated that the after-fatality injury death celebrations are mostly perceived as a ritual ceremony and celebration, which contrasts sharply with the mood of death and a burial in the South Sudan traditional context. The results also indicated that the aim of people was to offer comfort and support to the deceased person's family and assist them to cope with the effect and impact of death.

The house of the Rek Apuk family, in the Jieng community, is not lonely in its sorrow but is supported by the general clans. At a certain point, death becomes a collective event, both in requiring a house to live up to its obligations and in supplying it with its due. First a sick clan member, then a dead clan member, become the center of the community. Notably, the expression of care is similar: a visit and offerings, for those who are born and those who are dying within clan families. Complex transactions are organized between the family house and those from outside. The doors of a family house are open, and so its store varies more or less according to the different levels of social collaboration and topographical vicinity. In the burial procedure all levels of social relation are present and openly distinguished.

As an example, family members and neighboring communities all rushed to the road where Mangong Akol died. Community members acted as bonesetters and fracture specialists who appeared to make the arrangements after death. People helped in many different ways. There were people who wrapped the blanket around the child, prayed, cooked, distributed food, and constructed the coffin. Their help was evident, not only of solidarity, but also out of necessity. There were no commercial changes in the burial procedure. In addition to the nurses, Palakyow clan family, Padok clan family, Zande clan family and other burial specialists, there were other, less visible helpers.

The continuity of the cooperation between the living and the dead is a result of their mutual dependence as well as their mutual identity. For instance, what remains of the dead in the surviving clan family house and what the dead have taken away in surviving clan family house that is theirs.

APPENDIX: A

Table: Focus Group Committee for Claim Blood Life Wealth
Table showing focus Group-Committee of Representatives

S/No.	Name in Full	Civil Service position	Committee
1.	Wek Deng Kuanyin	Executive Director, Local Government	Chairperson
2.	Giir Thiik Riny Madut	Paramount Chief, Apuk South County	D/ Chairperson
3.	Lual Dhel	Court Clerk, Apuk South County	Clerk
4.	Madut Manyuat	Chief, Apuk South County	Member
5.	Angelo Kom Agoth	Insurance South Sudan Company Ltd.	Member
6.	Aru Madau Aru	Nephew to Mangong Aluel Deng (known as Mangong Akol Akot Anei (no. 7)	Member
7.	Akol Akot Anei	Father of Mangong killed in car crash	Member
8	Mayuot Deng	Relief & Rehabilitation Commission (RRC) for Humanitarian Officer	Member

Blood life Wealth 'Apuk Riem' in Cattle Equivalent

Paramount Chief: Giir Thiik Ring Madut, Apuk County, Gogrial East.

Paramount Chief Giir Thiik walking to check the cows paid as blood life wealth for the death of child Mangong Akol, killed in collision crash by the Azande driver Jackson Gelua Anthony.

The person standing up is Aru Madau Madut, nephew of the minor child Mangong Akol who died in collision crash on road traffic. They have discussed the quality and number of blood life wealth paid.

Blood life Wealth 'Apuk Riem' in Cattle Equivalent

Lual Dhel, Court Clerk seen checking for quality and number of blood wealth paid in cattle herds equivalent of monetary money currency. As prescribed by the Judge according to Wanhalel Traditional Customary Law and demand from the victim party. Madhel Malek Agei (writer of this Book) at the far end, on his left hand is Angelo Kom representing an Insurance Company and driver guilty of carelessness, negligence, and ignorance of road traffic rules. Another person with red shirt and woman with blue cloths are relatives of the deceased child who are here to check quality of cattle numbering thirty-one cows as 'apuk riem' translated as blood life wealth. Based on a verdict in the Apuk Law Court under the judge from Balanda clan in Wau.

Blood life Wealth 'Apuk Riem' in Cattle Equivalent

Checking of 'Apuk riem' cattle numbering thirty-one cows equivalent was confirmed according to the court sentence fine.

Picture to Check Quality of Cattle Herders Paid as 'Apuk Riem'
The Rural Highway Traffic Patrol Police Officer Master Sergeant Aduol Wol, asked by the Apuk Court Judge to inspect the quality of cattle herders before they are collected by the surviving members of the deceased child who died in fatal roadway collision crash in Apuk Lith community.

Picture of Divine Master, vehicles and drivers
Divine Master of the Fishing Spear Performing Ritual Prayers for Purity
Here are the Divine Masters cleansing drivers, cars, employees, residential areas, administration offices, buildings, new Rural Highway Road in Apuk County and living environment from evils, bad happenings, evil eyes and misfortunate.

The guilty family of Azande accepted the verdict of the Committee for Traditional customary courts, and paid the traditional court penalty fines of blood life wealth in cattle numbering thirty-one cows.

Picture of Bull in Sacrifice in 'Apuk Riem' Cattle 31 cows.
Divine Master performing peacemaking ceremony between guilty and victim families of the two communities.

The 'apuk riem' ceremony is a demonstration sign for a peacemaking ceremony between Azande and Apuk Lith communities and families, after a fatality criminal homicide act had taken place.

Azande and Apuk families sat apart, about 20 yards apart. His Azande kin represented the killer driver Jackson Gelua Anthony.

The 'apuk riem' cattle numbering thirty-one cows, payable to the family of the victim, which were to be collected after performing peacemaking ceremony, were placed between the Azande and Apuk families of the two communities with a small bull. The divine master who is seen directing the ceremony was invited from clan divinity spiritual powers. He was not related to either Azande family or Apuk family. Madhel Malek Agei highlighted that the clan family uses other spear masters to reconcile clan spirits and the creator of ancestors who chooses to empower the spear master to possess supernatural spirits. This enables healing for spiritual crimes, divine disputes, devil offences, oaths, homicides, bewitching, fatalities, wrongdoings, and evil eyes that people perceive to have come through the creator. The Divine master collects the divine wealth dona-tions, translated as apuk, payable to the clan spiritual priest and ranges in accordance with the retaliatory penalty for the specific spiritual crime and the circumstances of the victim party or family or community. 'Apuk' or 'apuk riem' compensation is well defined. The divine wealth to be received by the spear master varies. He is called upon to settle disputes, fatal acci-dents and crimes and shall receive his divine wealth. This is deemed as the 'apuk spiritual' price determined by the level of disputes and crimes that may cause social unrest, victim disability, death, or imprisonment.

The kin of the killer driver Azande Jackson seized the forelegs of the bull, and those of the victim child Apuk Mangong Akol who was killed in fatal road collisions seized the hind legs.

Madhel Malek Agei highlighted that clan spiritual law explicitly states that where the settled punishment is not carried out, the clan spirit will act against that person and his kin by ostracizing them. Divinity clan spirit retaliation punishment is certain and is consequently a very effective deterrent. The omniscient spirit will not endure its Laws to be disobeyed with impunity[284]. Agei emphasized that clan divinity spirit punishment is

---

284   Agei, Madhel Malek (2020). *Apuk a State in Waiting*, Africa World Book Company Lt. Australia. Pages

expressed in terms of simple death as well as of bearing one's evil or guilt. Sometimes "man shall bear his guilt" is followed by "and he shall die". Sometimes it is combined with the threat "to be cut off". This is sometimes joined with the threat of childlessness, deathlessness, mysteriousness, etc. Where the "bearing of guilt" stands alone, it is meant to impose the duty to bring a sacrifice to a divine spirit, Ancestor, Creator and Creator Law. This is defined as spiritual wealth or divine wealth by the Apuk Lith. Agei personally finds it appropriate. He had adopted and used it throughout the book, *Apuk: a State in Waiting*.

Madhel Malek Agei concludes that the biting of the spear symbolized an oath swearing to abide by the settlement. He interprets the spitting, scattering with entrails, and dusting with ashes as forms of purification, cleansing and blessing.

As a tradition, one bull is usually sacrificed for peacemaking ceremonial celebration party of purification, cleansing, healing, repenting, reconciling, harmonizing and forgiving for wrongdoing or sinning.

In other oath service occasions, all members representing both communities licked the bile of the animal and spit: From then on, all bitterness should be forgotten. Where there is a bamboo, both parties will hold one piece together and bite, then spit left, right, upward and downward.

Table For Cultural Identity

Rek Language	Location	Nationality	Identity	Rek identity Name
Jaang or Muonyjang or Muonyjieng (Jieng) Rek	South-Western Jieng Rek (Dinka)	Aguok, kuac, Lou, Kong-goor, Abiem, Abuok, Awan: all are sharing identity Kuei of Rek	Eagle (Fishing Eagle)	Kuei identity
Rek Jieng	South-Western Jieng Rek	Apuk	Eagle (African Eagle, or Martial Eagle, Crowned Hawk Eagle	Apuk-Lith
Rek Jieng	South-Western Jieng–Dinka	Apuk	Eagle	Apuk-Lith
Rek Jieng	South-Western Jieng-Dinka	Apuk	Eagle	Apuk-Lith
Rek Jieng	South-Western Jaang/Jieng Rek	Malual	Gier-Nyaang (Buothanyar)	Malual Giernyaang
Rek Jieng	South-Western Jaang/Jieng Rek	Tuic or Twic		Twic Mayardit
Agar	South-Central Jieng	Agar		Agar-Marol
Gok	South-Cenral Jieng/Jaang	Gok		Gok-Ayiel
Aliap, Ciec, Atuot	South-Central Jieng/Jaang	Ciec		Ciec
		Aliap		Aliap
		Atuot		Atuot

APPENDIX B

Differences of Criminal Offences in Azande, Balanda, Jieng And Nuer Customary Law Codes[285]

Offence	Azande/Zande	Balanda Bviri	Jieng/Jaang	Nuer
Murder, or fatality	Blood compensation payable for survivors: money	Blood compensation payable for survivors: - money	*Apuk or apuk riem: defines* Blood compensation, or reparation: payable in numbering cattle 31 cows or cattle herders	Blood Compensation or Reparation: – cattle (80 cows or cattle herders)
Robbery	Refund property, plus fine	Refund property, plus fine	*Acut or cuot:* defines Refund property, plus fine or imprisonment	Refund property, plus fine or imprisonment

---

285 Most of Criminal Offences can also be dealt with under Statutory Law.

Adultery	Compensation for husband: - money	Compensation for husband: --money, plus fine	*Aruok or rook:* defines Compensation for husband: numbering cattle 2 cows, 3 cows, 7 cows or 11 cows, plus fine or imprisonment	Compensation for husband: - (cattle plus fine or imprisonment)
Rape	Compensation for father: --(money, plus fine or imprisonment)	Compensation for father: -- (money, plus fine or imprisonment)	*Aruok or rook:* defines Compensation for father: numbering cattle 1 cow, 2 cows or more, plus fine or imprisonment	Compensation father: - cattle, plus fine or imprisonment
Incest	Not an offence common between girl and father	Law is silent	Ritual cleansing; recently fine or imprisonment	Ritual cleansing; recently fine or imprisonment
Theft	Refund property + fine or imprisonment	*Acut or cuot* -Refund property + fine or imprisonment	*Cut or cuol or cuot:* defines Refund property + fine or imprisonment	Refund property + fine or imprisonment

A Comparison of Different Civil Cases in Azande, Balanda Bviri, Jieng, and Nuer Customary Law Codes

Case	Azande/Zande	Balanda Bviri	Jieng/Jaang	Nuer
Divorce	Dowry returned to husband	Dowry returned to husband	Dowry returned to husband	Dowry returned to husband
Custody of children	Children remain with father if dowry paid. With maternal uncles if not	Children remain with father if dowry paid. With maternal uncles if not	Children remain with father if dowry paid. With maternal uncles if not.	Children remain with father if dowry paid. With maternal uncles if not.
Wife Inheritance	Not Practiced	Not Practiced	Practiced and fully enforced	Practiced

Laws of Obligation and Tort

Offence/ Event	Azande/Zande	Balanda Bviri	Jieng/Jaang	Nuer
Defamation	Payable compensation in monetary money	Payable in monetary money as compensation	Payable apuk or compensation in goats, sheep, cows to be determined by Judge/chief	Payable animal or monetary equivalent as compensation to be determined by judge/chief
Mishap by Fire	Refund of property and fine	Payable in monetary money as compensation	Payable compensation in livestock, cows or monetary equivalent	Payable anima or monetary equivalent l as compensation to be determined by judge/chief

Injury/ Death by Cattle/Goat/ sheep	Payable in Monetary compensation	Payable in monetary money as compensation	Apuk riem payable in animal involved given as compensation or equivalant	Payable animal or monetary equivalent as compensation to be determined by judge/chief
Injury/ Death by Horse/ Donkey/Dog	Payable in Monetary compensation	Payable in monetary money as compensations	*Apuk riem* or blood life compensation payable in cows equivalent determined by judge in cities	Payable in cows equivalent as compensation determined by judge in cities.
Death, Injury, crash, and/or collision by Car, Boda Boda, Bicycle in Roadway Accident Fatality	Payable in Monetary compensation	Payable in monetary money as compensation	*Apuk* blood life compensations payable in cows equivalent determined by judges in cities	Payable in cows equivalent as compensation determined by judge in cities

Punishment of Common Offences Under
Domestic Statutory and Sharia Laws

Offence	Statutory Law	Shariah Law
Murder	Death or Life imprisonment	Death or Dia or compensation
Robbery	Death or life imprisonment	Death
Theft	Imprisonment or fine	Amputation of limbs, known as cross Amputation: Right hand and Left Foot are amputated from thieves.
Adultery	Imprisonment and or fine	Stoning to death of man and woman
Rape	Imprisonment and or fine	Stoning to death of man
Incest	Imprisonment and/or fine	Law is silent
Blasphemy	Imprisonment and compensation	Lashing around 80 lashes.
Death, crash, collision occasioned by Car, Boda Boda and or Bicycle Road Accident fatality	Death or Life imprisonment or imprisonment for years determined by judge	Death or Dia plus fine and imprisonment for number of years determined by judge or Kadi/Gadi.
Injury caused by Car, Boda Boda and or Bicycle Road Accident fatality	Imprisonment plus fine	Fine plus Imprisonment for number of months, year, years determined by Kadi/Gadi or Judge

These pictures of cross amputees sentenced in the Islamic Law Courts called "Shariah" in the 'Sudans' (or two Sudans). They were retrieved from the academic research paper entitled: "The Causes of Conflict in the Sudan" (1986) written by Madhel Malek Agei, as a thesis submitted in partial fulfillment of the requirements for the Bachelor of Arts Degree in Political Science, Public Administration and International Relations in the Department of Social Sciences, Cuttington University College, Liberia, West Africa (not published).

Picture 1: "Is this Islamic Justice?"[286] Or, I may ask same question this way: Is this a Social Control based on Informal Customary Codes of Behaviour Justice? Cross Amputee was sentenced for the act of stealing. Amputating in some countries such as Iran was proposed, was formerly used or is currently used to punish people who committed crimes. The amputated person is called Amputee.[287]

Amputee': A person who has had one or more limbs removed by amputation.

Cross Amputee sentenced in the Shariah Law Courts in the Sudan, 1984. *(Middle East (The), No. 20, October 1984, Pages 20-21).*

---

286   Middle East (The), No. 20, October 1984, Pages 20-21.

287   "Definition of Amputee" www.merriam-webster.com, Retrieved 2018- 11-30

Picture 2: "Is this Islamic Justice"[288] Or I may ask same question this way: Is this a Social Control Based on Informal Customary Codes of Behaviour Justice?

This cross amputee has had his right hand and left foot amputated by amputator for stealing or theft, which is punishable by cross amputation sentenced in the Islamic Law Courts in the Sudan as a response and deterrent to thief or thieves or stealing actions or behaviour that deemed undesirable and or unacceptable according to Islamic norms, values and culture[289].

Cross Amputee sentenced in the Shariah Law Courts in the Sudan, 1985. *(Africa now, No. 52, August 1985 page 31).*

Cross Amputation here is done by amputating right hand and left foot of a victim. Sharia law of the Afro-Asiatic and Arab Muslims sentenced violated human rights more than what a civilised world might think, and plates number 6 (a), (b), and (c) of amputation could prove it rightly.

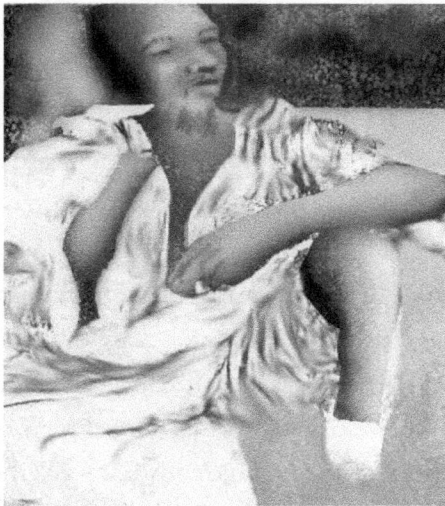

---

288   Africa now, No. 52, August 1985 page 31

289   Lee Hansen, Marcus (1918). "Old Fort Snelling, 1819-1858". Mid-America Series. State Historical Society of Iowaa, 1918. Page 124.

Picture 3: "Is this Islamic Justice?" Or I may ask same question this way: Is this a Social Control Based on Informal Customary Codes of Behaviour Justice? Cross Amputee sentenced in the Shariah Law Courts in the Sudan, 1985, *(Africa Now, No. 52 (August 1985), page 31).*

The victims of Sharia Law were estimated to be about 215 after the regime of President Nimeiri felt on April 6, 1985. The Association of Sharia Amputees (ASA) established in 1985 stated that memories of the regime were "revived of the hell".[290]

Expansion of Islam, Quran or Koran and Sharia laws

Religion of Islamic and Koranic Shariah Law of afro-Asianic speaking languages has destroyed and replaced, ritual, rite, ceremony, service, sacrament, formality, burial, mourning, formal procedure, custom, and practice of afro-African traditional religion in many parts of "the Sudans" or "two Sudans":- namely Sudan and South Sudan countries with multi-cultural and multi-religious societies in the African continent.

---

290   Mahmoud, Mohamed, "Sharia Victims United", Africa Now, No. 52 (August 1985), page 31.

Laws of Islamic Sharia in "The Sudans"

The name "Sudan" derives from the Arabic bilad as-sudan, or "the lands of the Black", referring to northern and Southern Sudan[291]. It was historically understood to denote the western part of the Sahel region. It roughly encompassed the geographical belt between the Sahara and the coastal West Africa.

The name "Sudan" in modern usage is also used in a separate context to refer to the geographic region comprising the present-day countries of the Sudan, including its western region which forms a part of the country, and South Sudan, which gained its independence in 2011. The name "the Sudans" is becoming the preferred option to avoid confusion in the explanation in the modern usages.

Sudan is marked by straw, forest cliffs and gallery forests along the rivers. Drought and livestock grazing threaten the area with desertification. The area is predominantly a plateau with river valleys of the White Nile.

Sudan is a transition zone between the Sahelian dry desert climate and the dense humid equatorial rainforest. Average annual temperatures vary between 23 and 29 degrees. Temperatures in the coldest months are above 20 degrees Celsius and over 30 degrees Celsius in the hottest months. Daily temperature fluctuations are up to 10-15 degrees. The summer monsoon brings rain from the equatorial. Precipitation ranges from 100-200 mm in the north to 1,500-2,000 mm in the South Sudan.

It extends in some km and stretches from the border of Kenya through southern Uganda, Congo, Central Africa, the Western Darfur region present-day Sudan, and South Sudan.

To the north of the South Sudan lies the Sahel, a more arid Acacia savanna region that in turn borders the Sahara Desert further north, and to the east the Ethiopian Highlands. In the southwest lies the West

---

291   *International Association for the History of Religions* (1959), Numen, Leiden: EJ Brill, page 131, West Africa may be taken as the country stretching from Senegal in the west, to the Cameroons in the east; sometimes it has been called the central and western Sudan, the Bilad as-Sūdan, 'Land of the Blacks', of the Arabs

Sudanian savanna, a wetter, tropical savanna region bordering the tropical forests of western Equatoria. In the center are lakes, swampy land and the more fertile region around the lake, while to the south of there are three highlands. To the southeast is the East Sudanian savanna, another tropical savanna region, bordering the forests of central Africa. This gives way further east to the Sudd, an area of tropical wetland fed by the water of the White Nile.

Many people were used as "a steady stream of slaves for the Mediterranean world" in the Sudan slave trade in the first millennium. With the arrival of the foreigners in the fifteen centuries, "people were directed to the Atlantic Slave trade," totaling over a thousand years for the Saharan and four centuries for the Atlantic trades. As a result, slavery critically shaped the Arabic, Islamic, Quranic and Shariah laws as institutions and systems in the Sudan. When foreigners first arrived at the region and found that slavery was "well established" in the region, used to "feed the courts of coastal kings as it was used in the medieval empires of the interior". Between the process of capture, enslavement, and "incorporation into a new community, the slave had neither rights nor any social identity." As a result, the identity of people who were enslaved "came from membership in a corporate group, usually based on kinship."292

In the 16th and 17th centuries slave raiders began to raid the region as part of the Islamic and Qur'anic Shariah expansion period and Nile River slave routes293. Their captives were enslaved, Islamized, converted into Islamic cultural practice and shipped to the Mediterranean coast, Europe, Arabia, the Western Hemisphere, or to the slave ports and factories along the west and north Africa coasts or Southeast and along the

---

292   Klein, Martin A. (1998). *Slavery and Colonial Rule in French West Africa.* Cambridge University Press. Page 1.

293   International Business Publications, USA (7 February 2007). Central African Republic Foreign Policy and Government Guide (World Strategic and Business Information Library). Int'l Business Publications. page 47. ISBN978-1433006210. Retrieved 25 May 2015.

Congo rivers[294], northwards through western Bahr Al-Ghazal to the Red Sea and Mediterranean.

The indigenous slave agents who are kings and warriors facilitated, taxed and partly organized the trade from the south, along the Mediterranean and trans-Saharan trade routes. In the 1830s, over 2,500 slaves were shifted across per year when slave trade, 'Sharia laws', and Arabic as Islamic languages of Afro-Asiatic classes flourished295. Even though the slave trade was officially abolished in 1853, in practice it continued until the 1890s296.

The southwards slave raid and Islamic expansion pressure increased in the early 17th century from the north with the rise of the Dar Fur Sultanates, who established Islamic center in Deim Zubeir, created "Dar Fertit"297 and introduced the first Islamic law courts in the South Sudan western region. The word 'Dar' means "home of", and "Fertit" does not define or portray any ethnic group, but was at the time a downgrading or harsh "word for non-Fur, non-Arab, non-Dinka or non-Jieng or Jaang and non-Luo groups in Western Bahr Al-Ghazal".298 Fertit is false word coined by slave owners as a name for their slaves and "Dar" as a name for 'the home of captured slaves' at the time. According to Rex Sean O'Fahey, "it was not so much a place but rather a state of mind. As the slave raiders

294   Alistair Boddy-Evans. Central Africa Republic Timeline- Part 1:

295   K. S. McLachlan, *"Tripoli and Tripolitania: Conflict and Cohesion burning the Period of the Bar nary Corsatris* (1551-1850)' Transactions of the Institute of British Geographers, New Series, Vol. 3, No. 3, Settlement and Conflict in the Mediterranean World. (1978), pages 285-294.

296   Lisa Anderson, *Nineteenth- Century Reform in Reform in Ottooman Libya,* International Journal of Middle East Studies, Vol. 16, No. 3. (Aug., 1984), pages 325-348.

297   Sikainga, Ahmed Alawad (1989). *"The Legacy Of Slavery And Slave Trade In The Western Bahr Al-Ghazal*, 1850-1939". Northeast African Studies. Pages 75–95.

298   Thomas, Edward (2010). The Kafia Kingi Enclave. People politics and history in the north-South boundary zone of western Sudan. London, Nairobi; -Rift Valley Institute. Pge 36, 103, 116.117. ISBN 9781907431043.

moved southwards, so Dar Fartit or Fertit moved south".[299] Colonizers and locals called the Deim Zubeir town as "Juku"[300] or "Uyujuku"[301] town located in Western Bahr Al-Ghazal.

The people in Dar Fertit came under pressure from systematic raiding by Zande chieftains and king[302]. The Deim Zubeir residents included a substantial number of ex-soldiers and former slaves, who had lost their ethnic ties and converted to Islam with Arabic as lingua franca.[303] Living conditions were particularly hard, since the area of Deim Zubeir was heavily infested with tsetse flies, which transmits the sleeping sickness[304]. Zubeir establishment of his rule was a civilizing mission in the name of "Islam" and for life service. Deim Zubeir town holds significance not only as a cultural site of interest for the physical location where the slaves were held during their grueling journey into Northern Sudan and on to Egypt to Arabia, but it also reflects the memories related to this challenging time in human history. Deim Zuber town gives an opportunity to remember this historic moment in South Sudan.

Of all the regions of South Sudan, Deim Zubeir called Uyujuku in western Bahr Al-Ghazal "is the first one which has seen the longest development of ivory and ostrich feather markets, Islamic expansion and

299   O'fahey, Rex Sean (1982). Mack, John; Robertshaw, Peter (eds.). *Fur and Fartit: the history of a frontier* (PDF). Nairobi: British Institute in Eastern Africa. Pages 75–88. ISBN978-1872566047.

300   Sharpe, R. Bowdler. *"Note on a Collection of Birds made by Herr F. Bohndorff in the Bahr Al-Ghazal Provice and the Nyam-Nyam Country in Equatorial Africa"* (PDF). Zoological Journal of the Linnean Society. Pages 17- 103 -421.

301   *"Deim Zubeir, Sudan- Geographical Names, map, geographic coordinates".* Geographic.org. 24 September 1993. Retrieved 31 July 2016.

302   Collins, Robert O. (1971). *Land Beyond the Rivers: The Southern Sudan* 1898-1918. New Haven / London: Yale University Press. Pages 219.ISBAN 978-0300014068.

303   Sikainga, Ahmad (1996). *Slaves into Workers: Emancipation and Labor in Colonial Sudan.* Austin. Pages 53–54.

304   Lewis, D.J. (1949). *"The Tsetse Fly Problem in the Anglo-Egyptian Sudan".* Sudan Notes and Records. 30: 189 – via Sudan Open Archive.

long-distance trade, and of complex political systems" institutionalized by Sultanates of Dar Fur from western Sudan. Deim Zubeir city in western Bahr Al-Ghazal is also the first region Islam, Qur'anic or Koranic teaching and Shariah laws" took root and flowered"[305]. When the Sundanese President Nimeiri imposed the Holy Sharia Law on September 26, 1983, which he called the "Islamic revolution", he stated that "With the proclamation of the Islam laws, the rule has become God's or Allah's rule and disobedience to the ruler, disobedience to God or Allah."[306] Islam did not demand much from a non-Muslim or an African to be converted into Islam. He or she will not study deeply the teachings of Islamic faith before he or she could be a Muslim. The required affirmation was that: "There is no Allah, but 'Allah' and Muhammed is the messenger of Allah". All African Muslims replace their own custom, value, culture and traditional religion with the "five pillars:"

1. The profession of one Allah
2. The fast of Ramadan
3. The giving of alms
4. The making of the five daily prayers and
5. Going on the great pilgrimage to the Holy cities of Mecca and Medina.[307]

In practice, being a Muslim means attending Koran or Qur'anic schools, going to the Friday prayers, keeping the fast of Ramadan, participating in public festivals and observing some of the rules governing naming and funeral ceremonies, marriage, inheritance and the conduct of women. Islam is found in towns in many parts in South Sudan because

---

305   Klein, Martin A. (1998). *Slavery and Colonial Rule in French West Africa.* Cambridge University Press.

306   Le Moy, Pa Scale Villiers, *"Nimeiri plays the Islamic Cord"* Middle East (The), No. 112 (February 1984), pages 22-23.

307   Gilsen, Michael, *Recognising Islam: Religion and Society in the Modern Arab World,* Pantheon Books, New York, 1982, page 219.

its practices are unpopular and are strongly opposed in the rural areas of South Sudan.

Middle Ages: Its medieval history is marked by the caravan slave trade[308] lead by the Sultanates of the Western Darfur and kings of central Sudan. Prisoners of war were a regular occurrence in the ancient Nile Valley and Africa. During times of conquest and after winning battles, the ancient Nubians were taken as slaves by the ancient Egyptians[309]. In turn, the ancient Egyptians took slaves after winning battles with the adversaries[310].

During the colonization period, the Sudan was created and Anglo-Egyptian Sudan was named after the present-day Sudan and South Sudan, which gained its independence in 2011.

---

308   Encyclopedia of Islam IX. p. 752, 758.

309   Redford, D. B. *From Slave to Pharaoh: The Black Experience of Ancient Egypt*. Baltimore: The Johns Hopkins University Press, 2004. Project MUSE

310   *"Ancient Egypt: Slavery, its causes and practices"*. Reshafim.org.il. Retrieved 13 March 2014.

APPENDIX C

Evaluation of the Study

This section evaluates the current exploratory investigation by explaining the research methods and design used and the procedures followed to gather data and analyze it. It also explains the extent to which the objectives were obtained. The investigation will then be evaluated in terms of its limitations and suggestions for further research.

Methods

The investigation used phenomenology and thematic content analysis in analyzing the narratives of individual respondents and focus groups. Thematic content analysis was used to explore issues presented while phenomenology was used to find the meanings from the respondents' point of view. New themes were derived. The themes were also interpreted in relation to the available literature and the Social Learning Theory as a theoretical approach used in the exploratory investigation.

The research instrument was a questionnaire consisting of open-ended questions to enable the respondents to mention any related issues that were believed to be relevant to the current exploratory investigation.

Limitations of the study
Sample size

The sample size that has been used according to qualitative research does not easily allow for generalization. The respondents in the current investigation are from townships in the Bahr Al-Ghazal and Equatoria regions.

It would be interesting to explore the trends in rural townships from other urban township areas across the country.

Literature

The available literature that specifically focuses on issues of mourning and bereavement in South Sudanese rural and urban township environments seem to be limited, thus there were not enough investigations to compare with the findings of the current exploratory investigation. Some parts of the literature were based on the researcher's own observations of some of the practices in the rural and urban township environments which very little has been documented in the literature.

Theoretical Framework

The theoretical framework used in this study is the social learning theory to describe how the 'phenomenon' of the 'after fatality road accident-death tears' party ceremony celebration was adopted and gained popularity in the rural and urban township areas of South Sudan. Even though some concepts such as social diffusion and innovation were highlighted in the exploratory investigation, concepts such as positive and negative reinforcement in the theory that influence learning could not be clearly accounted for in the study as to the reasons for the continuation of the practice.

Data Collection Instrument

The instrument used to collect data could have also focused on the rural and urban township people's experiences of and the meaning they attached to strict adherence to traditional mourning and bereavement rituals in a rural and an urban township environment.

The exploratory investigation could not also uncover the relationship between coping on a long-term basis and The 'after fatality road accident-death tears' ceremony celebration party. As this practice is a 'once off' occasion that occurs immediately after the funeral, it is still questionable if the intended effects are long lasting.

Recommendations for Further Research

A follow-up for exploratory investigation is recommended on the effectiveness of the On the effectiveness of the 'after fatality road accident- death tears' party in ceremony celebration if used as a coping mechanism for the people in the townships on the longer term.

A follow-up for exploratory investigation on the experiences of the rural and urban township people of the traditional mourning rituals and the meaning they attach to them with Their current experiences of the 'after fatality road accident- death tears' ceremony celebration parties.

A comparative investigation between the people who live in South Sudanese townships and those who still live in the rural villages on their perceptions of The 'after fatality road accident-death tears' ceremony celebration parties and adherence to traditional bereavement practices.

Other population groups such as older members of the society who have lived in the rural and urban township environments. It would be interesting to hear their experiences of the burials in the rural township and urban township environments.

An exploratory investigation that would highlight the relationship between the 'after fatality road accident-death tears' ceremony celebration parties and increased reported psychological problems or unresolved grief due to abridged traditional mourning practices (Kilonzo & Hogan, 1999).

Based on the findings of the current study on the description of the respondents on the use of alcohol at the 'after fatality road accident-death tears' ceremony celebration parties, a follow up investigation could explore the relationship between the use of alcohol as a possible defense mechanism in dealing with the grief reactions after the loss of a loved one.

Conclusion

The mourning rituals currently practiced in Most South Sudanese contemporary rural and urban township environments highlight the needs of the bereaved people living in those environments. Adherence to strict traditional mourning practices may not always be possible because of The new ways of living in that rural and urban township environments demand from the rural and urban township dwellers. The environment demands that mourning should be brief and intense so that people can go back to their normal lives as soon as possible (Dlukulu, 2010). The practice of the 'after road fatality accident death tears' ceremony party' seems to reflect this. The nature of the urban environment may also not completely allow and accommodate strict adherence to some of the traditional mourning practices. This confirms Parkes *et al.* (1997) assertion that adherence to traditional bereavement practices may not always be possible in strange environments that people currently find themselves. There may not be enough time, relevant resources and also familiar people to offer support in carrying out traditional mourning practices.

Even though performance of traditional mourning practices may seem to have been adapted, the people are aware of issues such as respect which Magudu (2004) highlighted as 'ukuzila' which is avoidance of certain practices to show respect. There was a general wish that the people could go back to original practices which would restore order in South Sudanese rural and urban township burials or funerals.

INDEX

Psychology 5, 37, 39, 54, 56, 202, 204, 206, 212

Pty 30, 122, 129-130, 276

Purity 296

Quran 308

Quranic 164, 166, 168, 170, 176, 310

Raan 106

Radzilani 152

Rahma 167

Ramadan 169, 313

Randall 79, 84, 143

Rando 51, 133

Rationalizing 185

Raymond 83

Rebecca 92-93

Redford 314

Rehabilitation 248, 290

Reimer vii, 21, 72

Rek 6-7, 9, 19, 27, 32, 40, 45, 49, 55, 57, 60-2, 66, 69-70, 73-5, 78-9, 82, 84-7, 89, 91-3, 99-100, 103, 106-7, 116-7, 117, 121, 124, 126, 128-9, 136, 141, 143-5, 148-9, 151-5, 161-2, 179, 189, 196, 199, 216, 218-9, 227-8, 237-9, 249, 252, 256-8, 260, 264, 270-1, 280, 283, 290, 300

Renk 99, 101-2

Reptools 37

Reshafim 314

Rex 311-312

Riders 3

Riem 76, 95, 270

Rinehart 38-39, 54

Riny 290

Roach 73

Roadway 22, 29, 200, 204, 282, 304

Robert 41, 66-7, 79, 143, 245, 247, 251, 279, 312

Robertshaw 101, 312

Robertson 29

Rochester 82

Roger 80, 90

Rogers 35

Roland 82

Roman 216-217, 280

Romanoff 39, 52-4, 134

Rooyen 15, 206, 280

Rosenberg 79, 143

Rosenblatt 2, 6, 37-8

Ross 24, 198

Rotledge 68

Rum 84, 89, 117, 124-5

Rumbeek 101

Rumbek 283

Rut 100

Ruweng 100

Sage 203-204

Sahara 102, 309

Saharan 101, 310

Sahel 309

Sahelian 309

www.ingramcontent.com/pod-product-compliance
Lightning Source LLC
Chambersburg PA
CBHW021849020426
42334CB00013B/251